Russia in Search of Itself

Russia in Search of Itself

James H. Billington

Woodrow Wilson Center Press
Washington, D.C.

The Johns Hopkins University Press
Baltimore and London

EDITORIAL OFFICES
Woodrow Wilson Center Press
One Woodrow Wilson Plaza
1300 Pennsylvania Avenue, N.W.
Washington, D.C. 20004-3027
Telephone 202-691-4029
www.wilsoncenter.org

ORDER FROM
The Johns Hopkins University Press
Hampden Station
P.O. Box 50370
Baltimore, Maryland 21211
Telephone 1-800-537-5487
www.press.jhu.edu/books

Library of Congress Cataloging-in-Publication Data

Billington, James H.
    Russia in search of itself / James H. Billington.
        p. cm.
Includes index.
    ISBN 0-8018-7976-0 (cloth : alk. paper)
1. Russia (Federation)—Civilization—Philosophy. 2.
Russia—Civilization—Philosophy. 3. Nationalism—Russia (Federation)
4. Post-communism—Russia (Federation) 5. National characteristics,
Russian. I. Title.
DK510.32 .B55 2004
947.086—dc22

                                        2003025484

About the Center

The Center is the living memorial of the United States of America to the nation's twenty-eighth president, Woodrow Wilson. Congress established the Woodrow Wilson Center in 1968 as an international institute for advanced study, "symbolizing and strengthening the fruitful relationship between the world of learning and the world of public affairs." The Center opened in 1970 under its own board of trustees.

In all its activities the Woodrow Wilson Center is a nonprofit, nonpartisan organization, supported financially by annual appropriations from the Congress, and by the contributions of foundations, corporations, and individuals. Conclusions or opinions expressed in Center publications and programs are those of the authors and speakers and do not necessarily reflect the views of the Center staff, fellows, trustees, advisory groups, or any individuals or organizations that provide financial support to the Center.

Contents

Preface

This book is an account of how Russians have been thinking about the nature and destiny of their nation since the collapse of the Soviet Union. It is not a history of the Russian nation itself during this period, but rather an attempt to chronicle how the heirs to a great intellectual tradition are grappling under new conditions of freedom with the classic question of Russian identity.

Ever since *glasnost'*—freedom to "speak out"—became a reality under Mikhail Gorbachev in the mid-1980s, the discussion of Russia's identity has been more open than ever before. Ideas are not only brought in from the contemporary West but also dug up from the Russian past.

Long-suppressed groups of people have found their voices and entered the debate. This debate is conducted in a variety of ways that would have been unthinkable only a few years ago: on television, the

Internet, and public roundtables, by polling agencies, nightclub enter-
tainers, educators crafting curricula, and organizations sponsoring
essay contests. All of this streams into an already flooded river of journalism that has by now publicized both popular and academic arguments for almost every conceivable point of view.

This discussion about what it means to be Russian occurs within a
political entity that—for the first time in its history—has become just
a *nation* rather than an empire, and a *democracy* rather than an autocracy. Communist totalitarianism had extended both the imperial and
autocratic powers of the state so far that it became an unprecedented
phenomenon in human history. Equally without precedent has been
the process of its devolution.

Much of what had been planted in the Soviet Union over the killing
fields of Stalinism had gone to seed, slowly decomposed, and in the
1980s began to provide humus for fresh growth. A thousand new flowers and as many weeds sprang up from below or were transplanted
from the outside. But old roots were never systematically dug out. It
did not immediately become clear which sprouts would ultimately
blossom and bear fruit in the depleted soil and unforgiving cold of the
new Russian Federation.

A certain human resilience and warmth, however, somehow survived the Soviet era, and the population had become better educated.
When communism collapsed, Russians were suddenly freed from the
pretension of being the dominant force within a world empire—and
from the all-permeating fear of a capricious and intrusive tyranny.
Thinking Russians were searching for truths about life in general and
their common national life in particular.

Russians have traditionally conducted such searches in the face of
awesome central power over which they have no control. There are
many Russian words for this force that has so long ruled over them and
pervaded their consciousness: *vlast'* suggests pure, raw power; *sila*,
physical strength; *derzhava*, power that imposes direction; *gosudarstvo*,
sovereign power; and *pravitel'stvo*, governing power.

The Russian word for the limitless power of a single leader, *samod-
erzhavie*, is the indigenous Slavic version of the Byzantine Greek

autokrates that had originally been rendered simply as *autokrator*. And imperial Russian rulers layered Mongol and early modern Western European authoritarian practices on top of their original Byzantine model to produce an autocracy more absolute than any other in northern Europe.

But the power traditionally exercised by an unaccountable single ruler in the Russian empire was always a thin external shell that covered vast spaces and covered up internal struggles. It was never an empty shell. Rather, it was like the outer doll on one of those dolls-within-dolls that the Russians call a *matryoshka*—the kind that foreigners on short visits buy when they want to take away something faintly amusing that they consider uniquely Russian.

Those who stayed a little longer or looked a little deeper inside that outer face of power saw other dolls with other faces. Russian culture, through its many mutations from frontier monks and holy fools to lonely artists and heroic dissidents, has always produced those who seek and speak truth to power. As Russia became less powerful but more free, its people began openly to express thoughts they had previously held within themselves and discussed only within small circles of trusted friends.

But just as Russians began to recover their public voices under Gorbachev's *glasnost'*, they began to lose their inner confidence in who they were and where they were going. The excessive centralization and enforced certainties of the Soviet system gave way to the fragmentation and uncertainties of a porous Russian Federation.

Uncertainty in a time of drastic change has produced a kind of cultural-psychological nervous breakdown. A rich and variegated torrent of words has poured forth, but it is not clear where the noisy conversation—let alone Russia itself—is heading. The agenda has not been set by any giant like Andrei Sakharov or Alexander Solzhenitsyn. It has not been controlled—or even framed—from the top down and center out as in the Russian past. Russians are not even sure that their own explosion of ink on subjective matters has much historical importance compared with the dismal realities created by the objective factors of geopolitics and economics.

So how can someone from a distant, once-rival country presume to describe the deep and often distressing dialogues unfolding within this very different culture? Americans have never fought Russians, but we were interlocked with them for more than a half-century in a new kind of conflict that had the potential to destroy the world. That face-off ended a dozen years ago in a sudden, peaceful way that neither country had foreseen.

Since then, the ideals of the one country have been dramatically adopted by the other. But those ideals—of freedom, democracy, and a market economy—have been planted among a people with a very different past history facing a bewildering host of present problems. And ordinary Russians are in some ways transferring the mixture of fascination and resentment that they used to feel about their own remote, unaccountable leaders to the sole remaining superpower, the even more distant America.

I continue to wade into these troubled waters because of a life-long scholarly fascination with Russia—and because, as an American, I am concerned that the Russian experiment in creating democracy contains greater potential for building a better world than we have yet appreciated—but also more continuing dangers than we have generally realized. My method of research lies in the madness of immersion—not, alas, from long residence in Russia, but from innumerable visits over forty-five years and many recent conversations with Russian participants in new Congressional programs for which I am responsible.*

My interest in Russia began by discovering Leo Tolstoy's *War and Peace* as a schoolboy while the battle of Stalingrad was raging. I vaguely sensed then that yesterday's novel had more to say about what tomorrow might bring than today's newspaper. I have subsequently explored

---

* Either a disintegration or an authoritarian resurgence in Russia could reactivate strategic dangers from the still vast Russian arsenal of weapons of mass destruction, and/or revalidate the classic geopolitical danger of tyranny prevailing in the dominant Eurasian landmass (whether through new conflicts or new alliances with the two forces with which it shares its largest borders and which are often seen as the most potentially threatening to peace and freedom in the early twenty-first century: authoritarian Islam to the south or China to the east).

in a variety of ways the sounds, pictures, and—above all—written words of Russians.

In my two major books, *The Icon and the Axe* and *Fire in the Minds of Men*, I tried to create a narrative first of Russian culture as a whole (emphasizing its distinctive religious and indigenous elements) and then of the force that largely destroyed it (the revolutionary faith transplanted from the West). Since becoming Librarian of Congress in 1987, I have written two smaller books: *Russia Transformed: Breakthrough to Hope*, describing the final overthrow of communism that I witnessed in Moscow in August 1991; and *The Face of Russia*, tracing how Russians went from wholesale imitation to creative innovation in adopting as their own, six successive foreign art forms with which they had no serious prior experience.

Their record of unexpected creative breakthroughs in the arts led me to wonder if the Russians could ever succeed in the difficult art of building a constitutional democracy. Here again was a form of creativity with which they had little prior familiarity. They had begun with the precipitous, large-scale importation of foreign political and economic models—as they had a millennium earlier with the sudden adaptation of Byzantine religious and artistic models. Would the Russians now succeed in creating innovative versions of their own in secular politics, as they had done in the fourteenth century with religious painting? Or would their adopted new models for society break down and break up as icon painting suddenly did with the advent of Western naturalism in the mid-seventeenth century?

New freedom in post-Soviet Russia permitted a much wider range of thinkers than ever before to participate in the most many-sided public discussion in history of the nature and destiny of Russia. Advocacy journalism (*publitsistika*) replaced prose fiction (*belletristika*) as the medium for conveying messages. Publitsistika became, in effect, the reigning art form of a fledgling democracy. The traditional creative arts, having been crippled by Soviet censors, were now weakened in new ways by the removal of state support in the new economy.

The new "publicistics" dominated not just the established print culture but also the new forms of multimedia, electronic communication.

I ventured into this world by creating a television series on Russian culture under the same title as my last book, *The Face of Russia*. And the Congress made it possible for us at the Library of Congress to create "Meeting of Frontiers" on the Internet, a bilingual, educational library of rare primary documents from both the United States and Russia illustrating parallel themes in the history of both countries.

This book is an attempt to mine the rich and varied body of publitsistika in an effort to determine how post-Soviet Russia is both defining its identity as a nation and relegitimizing the exercise of authority within its reduced but still capacious borders. My interpretation attaches more historical importance than others in American academia might to the moral passion and religious dimension of Russian culture. But I would contend that those involved or immersed in Russian culture often foresaw the impermanence of the Soviet system more clearly than those preoccupied with economics and politics.

It does not, of course, necessarily follow that studying intellectual and cultural expression in the more open, post-Soviet era will help anticipate future developments in the new Russian Federation. What seemed important was to consider a wide range of materials and opinions, to document them in footnotes, and to press on with a narrative text that might point toward some tentative conclusions. I have attempted to derive such conclusions from primary Russian sources—rather than to develop them through argumentation with the views of other outside observers.

Three provisional conclusions will emerge for those patient enough to follow the complex and often paradoxical trains of thought that I have found in the Russian record. None of these three seems to be part of the current consensus thinking—such as it exists—about Russia today. These conclusions result from taking seriously what important Russian thinkers are saying about their own nation. I do not presume that such thinkers will, by themselves, decisively influence, let alone define, the future of Russia. But I do believe that they reflect the psychological state of the Russian people out of which emerging political leaders will have to shape that future. I also hold that matters of belief and conviction are important determinants of major changes in history, and, particularly in the Russian case, that these matters are often decisive.

The first suggested conclusion is that the range of distinctly possible future identities for Russia should include alternatives that are both far better and far worse than any presently anticipated. Second, I believe that the balance of probabilities points toward an eventual outcome considerably better than is generally thought possible—provided that there is no major international war or internal upheaval. Finally, I believe that an enduring positive identity will be possible only if Russians are able harmoniously to synthesize Western political and economic institutions with an indigenous recovery of the religious and moral dimensions of their own culture.

The risk is that postcommunist Russia may not succeed either in fully institutionalizing an effective, yet limited government of laws or in developing the deep moral and spiritual underpinnings for a more modern and pluralistic society. The likely result of such a failure would be yet another version of Russia's historic hypercentralized autocracy, modernized by increased foreign trade and importation of useful technologies from Western economies. Russia will not return to the Slavophile, the Tsarist, or the Soviet past. The struggle for the future of Russia is not between "East" and "West" in the legendary Russian soul but between two very different syntheses of Eastern and Western elements in the emerging body politic.

* * * * *

I first planned to study Russia's search for a new identity in the late 1980s when the Soviet empire was beginning to crack. I was preparing to take a half-year sabbatical in 1987 to conduct research in Russia on a grant from the Carnegie Corporation of New York after thirteen uninterrupted years as director of the Woodrow Wilson International Center for Scholars. My appointment as Librarian of Congress canceled out the leave and put the study on a slower calendar as I began sixteen years of equally uninterrupted service directing a much larger institution.

The collapse of communism and implosion of the USSR made the subject both more complex and more urgent. Somewhat surprisingly, my new position multiplied rather than diminished my contacts with the processes of change in Russia. I made substantive trips to many parts of the Russian Federation, sometimes with congressional, presidential, library, and church groups and sometimes to advance acquisitions, exhibits, and interlibrary links with sister institutions.

I decided to move toward concluding my continuing inquiry into the Russian search for identity by organizing a series of conferences— small ones at first with American and Western colleagues at the Library of Congress and then three longer and larger ones with leading Russian thinkers in Istra, Tomsk, and Moscow. I was extraordinarily fortunate in being able to enlist Professor Kathleen Parthé of the University of Rochester as my collaborator in this phase of the project. Her important research on village writers and nationalistic publicists drew widely on primary sources. And her writings were remarkably free of either the reflexive condemnation or the sentimental glorification with which Western observers often approach distinctively Russian phenomena. She helped frame the questions for the three colloquia in Russia and did a masterful job of translating their entire proceedings from the original Russian and editing them for separate publication with supplementary commentary.*

I had originally intended to include in that publication an essay combining reflections on those meetings with my conclusions about Russia's search for identity, drawn from a decade of extensively reading and intensively talking with Russians. But the essay grew into a book. Its completion was delayed but enriched by the swelling volume of millennium-inspired polemics and prophecy—and by the more than 7,500 young Russians who came to America between June 1999 and December 2003 under the congressionally created Open World/Russian Leadership program of which I have been the chairman.

---

* James H. Billington and Kathleen Parthé, *The Search for a New Russian National Identity: Russian Perspectives* (Washington, D.C.: Library of Congress, March 2003). Available online at: www.loc.gov/about/welcome/speeches/russianperspectives/index.html. Professor Parthé also kindly read the manuscript of this book and provided valuable suggestions. I first wrote on this subject in 1990 in the *Washington Post* ("Russia's Quest for Identity," January 21; and "Looking to the Past," January 22). I subsequently lectured on the subject in Moscow (published as "Rossiia v poiskakh sebia." *Nezavisimaia gazeta*, June 4, 1991).

I alone bear the responsibility both for the choice of the primary materials I have winnowed out to use in this book and for the interpretations that I have tried to induce from, rather than impose on, the Russian record. But I owe a number of deep debts—first and foremost to the Congress of the United States. On a continuing and bipartisan basis, it has supported the Library of Congress institutionally in a variety of projects to help with the process of democratization in Russia, and has encouraged me personally to continue writing on Russia. Above all, I thank the Congress for creating and sustaining its library as a universal collection of the world's knowledge in almost all languages and formats. Almost every item referenced in my footnotes can be found in the Library of Congress. I could not have written this book without these resources, but my debt to this institution only begins with the collections.

I am indebted in a variety of ways and over a long period of time to two colleagues at the Library in the Russian field: Irene Steckler and Harry Leich. They exemplify the dedication and scholarly skill of our gifted staff at its best. I greatly appreciate Mikhail Levner's help in finding materials for this study in and beyond Moscow. I am deeply grateful to former U.S. ambassador James Collins, who, like his cultural attaché John Brown, participated in the colloquia—and to Alex Khilkov and to many in the U.S. Embassy in Moscow and the U.S. Consulate in St. Petersburg who have supported the Russian projects of the Library of Congress.

I thank the many, many Russians with whom I have discussed this topic. I especially appreciate the help and friendship of the late Dmitry Likhachev and Ekaterina Genieva. Among the many at the Library of Congress I should properly thank, I particularly want to acknowledge the helpfulness of my excellent special assistant Tim Robbins and the outstanding work of my incomparable former secretary Barbara Sakamoto in preparing the final version of this manuscript for publication.

Dmitri Glinski has made a particularly important contribution to this study. He has been an invaluable and imaginative research associate—scouring obscure publications, Internet websites, and popular television shows in order to find, describe, analyze, and critique many of the attitudes I sought to canvas for this study. I also thank him and Caron Cadle for reading and critiquing the final manuscript.

I thank the Carnegie Corporation of New York both for its generosity in funding this project—and for its patience in waiting for its completion. I appreciate the moral as well as intellectual force of the corporation's two most recent presidents: Dr. David Hamburg, a visionary who made the original grant and has continued to be interested in the project; and his successor, Dr. Vartan Gregorian, a great educator who has continued to be supportive of this project and gracious in extending deadlines for its completion. I am deeply grateful for the example and inspiration of my brother David P. Billington.

Finally, I express my enduring appreciation and affection for my wife Marjorie. Her familial dedication, unfailing cheerfulness, and intuitive good sense have supported me in innumerable ways in this and all my undertakings.

James H. Billington
McLean, Va.
December 9, 2003

I. The Long Prologue

The large political units known in the modern world as nation-states define their identity basically in three ways: geographically, historically, and culturally. In all three of these categories, Russia is utterly unique.

Geographically, the Russian state—even within its reduced, post-Soviet borders—covers the largest land-mass of any nation in the world. It also contains the world's largest supply of undeveloped natural resources. Yet in the north and east, Russia has some of the world's harshest climatic conditions; and in the south and west, it has long, largely unprotected borders with a variety of very different, often hostile, civilizations.

Historically, Russia has been unified and governed by an autocratic single ruler supported by large military and security forces and an immense state bureaucracy. Centralized and almost unlimited power has been legit-imized by an ideological institution (the Orthodox Church, the Communist Party) whose claims have tran-scended traditional bonds of language and ethnicity and invested the ruler with god-like attributes. All of this made Russia, for most of its history, more like an ancient empire than a modern nation-state.

Russians have only rarely and recently described their country as a "nation" (*natsiia*), and the word still used for "state" (*gosudarstvo*) is derived from the term historically used for an autocratic "sovereign" (*gosudar'*). Until the twentieth century, Russian historians almost always focused their attention mainly on the "great sovereign" (*velikii gosudar'*) at the top. And even in the Soviet era, when the general secretary of the Communist Party replaced the tsar, there continued to be little historical attention paid to state institutions other than the secret police.

Seeking to preserve unity and maintain control over a vast and exposed territory, the Russian empire was frequently at war with its neighbors. The Russians' basic understanding of all this recurrent conflict has been diametrically opposite to that of their principal neighbors. Russians have generally seen themselves as perpetual victims of foreign predators, building on the fact that rival empires have invaded their land from the Mongols and Teutonic knights to Napoleon and Hitler. Most of Russia's immediate neighbors, however, have seen themselves as victims—smaller nations threatened with conquest by the relentless expansion of a much larger power armed with unlimited ideological justification for extending its empire.

Culturally, there really was no broad sense of national identity in the Russian empire before the nineteenth century. The overwhelmingly peasant population was basically enserfed, illiterate, and loyal to the tsar and to the Orthodox Christian faith. The peasantry was generally obedient to—if resentful of, and occasionally rebellious against—the governmental and bureaucratic institutions that intruded into their local way of life in the name of distant, higher authorities.

There was neither ethnic nor linguistic unity within the empire. As it expanded territorially to the east, it added native Asians as subjects even as it quietly absorbed people and ideas from Western Europe. This process of internal Europeanization began in the sixteenth century. Subsequently, Orthodox Russia largely built its military, governmental, and commercial institutions on Protestant models, and its aristocratic artistic culture on Catholic models.

Peter the Great basically adopted the Swedish form of government and modeled his new capital of St. Petersburg on Amsterdam. He personally visited and extensively borrowed from the Protestant countries of Northern Europe. The generic Russian term for "foreigner" was the word for "German": *nemets.*

Russia's modern artistic culture was, however, largely shaped by Catholic Europe. It had started to become semi-Polish under Peter's father, Tsar Alexis, in the old capital of Moscow in the late seventeenth century after the Russian empire absorbed much of the Western Ukraine and Belarus, which had been governed by Poland and influenced by its culture. In the new capital of St. Petersburg, the two dominant rulers of the eighteenth century, the Empresses Elizabeth and Catherine the Great, created a new aristocratic culture that was audiovisually Italian and linguistically French.

Not until the nineteenth century was there any widespread consciousness that Russia had a distinct national identity defined by secular criteria such as ethnicity and language. The concept of Moscow as "the third Rome" had rarely been mentioned until then—even in the monastic culture, where it originated in the early sixteenth century. Nor did the panegyric court literature in "the new Rome" of St. Petersburg have much impact even within the aristocratic culture that produced it. Written in a stilted Russian laced with Church Slavonic elements, eighteenth-century literary rhetoric basically appealed neither to the nobility who preferred to speak French nor to the peasants who spoke an unliterary Russian or Ukrainian. Both groups defined their identity by service to the tsar, adherence to the Orthodox Church, and residence on the land.

All of this changed beyond recognition in the last two centuries. An often-bewildered people sought to define for themselves a place in the modern world commensurate with the immense physical space that they occupied. Their search for identity produced intense intellectual debate in the nineteenth century and unprecedented social upheavals in the twentieth. All of that was prelude to the dramatic, if chaotic, new search for national identity that followed the collapse of communism, which is the main subject of this book.

1 | The Nineteenth-Century Discovery of Identity

R ussian self-consciousness was dramatically changed in the early nineteenth century by the intoxicating experience of repelling and defeating the largest and best army in the world. Napoleon's *grande armée* had occupied Moscow in 1812 but was then ground down and pursued all the way to Paris. The accompanying upsurge of patriotic feeling among all social classes in Russia sought to find public expression first in the dominant art form of the eighteenth century: monumental architecture. The rebuilding of burnt-out Moscow was itself a monumental undertaking. The flammable wooden buildings of the old city were replaced by neoclassical stone structures, and popular interest grew in the public discussion of an official national monument to commemorate the victory over Napoleon.

It took nearly the entire century to conceive, build, and dedicate the memorial. The process began in the second decade of the century with the megalomaniacal plans of a Swedish architect to reconstruct the hill from which Napoleon had first seen the city into a three-story megachurch. (A subterranean, triangular base was to symbolize the body; a ground level, cruciform church, the soul; and a huge hemispheric dome on top, the spirit.) The project ended in 1889 with the dedication of an altogether different building: the gigantic, neo-Byzantine Church of Christ the Savior designed by another Swedish architect. This edifice was capped by a dome more capacious than St. Peter's in Rome and higher than the bell tower of Ivan the Great in the Kremlin.[1]

Tsar Alexander I (1801–1825) had already decreed in 1812 that the memorial should "speak in stone" to future generations; but the stone was cold, and monumental architecture was an aristocratic art form. The quest for a cultural evocation of the victorious struggle eventually produced the greatest epic novel of the modern era: Tolstoy's *War and Peace*. And it was through the new artistic medium of vernacular literature that Russians began to discuss the nature of the nation that had come together to defeat the most powerful army in history.

A more flowing form of the Russian language came into being to express the Russians' sense of shared pride and to retell and embellish the stories embedded in their secular folklore and historical chronicles. The key moments in this sudden flowering of a self-conscious, written Russian culture were Nicholas Karamzin's elegant, twelve-volume apologia for autocracy, *History of the Russian State* (1819–1826), and Alexander Pushkin's rich poetry and panoramic evocation of Russian life and history.

Increased contact with the West and the spread of both higher education and accessible journalism within Russia deepened the desire to define how Russia related to Europe. Continuing dynastic intermarriages with other royal houses were no longer a sufficient means of relating to a Europe that was now using the relatively new term "nation" to legitimize state power. The "nation" was a secular ideal shaped and spread by the rhetoric of the French Revolution. It became the rallying cry of non-French peoples resisting Napoleon's imperial distortion of that ideal. German romantic philosophy gave added intensity to the new idea by suggesting that different ethnic-linguistic peoples are, in fact, organic bodies, and that individuals can truly fulfill themselves only as subordinate parts of that greater whole.

La nation suggested a community that was more participatory and less patriarchal than la patrie, the fatherland. The nation was the entity in which liberty and equality could be realized by intensifying feelings of fraternity, the third ideal in the revolutionary trinity. The nation was sanctified by the imagined brotherhood of all the people within it. States were no longer to be held together by the differentiated allegiances of a stratified population to a monarch.

The Russian imperial establishment initially tried to combat the revolutionary appeal of liberty-equality-fraternity with a reactionary trinity of its own. Tsar Alexander I proclaimed that the three monarchs who had combined forces to defeat Napoleon were, in fact, a Holy Alliance destined not only to restore monarchy in Europe but also to reunite Christianity as three parts of a holy trinity: an Orthodox Romanov, a Catholic Hapsburg, and a Protestant Hohenzollern.

After crushing a nationalistic revolt in Poland in 1831, the successor of Alexander I, Nicholas I (1825–1855), tried to co-opt the appeal of this new ideal. He added the word "nationalism" to two other traditional terms, "autocracy" and "orthodoxy," in setting forth the trinity of ideals that became the official ideology for his empire in 1833. Since the Russian word used for "nationalism" in this formula (narodnost') was derived from the term for "the people" (narod), it carried inherently anti-authoritarian overtones. The revolutionaries who rose up under Nicholas's reformist successor, Tsar Alexander II, drew on the emotional appeal of the same core word by defining their cause as narodnichestvo, "populism."

The cultural question of Russian national identity arose in the nineteenth century in part out of the Russian aristocracy's social and psychological search for its own identity. The aristocracy had depended for its privileges on the imperial court (its very name, dvorianstvo, was derived from dvor or court), and for its daily bread on the peasantry. But Russian literature early on made the aristocratic "superfluous man" one of its main stock characters. And, after the emancipation of the serfs in 1861 and the rapid development of a less stratified, more

urban culture, aristocratic identity lost much of its practical significance. Many aristocrats felt discomfort or guilt over continued privilege
and/or a need to sustain their preeminence by helping to define a
noble and inclusive identity for the Russian people as a whole.

But it was difficult to speak for the nation when aristocrats usually
spoke the Russian language only with servants in the city and with
peasants in the countryside. Noblemen spoke French to one another,
cultivated Italian music and architecture, and—most fatefully of all—
thought in German.

The Hegelian Infatuation

Russia, like awakening Prussia, had felt compelled to find a new
national identity in the wake of their common victory over Napoleon.
The engine of reform that propelled young Prussians into a new kind
of national service was the first great modern research university created at Berlin in 1809. The new University of Berlin was designed to
serve a secular state and was built around the library and laboratory
rather than the classroom and catechism. Berlin and the other great
German universities that soon imitated it gave birth to a revolution in
thought that shaped Russia's sense of itself far more than either the
French Revolution in politics or the English Industrial Revolution.

The romantic idealism of the German universities inculcated the
belief that great changes were inevitably coming out of history itself.
Humanity was seen as progressing toward a total liberation that would
be—at one and the same time—spiritual, secular, and political. History was propelled forward by the human mind and spirit (the German word *Geist* having both meanings). History was a metaphysical
process with physical consequences, and its most important end product was the realization of an ideal nation-state.

Philosophy replaced theology as the dominant discipline at the University of Berlin. Johann Fichte became both rector of the university and
professor of philosophy after sounding a clarion call for a new secular
nationalism in his *Lectures to the German Nation* of 1807–1808. Georg
Hegel, who held the chair in philosophy from 1818–1830, taught that

present setbacks could lead to future gains, since history advanced—like human thought itself—through a process of contradictions.

Young Germans were encouraged to believe that this "dialectical" advance of the world's mind/spirit (*Weltgeist*) would be fulfilled by the creation of a new type of German nation. Germans from many divided principalities were inspired by this train of thought to come to Berlin and serve the reformist state of Prussia. They began the process by which traditional Lutheran Prussia grew into a new kind of secular nation-state that was to supplant the multiethnic Hapsburg empire as the dominant force in central Europe.

Unlike their counterparts from Prussia, the young aristocrats from Russia who flocked to German universities could find no practical outlet at home for attempting to realize their ideals. The Russian empire under Nicholas I was the bastion of political reaction in Europe, resisting reform of all sorts after crushing first their own moderate Decembrist reformers in 1825 and then the Polish uprising for independence in 1831.

Unable to reach out broadly into society, educated young Russians delved deeply into themselves, meeting within small circles for philosophical speculation in the 1830s and 1840s that raised utopian hopes for the future and generated extraordinary emotional intensity. Metaphysical philosophy had been almost entirely absent from both the monastic culture of Moscovy and the aristocratic culture of St. Petersburg. But the historical theology of Russian Orthodoxy inclined Russians to the view that history assigned a special role to Russia. German romantic thought was piled on top of experience in Masonic lodges, conditioning young Russians to believe that their own newly found identity as thinkers of great thoughts might enable them to provide a new kind of leadership for Russia. Their task was to think more deeply within a secret circle that would ultimately share its purified insights with a broader public through a new kind of "thick journal." Its publication would not so much entertain as transform the society.

For young aristocrats, a secret circle was a kind of "liberated zone" in which to discover their own version of the "freedom, equality, and fraternity" talked about in Europe but unobtainable in Russia. Denied any outlet for practical reform and unsatisfied with "the freedoms of the ballroom" (*bal'nye vol'nosti*), they poured their aesthetic imagination and moral passion into often-utopian visions of a better society. They began to ask what Russia as a whole had been and what it might become. Past history was seen as defining future destiny, and questions about both past and future soon merged into the single issue of determining Russia's distinctive national identity.

No nation ever poured more intellectual energy into answering the question of national identity than Russia. A nonaristocratic, self-taught journalist from Irkutsk, Nicholas Polevoi, pointed the way to a broader concept of Russia as a nation by writing a six-volume *History of the Russian People* (1829–1833). The title was a rebuke to Nicholas Karamzin's (*History of the Russian State*) focus solely on the government, and to another conservative historian, Mikhail Pogodin, who predicted a "grandiose and almost infinite future" for Russia in his inaugural lecture as professor of history at Moscow University in 1832.

The euphoria articulated by Pogodin was broken by the publication in 1836 of Peter Chaadaev's *Philosophical Letter*, which shocked the imperial establishment by describing Moscow as "Necropolis" (city of the dead) and Russia as a part of geography rather than history with no real identity of its own. Pronounced insane, he replied with his *Apology of a Madman*, suggesting that Russia's very lateness in development would enable her to do better than Western nations. This was, in essence, the basic prophecy/hope/conceit that ignited the debate that followed between Slavophiles and Westernizers.

The Slavophile/Westernizer debate was the first open discussion ever held in Russia on the subject of national identity—and perhaps the most famous and seminal of all such debates in a traditional country confronting the intrusion of more advanced foreign models. Both of the contending parties were deeply influenced by Western thought. Both believed that Russia had a unique role to play in history that differed from the official nationalism and militarism of Nicholas I.

The Slavophiles saw Russia as a unique civilization combining the virtues of the Orthodox faith, Slavic ethnicity, and the communal institutions and decision-making procedures of an overwhelmingly peasant population. For them, Russia was a suprapolitical force, capable of healing by the power of its example both the social divisions within Russia and the spiritual wounds of a Europe ravaged by revolution and war. They saw all of human history as a struggle between spiritual and material forces. The poet Fedor Tiutchev described it as cosmos versus chaos; the philosopher Alexis Khomiakov, in his *Sketches of Universal History*, as a perpetual struggle between the spirit of Iran and of Kush.[2]

In Khomiakov's view, Iranians believed in God, inner freedom, and artistic creativity; Kushites, in material force and sensual gratification. The latter had triumphed when Rome conquered Greece and when Byzantine formalism and Prussian militarism were superimposed on Slavic spontaneity. The Jews, the original bearers of the Iranian spirit, had now passed on their role as a chosen people to the unspoiled Russians, whose family feeling, closeness to nature, and oral folklore kept alive the possibility of a future harmony among all people.

The Westernizers sought to bring the search for a new Russian identity down "from the blue skies into the kitchen" in the words of radical journalist Vissarion Belinsky.[3] With the coming of railroads, telegraphy, and the steam-driven printing press in the 1840s, St. Petersburg's "window to the West" widened into a broad gateway. Many new Western answers to Russian problems streamed in to challenge the romantic theories of the Slavophiles.

Their leader Timofei Granovsky suggested a new Westward-looking approach to history in the elegant lectures he delivered during his long tenure as professor of history at the University of Moscow from 1839 to 1855. He inspired a new generation of students by bringing a liberal perspective into a bastion of traditionalism.

Granovsky had studied in Berlin and accepted the basic Hegelian concept of history as a rational process through which the dialectic of thought leads to the liberation of society. But he was also fully conversant with the works of English and French liberal historians. He introduced in his lectures a comparative perspective that seemed to suggest that constitutional monarchy was preferable to autocracy and that there were precedents in Russian history for outcomes other than the repressive rule of Nicholas I.

Broadly speaking, the Slavophiles argued that the identity and destiny of Russia lay in faith and family and in the spiritual values and communal institutions of rural Russia. The Westernizers stressed the desirability and inevitability of more individual freedom, legal accountability in government, and greater openness to the international commerce in which Russia was, in any case, increasingly involved.

The issue between the two camps was not just East versus West or the past versus the future. Each camp found models to praise in both the Russian past and the contemporary West. The Slavophiles idealized the religiosity of pre-Petrine Moscow and the reflective tranquility of contemporary Oxford. The Westernizers idealized the proto-parliament of medieval Novgorod and the bustling vitality of contemporary London.

The liberal Westernizers seemed to have been vindicated by the sweeping reforms introduced by Tsar Alexander II (1855–1881). He freed the serfs and instituted trial by jury and a measure of local self-government in the early 1860s. But two new and deeply divergent views of Russian politics arose from the left and the right to challenge the moderate, liberal identity that the Anglophile Alexander initially seemed to be constructing.

A socialist path on the left was opened up in the emigration by Granovsky's student and lifelong friend Alexander Herzen.[4] Herzen saw the Slavophiles and Westernizers as two heads of a single Janus, whose common heart beat for the Russian people in opposition to the heartless rule of Nicholas I. But he wanted to go beyond the legal reforms of Alexander II to realize in Russia the socialist society that the West itself had failed to produce in the unsuccessful revolutions of 1848.

Herzen came to believe that his radical, Westernizing ideal might be advanced in Russia by using the peasant commune as the vehicle for a socialist transformation. The revolutionary populism that subsequently developed in Russia was inspired by the inherently implausible idea that a Russian institution beloved by conservative Slavophiles could help realize in Russia a radical Western ideal that had just been rejected by the West itself.

After and beyond the liberal and populist stages of the Westernizing movement, yet another, revolutionary, wing emerged from the detritus of Russian Hegelianism. Like the second, radical generation of young Hegelians in Germany, the literary critic Belinsky and the explosive anarchist Mikhail Bakunin rejected Hegel's idealism but saw revolutionary change coming in a dialectical, Hegelian manner. The present, seemingly victorious social "thesis" (the rule of kings and commerce) was to be destroyed by its revolutionary "antithesis" (thinkers in tune with history). This heroic process of "negation of negation" led by a new type of "world historical figure" would lift mankind up from the bonds of necessity to the realm of freedom.

The ultimate effect of Hegel's philosophy of history in Germany proved to be a "right Hegelianism" that glorified an idealized nation-state as the culmination of history. But Hegel impacted Russia primarily with his dialectical method, which was seen as legitimizing the total rejection of the existing Russian state. Hegel's dialectical idealism briefly tranquilized the notoriously "furious" Belinsky into a "reconciliation with reality" in the early 1840s, but subsequently led Belinsky and the next generation of Russian intellectuals to revolution through a kind of dialectic of its own.

The militantly materialistic "men of the 1860s" rebelled against all forms of idealism and were called "nihilists" by older liberals in Turgenev's classic novel of 1862, *Fathers and Children*. Yet another generation in the 1890s synthesized the old dialectical method with the new materialism into the revolutionary dialectical materialism of yet another left Hegelian product of the University of Berlin, Karl Marx.

The Rise of Nationalism

The new mass society and urban journalism gave birth in the late nineteenth century to a secular Russian nationalism within the multinational empire. A conservative view of Russian identity had opened up to the right of Alexander II's moderate liberalism and dominated Russian thinking and politics into the early twentieth century. This conservatism was most persuasively argued and responsibly codified in the longest and best-documented history of Russia ever written: the twenty-nine–volume work produced by Sergei Solovev between 1851 and his death in 1879, *History of Russia from the Most Ancient Times.*

Earlier semiofficial historians of Russia Vasily Tatishchev and Karamzin had basically written imperial histories "of the government of all the Russians" (*gosudarstva rossiiskago*). Pogodin's history of "the people" was the romantic tale of popular loyalty to imperialist policy. Solovev wrote an archivally based narrative of an organic nation as if it had a life of its own. The people within Russia's expanding borders were parts of a single body, and Solovev purported to tell how that body grew not just in physical stature but also in "national self-awareness" (*narodnoe samosoznanie*).[5]

This was classical nineteenth-century nationalistic history. But whereas most chroniclers of European nations in that era were legitimizing a struggle for freedom from oppression, Solovev's history basically praised the Russian nation for resisting change to its authoritarian government. Solovev criticized Alexander II's liberal reforms as attempting to ride a horse without the bridle and reins that a monarch should always have at his command. Solovev became the tutor of the future Tsar Alexander III (1881–1894), who attempted to rein in all pressure for change.

Whereas the relatively compact and ethnically homogeneous states of Western Europe turned outward to build new empires overseas in the 1880s and 1890s, Russia's already vast and multiethnic land empire turned inward in search of some unifying identity of its own. Italy and Germany had just unified by creating ethnic-linguistic nationalisms based on the raw power of Piedmont and Prussia rather than on the liberal idealism of the romantic revolutionaries of 1848. Under Alexander III, Russia attempted to create—for the first time in its history—a secular nationalism based on language and ethnicity.

"Russification" was an unevenly implemented policy designed to counter growing nationalistic and separatist sentiments on the periphery of the Russian empire. Poland, Finland, and the nations of the Baltic and Caucasus all spoke different languages and had prior histories of political independence. The enforced teaching of nationalistic Russian history and the Russian language provoked a nationalist reaction not only in these non-Slavic lands but even in the closely related Ukraine. There were also stirrings in relatively new areas of Russian rule in Central Asia, where a growing Muslim population was subject to a Christian tsar.

In an age of growing industrialization, literary realism, and philosophical materialism, romantic ideals had lost their appeal. The secular nationalism of late nineteenth-century Russians was increasingly defined negatively—in terms of the external enemies they opposed and the internal scapegoats they victimized. After revolutionary populists assassinated Tsar Alexander II in 1881, anti-Semitic pogroms began almost immediately, and the popular press began portraying Jews as opponents of—if not conspirators against—an authentic Russian identity. Russians were stung by the fact that Christian nations like England and France had joined Muslim Turkey in defeating Russia during the Crimean War. Russians were further outraged by the poor treatment they received at the Berlin Peace Conference of 1878 after defeating the Turks in the Balkans. Many Russians began to see Europe itself as their enemy.

Using sweeping ideological terms rather than the traditional language of diplomacy, the biologist and former radical Nicholas Danilevsky described Russia as locked in a Darwinistic struggle for the survival of the fittest with the "Romano-Germanic" West in his *Russia and Europe* of 1868.[6] Russia was the heir to a peace-loving and contemplative Greco-Byzantine alternative. To preserve its very identity, Orthodox Russia must prepare for war against Europe. The Slavic peoples of the Balkans must be defended not just against the Muslim Ottomans but even more against treacherous Austria, which had failed to support its Russian ally in the Crimean conflict. Danilevsky traced a multistaged pattern in history whereby the Slavs would ultimately prevail over the "Arians" of the West. The Russian victory in the Balkan war with Turkey in 1877–1878 seemed to vindicate this kind of cultural and racial nationalism.

A nationalistic mass journalism made various attempts to define Russian identity in terms of its external enemies. Kaiser Wilhelm II of

Germany, who was losing his alliance with Russia in the 1890s, personally encouraged Tsar Nicholas II to become a great Pacific power and help combat the "yellow peril." The completion of the Trans-Siberian railroad and victory over China in the war of 1894–1895 encouraged many Russians to think of themselves as the defenders of the white race, if not of European civilization.

At the dawn of the twentieth century, secular nationalism involved Russification at home and occasional dreams of pan-Asian, as well as pan-Slavic, expansion abroad. The radical-turned-reactionary, Moscow-based journalist Mikhail Katkov had made liberation of the Slavs under Turkish domination a popular cause in the twenty years between the government-sponsored Moscow Pan-Slav Congress of 1867 and his death in 1887. In the years that followed, the St. Petersburg-based journalist Esper Ukhtomsky championed a similar expansion into Asia while acting as director of the new Russo-Chinese Bank and serving as one of the directors of the Manchurian spur to the Trans-Siberian Railroad.

The emptiness of popular chauvinism and the overextension and fragility of the empire became evident when Russia began losing, rather than winning, wars. Russia's defeat by Japan in 1904–1905 and by Germany in 1914–1917 led to a series of revolutions and the eventual installation of a new communist system that purported to supersede nationality and nationalism altogether.

Defeat did not seem possible to most Russians in 1913 as they watched the Romanovs celebrate the 300th anniversary of their dynasty.[7] The economy had been growing and freedoms expanding. Mild constitutional limitations had been placed on autocracy and a kind of parliament created in the wake of the Revolution of 1905. Most leading revolutionaries had fled abroad, and the Russian people seemed united as they marched off to battle in 1914 against the Germanic oppressors of their Orthodox Slavic brethren in Serbia.

By that time, a nationalistic view of Russian history had been all but institutionalized in the popular journals and elementary schools of an increasingly literate population. Russians were encouraged to see themselves as a long-suffering people with much folk wisdom drawn

from their closeness to nature and their heroic history. Saints and soldiers were the designated heroes of a narrative stressing conflict with
both the East (Mongols, Muslims, and now China and Japan) and the
West (Teutonic knights, Poles, Swedes, Napoleon, and now the Germans). The deepest threats came from traitors, bad advisers, and petty
functionaries who stood between and thwarted the presumed goodness of both ordinary people and the tsar. Russian strength lay in the
native ingenuity of its people and the vastness of a land that provided
both physical protection and metaphysical inspiration.

There were, of course, a growing number of sophisticated discussions about which policy to adopt and which official was making this
or that mistake. But the prevailing popular view was essentially myth-
ical rather than critical. General indifference to social and economic
questions at the national level and naive idealization of past events
and heroes basically echoed the original monumental histories of Russia, which had rarely discussed policy questions of current relevance
and never carried the story to anywhere near the present.

From Tatishchev's panegyric *History of Russia from Earliest Times*
(1739) to Vasily Kliuchevsky's occasionally critical and sociologically
sophisticated *Course of Russian History* (1905–1911), the great historians
tended to avoid dealing directly with contemporary controversies. All of
them—implicitly, if not explicitly—legitimized "Russia" as a geographic
entity entitled to all the lands described in the lengthy imperial title.
This included "all the Russias"—Great, Small, and White—and all other
contiguous, non-Slavic lands that recognized the sovereignty of the tsar.
Great Russians were the main actors in the drama, with other Eurasian
peoples filling out a *dramatis personae* who were "of Russia" (*rossiiskii*),
not just ethnically or linguistically "Russian" (*russkii*).

While there was no real sense of secular national identity for Russia
prior to the nineteenth century, there had been a strong feeling of cultural distinctiveness.[8] It was based on both fidelity to the Orthodox
faith and the closeness to nature of a peasant culture. Already in the
popular culture of the late seventeenth century, Russian Old Believers
used the term *rusak* to describe those who resisted foreign ways of living and worshipping. The great martyr to the old church rituals, the

Archpriest Avvakum, used the term to suggest someone who is physically strong and spiritually faithful in his allegiance to indigenous Russian traditions. He addressed Tsar Alexis by his patronymic, appealing to familial as well as protonational loyalty in an unsuccessful attempt to fend off the reform of Russian church rituals according to Greek models: "You, Mikhailovich, are a rusak, not a Greek."[9]

"Rusak" is a now rare, but clearly protonationalistic word used to describe a variety of distinctive peasant foods as well as the gray hare that inhabits the deep Russian interior. The term seemed to express special endearment for those who cling to native Russian ways amidst foreigners. The familiar form *rusachok* was used to praise the "wise" and "dear" who "are thrust into the fire but do not betray the true faith."[10]

Various nouns and adjectives based on the root word "Rus" or "Ros" were used to describe Orthodox Eastern Slavs without any clear indication of their geographic location or ethnic identity. Beginning with the Muscovite conquest of much of the Ukraine and Belarus under Tsar Alexis in the third quarter of the seventeenth century, the modern forms of those roots (with two s's rather than one) began to be used to designate all Russian-speaking, Orthodox subjects of the tsar.[11] There was sometimes a presumption of geographic location in Great Russia to the north. Subjects of the tsar who were not necessarily from Great Russia or even Orthodox Slavs were sometimes called *rossichi;* European Russians, *rossiiushka;* and Russians who migrated east to Asia, *rosseiskie.*[12]

The single "s" form continued to be used, particularly by Eastern Slavs who fell under Western jurisdiction, became Catholic or simply felt more kinship with Kievan Rus than with the new Muscovite Rossiia. Those in Hapsburg-controlled Galicia used the term *rusin* for themselves; those in Polish-controlled Lithuania used *rusman* and *rusmanka* for Russian.[13] Many words and sayings were popularly employed to suggest that there was, indeed, something distinctive about being a real Russian *muzhik.* But people in imperial Russia tended to identify themselves more by rank, profession, family, and faith than by nationality.

The explosion of artistic creativity in nineteenth-century Russia—and particularly of a vernacular literature charged with moral and prophetic content—intensified feelings of cultured distinctiveness and national pride. But a clearly articulated and coherent secular nationalism never fully emerged before the twentieth century.

2 | The Twentieth-Century Search for Legitimacy

Tumultuous social upheavals and disastrous defeats in war deepened the search for identity into a search for basic political legitimacy during the first two decades of the twentieth century. An essentially archaic empire could no longer count on the passivity of its increasingly educated and restive population. Questions that had mainly involved a small group of intellectuals in the nineteenth century were taken up with greater urgency by a far wider range of participants. They were asking who should exercise what kind of authority over whom in the Russian empire.

Three new approaches to defining Russian identity appeared during this period, and have continued to develop during and after the Soviet era. First came a cultural and religious view that sought to transcend and avoid politics in the last years of tsarist rule. Second came a sociological and antireligious view that put its faith totally in political action and became the official, legitimating ideology for Soviet rule. Third came an ethnic-geographical view of a nonimperial Russian nation that struggled in the postcommunist era both to gain the spiritual sanction of the first view and to regain the political power and dexterity of the second.

The Russian Idea

A purely cultural view of Russian identity grew out of the sudden flowering of Russian artistic, religious, and philosophical creativity in the "Silver Age" at the beginning of the twentieth century. Dostoevsky originated the thought that "the Russian idea" could provide an identity and mission for Russia in the world. In 1861, he criticized both Westernizers and Slavophiles for lacking "a feeling for the Russian spirit" and closeness to the soil (*pochva*).

> We know that we will not cut ourselves off from humanity with what is now already a Chinese wall; that the character of our future activity can, in the highest degree, involve all humanity; that the Russian idea can be the synthesis of all those ideas that . . . Europe is developing in its separate nationalities [*natsional'nostiiakh*]; that perhaps everything that is hostile in these ideas will find its reconciliation and further development in the Russian nationality [*narodnost'*].[1]

Further definition of this "Russian idea" came later from the reigning thinker of the Silver Age, Vladimir Solovev. In a lecture in Paris entitled, "The Russian Idea," he declared in 1888 that "the idea of a nation is not that which it thinks about itself in time, but that which God thinks about it in eternity."[2] A nation, however, "may not understand its own calling." Solovev's Russian contemporaries might think that they are called to fight for the Slavs in the Balkans, but their real calling is to bring unity to Christianity and Christianity to the world. Artistic creativity was assumed to be a spiritual calling because—in the famous phrase of Dostoevsky—"beauty will save the world."

Solovev sought a peaceful and spiritual identity for a Russia that would exercise an essentially nonviolent and apolitical role among the nations. A more nationalistic twist was given to this belief in a distinctive "Russian idea" by Nicholas Berdiaev. In his *Fate of Russia*, an essay on war and nationality written in 1918, Berdiaev characterized Russia as a land of extremist contradictions: authoritarian and anarchistic impulses, rank chauvinism and deep embarrassment about one's country, paralytic servility before external authority and limitless internal, spiritual freedom.

Berdiaev had feared that the Russian nation would continue to be held back by the passivity of Russia's "eternally womanish" (*vechno bab'e*) population. He had hoped in 1915 that World War I would produce "a breakthrough of Russia's masculine spirit"[3]; but, when the "breakthrough" ended up producing a communist revolution, Berdiaev, like many other key thinkers and artists of the Silver Age, was summarily deported in 1922. Initially in Berlin but mostly in Paris, he became, until his death in 1948, the most prolific and influential writer on Russian identity among Russian émigrés.

From the beginning of World War I in his *Soul of Russia* until just after World War II in his *Russian Idea*, Berdiaev produced numerous writings suggesting that the essence of the Russian nation lay in the spiritual striving of its creative thinkers and artists. Russians were essentially pilgrims, "wanderers over the Russian land," who were inspired but left in disorder by Russia's vast expanses:

> In the Russian soul there is a sort of immensity, vagueness, a predilection for the infinite, such as is suggested by the great plain of Russia . . . , a vast elemental strength combined with a comparatively weak sense of form.[4]

The path to deliverance from Russia's various ordeals pointed beyond geography to history. Russia had—for Berdiaev as for Solovev—a providential mission and an ultimately Christian destiny. For Berdiaev, however, the end in view for Russia had become not so much Solovev's vision of universal confessional reconciliation but the more nationalistic belief that Russian society would somehow come to embody a Christianity more vital than that of any other existing Christian country.

> The New Jerusalem is not to be torn away from the vast Russian land . . . [and its] soil leads to the New Jerusalem.[5]

Unfortunately, Russia was producing in the interwar period not a New Jerusalem but a Stalinist dictatorship. Berdiaev, like many creative figures of the Silver Age, held a basically aesthetic and apolitical view of the world. He had been a key contributor to the landmark publication, *Vekhi* (Signposts), which had called the Russian intelligentsia back to philosophical idealism and religious faith; and he subsequently wrote an admiring biography of the reactionary neo-Byzantine thinker Constantine Leontiev.

Shortly after his forced emigration, he wrote in Berlin an anti-egalitarian *Philosophy of Inequality*,[6] and he later identified in Paris with French Christian personalism—the very opposite of Russian secular collectivism. But Berdiaev never shook off the predilection of the Russian intelligentsia for seeing history as a progressive process of secular deliverance. Precisely as Soviet rule entered its most repressive and inhumane phase in the 1930s, Berdiaev began to develop a more benign view of the Soviet regime.

In his influential *The Sources and Sense of Russian Communism* of 1936,[7] he portrayed Soviet communism less as an adaptation of Western Marxism than as a variant of historic Russian communalism, less as a militant atheistic system bent on destroying religion than as a kind of Christian heresy rising up against the unworthiness of nominal Christians. Although he himself never returned even to visit the USSR, he counseled many Russian émigrés to return to Stalinist Russia immediately after World War II.

In tracing a distinctive Russian genealogy for Soviet communism, Berdiaev listed many of the same radical thinkers that communist ideologists were using to legitimize themselves. The sacred lineage began with Radishchev's late eighteenth-century critique of Russian social conditions, continued through the time of the martyred Decembrists of 1825, gathered force with aristocratic radicals such as Alexander Herzen in the 1840s and 1850s, gained focus with the nonaristocratic "nihilists" of the 1860s, became revolutionary with terrorists (the first time that term was ever used as a badge of pride) in the 1870s and 1880s, and gained a coherent philosophy of history with the advent of Marxism in the 1890s and early 1900s.

Russian Marxism provided a fresh way of affirming the core belief of the alienated Russian intelligentsia: that history has a liberating destiny that can be realized by an elite committed to revolutionary change. In his later years, Berdiaev seems to have seen Marxism as a dialectically prerequisite phase for a purified Christianity. The New Jerusalem would occur in Russia precisely because the apocalypse foreseen in the Book of Revelations had prepared the way.

Utopian Ideocracy

Vladimir Lenin's Bolshevik variant of communism synthesized the conspiratorial political terrorism of revolutionary populism with the scientific pretensions of Marxism. Lenin's revered older brother had been a martyr of the terrorist tradition, and Lenin used the new weapon of Marxism to impose discipline and provide "scientific" legitimacy for the coup d'état that brought him to power amidst the chaos of 1917.[8]

The Russian intelligentsia's opposition to the existing order was useful in preparing society for a revolution but useless in preparing revolutionaries to govern. Lenin's "party of a new type" was conceived from the beginning as a kind of rival to the intelligentsia. In contrast to intellectuals who purported to speak truth to power but accomplished little for the people, Lenin focused his Bolshevik party on gaining power in order to bring truth to the people.

In his key treatise of 1917, *State and Revolution*, Lenin's only suggestion of how revolutionaries would govern after attaining power was that they could resolve conflicts "as simply and lightly as any crowd of civilized people, even in modern society, interferes to stop a scuffle or prevent a woman from being assaulted." Revolutionary rule would require "no special machine, no special apparatus of suppression."[9]

This astonishingly utopian view had a certain appeal for intellectual believers in total human perfectibility. And a good number initially accepted the Bolsheviks' invitation to join the "armed people" in the new life of revolutionary struggle. But the "party of a new type" soon began destroying not just the old intelligentsia but also all other pockets of resistance to its own self-appointed role as the vanguard leader of the "armed people."

Communist power was not fully secured until the end of the long "time of troubles" that began when the tsarist empire went to war in the summer of 1914 and ended with the formal establishment of the new Union of Soviet Socialist Republics in the winter of 1922. Moscow, once seen as the "third Rome" with a universal Christian mission, had become in 1919 the founding site of a "Third International" with a universal, revolutionary mission. The Leninist party in Russia literally became a branch of a new World Communist Party that repudiated the open democratic approach of the Social Democratic Second International. Although the new communist regime totally rejected past tradition, it had to use new versions of old symbols to gain popular legitimacy. The charismatic Lenin died in 1924, and his worshipful successors entombed him in an underground shrine in Red Square in much the way that the original saints of Rus had been preserved in the Monastery of the Caves in Kiev. Joseph Stalin, the former seminarian and future successor to leadership, intoned a set of catechistic pledges of fidelity to Lenin at his funeral. The first, most fundamental and most enduring element in the new legitimacy—a quasireligious cult of veneration for an allegedly infallible political leader—was thus established at the very beginning of the new political entity.

The dead Lenin became a kind of Christ figure for the new hagiography and iconography that replaced the old. He was later construed more as a John the Baptist preparing the way for a divinized Stalin. His successors as general secretaries of the Communist Party attempted to depict themselves as part of an apostolic succession of leaders delivering humanity from the bondage of feudalism through the ravages of capitalism to the earthly paradise of a supranational egalitarian society.

A major achievement of the new Soviet regime was its ability to create a measure of legitimacy for the inherently implausible idea that an absolute dictatorship could create absolute human happiness anywhere—let alone everywhere. Communist leaders provided a new materialistic and scientific garb for the Russian intelligentsia's basic

Hegelian belief that history is a rational process that moves through contradictory phases toward a liberating conclusion. This core view had been put in Marxist form for Russians in the 1890s by George Plekhanov, a former populist. His emphasis on the controlling power of economic forces had enabled a new generation of Russian thinkers to move once again "from the blue skies to the kitchen." The despair induced by the defeat of revolutionary populism and the growing inequalities imposed by early industrialization seemed to be dispelled by the heady idea that Russia's new capitalist phase would be short-lived and would "dialectically" produce a proletariat that would destroy capitalism and create a new classless society.

Lenin himself made the two essential modifications in Marxist ideology that enabled it to legitimize a revolutionary mission for Russia. He expanded, in his *Two Tactics of Social Democracy* of 1905, the concept of the "proletariat" to include poor peasants as well as the urban workers that Marx had envisaged as supplanting the bourgeoisie and ending all class warfare. And he suggested in *State and Revolution* that an interim "dictatorship of the proletariat" would be needed to prepare a still backward, largely rural Russia for the transition to a classless society. The dictatorship would soon thereafter, he insisted, "wither away" as the new communist society came into being. What withered away, of course, was the idea that a dictatorship would itself wither away in a country with an authoritarian tradition.

This allegedly temporary dictatorship was given a long-term lease by the second legitimizing instrument of Soviet rule: Lenin's concept of leadership by a secret, ideologically based, party elite. Lenin set forth this antidemocratic idea in his seminal pamphlet of 1902, *What Is To Be Done?*, proclaiming on the very first page that "a party grows stronger by purging itself." He brought such a party into being the next year by splitting his Bolshevik faction away from the more democratic Menshevik group within the rising Russian Social Democratic Party.

Lenin's new type of party appropriated, in effect, two roles that the radical intelligentsia had often claimed for itself: the exclusive right to speak both as an interpreter of historical truth and as a servant of the suffering Russian people. It followed inexorably that the old intellectuals, as rival definers of truth and pretenders to service, could have no place in a Russia whose ruling party called its daily newspaper "Truth" (*Pravda*).

The Bolshevik Communist Party was conceived by Lenin as providing "consciousness" for the workers and poor peasants. If left solely to their own devices, the lower classes would succumb to self-defeating "spontaneity," either lashing out with futile uprisings or settling for minor economic handouts. Lenin's new party sought to combat both "infantilism" and "adventurism" on the left and "trade unionism" and "tail-endism" on the right. His party focused on devising a strategy for gaining power and for imposing its secretly determined tactical imperatives on the masses and their inchoate revolutionary aspirations.

Once the Bolsheviks prevailed in the civil war that followed the revolution of 1917, they had to develop a political strategy for ruling Russia and for legitimating the authority they were imposing on a very large country. The Bolsheviks devised a way of both sustaining their pretension to being agents of historical inevitability while, at the same time, justifying all the zigs and zags that effective government would require. The "party line" became the key tool of governance. The party elite, the alleged executors of historical truth, defined it in secret conclaves and legitimized all its twists and turns as ways to avoid either "left" or "right" deviations.

The militant and hierarchical party in charge justified everything in terms of an allegedly scientific ideology, and it proceeded to build a far more totalistic and intrusive autocracy than had ever been seen before. The "general line of the party" was defined by the "political bureau" and imposed from the top down by party members animated by the supreme new virtue of *partiinost'* (sacrificial party spirit).

Stalin developed a new technique, an "artificial dialectic," for forcing one mass mobilization campaign after another on his brutalized subjects.[10] Whenever the party line began to change, the Bolshevik executors of the previous line were denounced, humiliated, and purged as a kind of consolation prize for the suffering masses. The way was then open for the next campaign and a repetition of the process by which both the party and the population were manipulated and controlled by small inner circles centered on the party's supreme leader. Party members lived in perpetual fear of being purged for Trotskyism, Bukharinism, or other heresies, which always bore the names of an allegedly errant former associate of the infallible leader.

These techniques continued to be used but lost their legitimizing force after the death of Stalin in 1953. His successor, Nikita Khrushchev, began to unravel the mystique of the omniscient leader in February 1956 with his partial denunciation of Stalin's "cult of personality" at the 20th Party Congress. The apostolic succession and myth of infallibility were broken, and it became progressively more difficult to sustain the other distinctive elements that had been used to legitimate communist rule.

The idea that the Soviet Communist Party was leading a global, revolutionary movement waned in the 1930s. An obligatory Russocentric view of history was introduced by Stalin to fortify the fading legitimacy of Soviet power based on communist ideology. He rejected Mikhail Pokrovsky's previously canonized Marxist approach that had emphasized impersonal class conflict and virtually eliminated any mention of individual leaders. To give human appeal to Russian history and to legitimize his own purges and calls for sacrifice, Stalin developed a new narrative depicting Russia as a perpetual victim of external invasions and internal betrayals.

The Party redefined its role as building "socialism in one country"; and Stalin forced unprecedented suffering and social upheaval on the people of the USSR through coercive collectivization of agriculture, ruthless industrialization, massive purges, and an "archipelago" of slave labor camps. Later ideological rationalizations under Leonid Brezhnev about the need to achieve "developed socialism" before reaching classless communism did little to camouflage the reality of an inward-looking, repressive totalitarianism presided over by a "new class" of party functionaries. The Third International (Comintern) had been dissolved in 1943, and its pallid, postwar successor, the Communist Information Bureau (Cominform), was shut down in 1956.

For more than thirty years thereafter, Soviet communism sustained its authority internationally by remaining a military superpower and by periodically staging, with its American rival, summits that focused attention on the one arena in which the two sides were evenly matched: weapons of mass destruction. Power was exercised within the USSR by an ever-growing bureaucracy of Communist Party *apparatchiks* and security forces. Communist ideology lost its legitimizing force as leadership passed from Khrushchev to evermore aged and infirm hands: Brezhnev, Yury Andropov, and Constantine Chernenko. Power was transferred from one leader to his successor by a grotesque ritual within the Politburo of the Central Committee (briefly dignified with the name "Presidium" under Khrushchev). The "black file" with all its potentially compromising information on all other party leaders (including the outgoing general secretary) was solemnly passed on to the incoming general secretary.[11]

The system had lost legitimacy with the populace it ruled, but elite opinion both inside and outside the USSR assumed that the Soviet system would remain basically unchanged for the foreseeable future. In one of the most ambitious studies ever made of the Soviet system, forty Western experts, representing many disciplines and points of view, published in 1983 a study that was summarized in the preface with these words:

> All of us agree that there is no likelihood whatsoever that the Soviet Union will become a political democracy, or that it will collapse in the foreseeable future, or that it will become a congenially peaceful member of the international community for as far ahead as one can see.[12]

Two years later, the new and much younger figure of Mikhail Gorbachev became general secretary and began the process of change that invalidated every one of these consensus conclusions.

Great Russian Nationalism

More than has been generally understood even in Russia, Great Russian nationalism was a driving force in creating Soviet totalitarianism, in propping it up and prolonging its life span, and even in eventually dismantling it. Nationalist belief in all things Russian became a major legitimizing factor for the Soviet empire under Stalin in the 1930s, once the initial belief in communist internationalism had faded. Then, after Stalin's death in 1953, Khrushchev combined a partial "thaw" in cultural controls with a kind of communist revivalism (more giant projects at home and new support for revolutionaries abroad). This unstable mix gave rise to a "primordial" nationalism in Russian culture that rejected the modernization imposed by communist central planners with their forced urbanization and destruction of traditional values.[13]

During the long period of stagnation under Brezhnev (1964–1982), Soviet leaders made serious attempts to co-opt the emotional appeal of this "village prose" and to fortify an ossified communist ideology with the flesh and blood of Russian nationalism.[14] When the Soviet Union itself began to lose cohesion in the course of the 1980s, a hitherto little-known figure from the propaganda department of the Communist Central Committee, Gennady Zyuganov, tried to forge a political alliance with extremist, nationalist ideologists who had been promoted to prominence by the Brezhnev regime.[15] This was the first of many efforts to forge a left–right or "red–brown" political bloc in opposition to liberalization. They did not succeed in blocking the Gorbachev reforms or in holding the Soviet Union together. But their coming together in 1990–1991 pointed to the nationalist direction that Zyuganov, the emerging new communist leader, would take in his continuing struggle against democratization in post-Soviet Russia.

It may seem paradoxical that a kind of Russian nationalism also helped to delegitimize the communist system in its last days, as well as to keep the final breakup of the USSR peaceful. But, in effect, the instrumental imperial nationalism that had been promoted for political purposes by communist ideologists proved far less popular than the quiet development of the gut conclusion that an artificial and inhumane imperial system was destroying the values, ecology, and economy of the core Russian nation itself.

In June 1991, the citizens of the Russian Republic of the USSR overwhelmingly elected as president Boris Yeltsin, who had already decisively repudiated communism. His firm presence in the Moscow White House, the government building of the Russian Republic in August

1991, anchored the resistance to the hard-line communist coup d'état that briefly claimed control of the entire Soviet Union in August 1991. Only when the Russian government faced down its nominal Soviet overlords and, in effect, seceded from the imperial communist state were the other national republics able to establish their own independence. Because the breakup of the USSR was achieved by Russians asserting their national pride (as well as their determination to gain the benefits of Western freedoms), other nations were freer to express similar sentiments; and the Soviet federation devolved peacefully into constituent nations rather than violently into Yugoslav-type ethnic warfare.

Political nationalism with imperial overtones has, however, not only survived, but has also become a growing rhetorical staple for ambitious politicians in post-Soviet Russia. While neither Zyuganov nor any other aspiring opposition leader was able to form a coalition capable of gaining power, Vladimir Putin increasingly co-opted nationalistic causes to sustain his power. The kind of primitive nationalism promoted in the Soviet era has persisted in popular thinking—and remains an important, if partly subliminal, legacy of the twentieth century and of Joseph Stalin, the non-Russian autocrat of the USSR, to those struggling to legitimize pluralism in a more ethnically Russian Russia.

* * * * *

In order to mount his internal social revolution of forced industrialization and agricultural collectivization, Stalin found that he had to motivate the predominantly Russian masses of the USSR with something more down to earth and close to home than communist theory. As he filled concentration camps and purged all forms of real and imagined resistance, Stalin also needed to sustain his authority. Increasingly, the ethnic Georgian dictator fell back on an ethnic Russian nationalism that cultivated fear of foreign enemies, focused hatred on alleged domestic traitors, and used Jews and other ethnic minorities as scapegoats.

The Union of Soviet Socialist Republics was the first significant sovereign power in the modern world that contained neither an ethnic nor a geographical designation in its official name. Stalin, a non-Russian from a small principality in the Caucasus, had studied, like Hitler, the role of ethnicity and nationalism in the multinational Hapsburg empire. Lenin chose Stalin to form a nationality policy for the multi-ethnic USSR; but, in a long-suppressed political testament written shortly before his death, Lenin warned against the secretive Georgian's inclination toward "Great Russian chauvinism." That, indeed, proved to be Stalin's fallback position in the late 1930s when his perpetual purges and mobilization campaigns threatened to paralyze or fatally weaken the USSR.

Stalin began to promote a superhuman image of himself as the greatest of all Great Russians, radiating omnipotence and omniscience out of the Moscow Kremlin, draped in the trappings more evocative of an emperor than a proletarian leader. Pictures of Ivan the Terrible and Peter the Great were hung in his office along with those of Marx and Lenin. Stalin directed the new art form of cinema away from depicting cardboard communists versus caricatured capitalists to the patriotic glorification of past Russian heroes resisting foreign invaders.

The great Soviet filmmaker, Sergei Eisenstein, had created in his silent films (*The Battleship Potemkin* of 1924 and *October* in 1928) a montage of images idealizing the proletariat's revolution against the bourgeoisie. Then, on the eve of World War II, he added the evocative power of Sergei Prokofiev's music to produce *Alexander Nevsky*, the compelling saga of a divided Russia coming together to repel a thirteenth-century Teutonic invasion, prophetically anticipating the new German invasion that was about to begin.

The political divisions (*guberniia*) of the old Russian empire had not been defined by ethnicity. But the divisions (union republics, autonomous republics) that Stalin had drawn up for the new Soviet Union were basically defined by their dominant ethnicities. There was considerable pretense, as well as some reality, to the Soviet accommodation of linguistic and cultural diversity. But Stalin had drawn the often-arbitrary borders of many of the major non-Russian republics to include substantial minorities of an ethnicity historically hostile to the dominant one. Large numbers of ethnic Russians were zoned into the two largest republics (Ukraine and Kazakhstan) and later resettled in Estonia and Latvia when they were reconquered. Religious minorities were inserted into the domain of independent-minded republics in the Caucasus (Christian Armenians in Muslim Azerbaijan, Muslim Ossetians and Abkhazians in Christian Georgia).

This structure was useful for imperial crisis management. A dictator in the Kremlin could manipulate ethnic groups against each other in restive provinces. Russian nationalism was used as an overall disciplinary device, and the Jews (who were given no territorial base except, belatedly, the small, bleak Jewish Autonomous Region on the Chinese border) were periodically offered as scapegoats for everyone else.

The Soviet Union was, in effect, relegitimized by a genuine patriotic revival during World War II. The successful resistance to the massive German invasion required the rehabilitation of previously proscribed Russian traditions. Tsars and their military leaders and symbols were lionized; and the Russian Orthodox Church, which had been persecuted to the verge of extinction, was given an enhanced status after Stalin visited the Patriarch in 1943.

Precisely because their casualties and privations were so great in what they called "the great fatherland war," ordinary Russians attributed the eventual victory to primordial Russian virtues: "heroic action" (*podvizhnichestvo*) sustained through "long endurance" (*dolgoterpenie*) and sacrificial suffering (*stradanie*). Positive patriotism was, however, soon turned once again into negative nationalism. Stalin used the "struggle for peace" against the alleged "warmongers of the West" to dampen the postwar hopes of his subjects for continued good relations with the USSR's wartime democratic allies. In his last years, Stalin whipped up popular hatred not just against former allies but also against "rootless cosmopolitans" in Westernized Leningrad, "bourgeois nationalists" in the USSR's non-Russian republics, Jewish "doctor-poisoners" inside the Kremlin, and "enemies of the people" who were potentially everywhere.

Russian nationalism was fortified in new ways during the 1950s by the detonation of a hydrogen bomb, the development of intercontinental rockets, and the launching of Sputnik, the first man-made satellite to orbit the earth in outer space. These genuinely positive accomplishments of Soviet science raised the danger of potentially deadly use against the American rival that Khrushchev promised first to "bury," then to "overtake and surpass."

Stalin had created a large working class through forced industrialization, but he and his heirs clearly ran a dictatorship *over*, rather than *of*, the proletariat. Real power came to be exercised not so much even by the Communist Party (which had 19 million members at the end of the Soviet era) as by a hard-core, highly privileged *nomenklatura* within the Party (estimated at no more than 3 million).

Alternative role models were needed to motivate the population once the gulags were largely emptied and fear diminished in the post-Stalin period. Individual heroes returned to dominate Russian history, and special prominence was retroactively assigned to earlier military leaders and to scientific innovators who anticipated the perceived needs of the eternally endangered Russian state. Stalin, whose inexplicable trust in Hitler had rendered Russia unprepared for the German invasion of 1941, assigned himself the title of generalissimo; and his successor Khrushchev legitimized himself by initially bringing into his new leadership team an authentic military war hero, Marshal Georgy Zhukov.

By the time Zhukov was thrust aside in 1957, Russia was present in outer space and a new parade of heroes began: scientists and astronauts. Not far from where Khrushchev was eventually buried in the cemetery of the Novodevichy Monastery in Moscow stands a one-of-a-kind memorial: an oversized stone statue topped by an array of miniature, metal rocket launchers, marking the resting place of the founder of Russia's rocket program. Metal monuments of space vehicles moving upward began to appear all over Russia along with heroic statues of those extending the "space" (*prostranstvo*) so idealized by the Russian people out to the cosmos.

Whereas Soviet exploits in space created genuine national pride, there was equally genuine resentment of the expensive attempts that began with Khrushchev to project Soviet power for ideological reasons to distant places (Ethiopia, Angola, Vietnam, Cuba) with which Russia had no historic links and which seemed to serve few national interests. The invasion of Afghanistan led to growing Russian casualties and disillusionment.

A basic nationalist-authoritarian view of Russian history became frozen into place by the late Soviet period. Rustic Slavic virtues were glorified as a kind of genetic gift that predated Christianity and produced a cultural-military flowering in Kievan Rus. Then began the endless tale of persecution and victimization of the virtuous Eastern Slavs, generally described as Russians rather than Ukrainians or Belorussians. The invasion and long overlordship of Mongols from the East was followed by an even longer procession of Western invaders supported by weak or treacherous Russians disloyal to the unifying Russian leader.

The inspiring "positive heroes" that Soviet ideological commissars had long hoped would emerge from the new literature of "socialist realism" were retroactively located instead in traditional Russian history. Warrior-saints such as Alexander Nevsky and Dmitry Donskoi and warrior-tsars such as Ivan the Terrible and Peter the Great were praised along with great scientists who served the state such as Mikhail Lomonosov and an ever-shifting pantheon of contemporary "heroes of the Soviet Union."

The long "period of stagnation" under Leonid Brezhnev (1964–1982) was succeeded by an era of even more ailing and aged leaders: former KGB head Andropov and former border guard in the Ministry of the Interior (Chernenko). Russian nationalism seemed less an ideal for the young than a security blanket for the old.

After many years of geriatric leadership (beginning with Brezhnev in 1964), the nomenklatura thought the future was secure and finally chose the much younger Mikhail Gorbachev in 1985. Gorbachev had been the energetic party head in Stavropol, where aging Politburo members had often gone for rejuvenating mineral baths. The veteran Stalinist Andrei Gromyko assured his colleagues that Gorbachev combined "a nice smile" with "steel teeth." Here, presumably, was a leader who could bring new legitimacy to communist governance without succumbing to what Soviet ideologists had long denounced as "toothless vegetarianism" in their conflict with the bourgeois Western world.

The subsequent collapse of communism and the Soviet empire resulted not just from the many failures of the Soviet system but also from its one great success: the spread of education. Gorbachev was the first ruler of Russia ever to have completed his university studies. He intended to rejuvenate the party by bringing in a new and better-schooled generation. They could accelerate the "scientific and techni-cal revolution" that communist ideologists had been calling for to sus-tain a lagging economy and an overextended empire. If his talk of *perestroika* (the restructuring of institutions) remained largely an ideo-logical slogan, his commitment to *glasnost'* (open speech) was real and transformative.

As the populace became better informed about disasters such as the nuclear contamination from Chernobyl and the military failures in Afghanistan, they became more openly critical of official policies. As they gained access to information previously denied them, they had a growing desire to *discover* more about the economic and political expe-rience of the outside world. But at the same time, they sought to *recover* what had been lost in their own heritage. This gave birth to a new kind of anti-Soviet cultural nationalism.

Recovery began—literally—in a down-to-earth way. The so-called "village writers" (*derevenshchiki*) in post-Stalinist Russia started to speak up for the fading memory of rural life and the despoiled and neglected Russian provinces. Popular anger grew at the urbanized cen-tral planners who had destroyed both the values of grassroots tradition and the ecology of the Russian land.

The industrial pollution of Lake Baikal, the world's deepest lake and greatest repository of fresh water, became a particular cause célèbre in the works of the most polemical village writer, Valentin Rasputin. A native of nearby Irkutsk, Rasputin made the flooding of a village in a river basin a metaphor for Soviet communism drowning Russia itself in his *Farewell to Matyora* of 1976. He subsequently portrayed a fire in a Siberian camp as a prophetic judgment on the Soviet system (in his *Fire* of 1985).[16]

In the late 1980s when Soviet planners put forward serious new blueprints for reversing the flow of rivers in Siberia, Rasputin suggested from his newly won seat in a hitherto docile Supreme Soviet that the Russian nation itself might have to secede from the Soviet Union. That is—as noted above—technically what happened in August 1991, when Yeltsin's government prevailed against the communist coup leaders of the USSR. Yeltsin's government thereafter rapidly assumed full sovereign power over what had been a Russian subdivision of the USSR—thus becoming, in effect, the enabler of peaceful independence for all the others.

The impulses to discover the outside world and recover their own heritage challenged the absence not just of political freedom, but also of moral responsibility in the Soviet system. Learning more about postwar Western societies fed the passion for freedom. Gaining access to long-proscribed aspects of their own religious and cultural heritage stimulated thinking about personal responsibility. The great mantra of Soviet officials from top to bottom had always been, "It doesn't depend on me" (*Eto ot menia ne zavisit*). People had to make real personal decisions in the late Gorbachev era when genuine elections began to be introduced, and especially during the hard-line communist coup attempt against Gorbachev in August 1991, when the outcome was in doubt.

A democratic Russian Federation emerged from the defeat of the putsch and the subsequent implosion of the USSR. Russians were beginning to experience freedom and to accept responsibility. But it soon appeared that the new freedom was bringing a new *irresponsibility* through confiscatory privatization, official corruption, and widespread criminality. And the political legitimization that democratization might have provided was severely undermined when Yeltsin suspended and shelled the Russian parliament in October 1993. Those supporting him were largely repudiated in the parliamentary elections of December 1993.

Yeltsin was reelected president in 1996; at the end of 1999, he picked a successor, Vladimir Putin, who was elected in 2000 and proved to be a popular leader. But the Russian people felt a continuing and, in many ways, increasing need to find distinctive national elements that could give both clear identity and moral legitimacy to the new Russia.[17]

II. The Quickening Quest

The new Russia's current search for identity began in many ways during the astonishing three days in Moscow in August 1991 when the Soviet Union simply disintegrated in a way and with a speed that no one had expected—and that no one has yet satisfactorily explained. The standard explanation has been that the new *glasnost'* generation simply wanted to share in the freedoms that had brought material prosperity to the postwar Western world. This truism, however, totally fails to account for any of the following implausible, central facts about the nature and outcome of the specific crisis that precipitated the change:

- The coup was carefully planned and initially supported by almost everyone in the top Soviet leadership.[1]
- There was no significant popular uprising in support of the resistance to the coup.
- A thin human ring around some 150 armed volunteers inside Yeltsin's White House nevertheless prevailed against the 5.5 million members of the armed forces arrayed against them, almost all the leaders of whom supported the coup.
- The only top Soviet leader who finally *did* resist (Gorbachev), who had created glasnost' in the first place, was totally rejected as a leader in the process.

Witnessing those fateful seventy-six hours in Moscow, I found the situation surreal and the atmosphere around the White House more carnivalesque than revolutionary. I described it then as a fever break (*perelom*) that ended the totalitarian system[2]; but it clearly did not ensure future health for the convalescent. The August events saw society reject one type of authority without entirely establishing another. The ensuing crisis of legitimacy has not yet been resolved in the new Russia. We may begin to find clues on how a new legitimacy might finally be secured by probing one last time into exactly how the old legitimacy was disestablished in those three days of the failed coup.

What happened was something like the "withdrawal of the mandate of heaven" that periodically occurs after long periods of autocratic rule in traditional China. It can perhaps also be described as a massive, nonviolent moral revolution—somewhat analogous to the changes impelled by Martin Luther King in the United States, Nelson Mandela in South Africa, and the Solidarity movement in Poland. But the resistance had no charismatic leader like King or Mandela nor any organization like Solidarity.

What unfolded was one of those rare, one-of-a-kind sequences in history: an entirely spontaneous movement, leading to profound and immediate political change, followed by a sustained debate about the very identity of the affected nation itself. In August 1991, no one clearly issued either an appeal to defend or an order to storm the White House. With the mass media silenced and no one quite sure what was happening, the outer conflicts *between* people in Moscow suddenly became less important than the conflicts raging *inside* them. Almost everyone—those standing on both sides of the barricades and those crouching on the sidelines—

shared certain elemental feelings. These common emo-
tions were layered inside almost everyone, like the dolls-
within-dolls of a *matryoshka*.

First came fear. Tanks rolled into Moscow on August
19, 1991, as they once had with murderous effect in
Budapest and Prague. But this intimidating face of
power had come to be seen as only the thin outer shell
of the Russian matryoshka. In the three days of uncertainty that followed, Russians of all persuasions experi-
enced within themselves what was for most an altogether new feeling: personal moral responsibility.

Russians did not yet feel free, but they had to decide
individually what they would or would not say or do.
Moral revulsion was felt by those who might be asked
to shoot, no less than by those who would be targets. In
their confusing inner search for guidance, many Russians were subliminally rediscovering a Russia far different from that of autocratic power lacquered over with
Russian nationalism.

The inner force of Russian culture was breaking
through the outer shell of Soviet power. The face of Gorbachev returning from house arrest after the collapse of
the coup briefly appeared on the next doll within the
Russian matryoshka. But his image was etched on a thin
shell between the geriatric outer face of power and the
inner layer of a young generation seeking freedom. The
dramatic siege of the White House indelibly engraved
the alternative figure of Yeltsin on that inner doll.
Unlike the in-between figure of Gorbachev, Yeltsin's
image seemed to stand on solid wood.

Yeltsin brought initial legitimacy to the new democratic regime not only by his courage in resisting the
coup but also because his key actions resonated with
the half-forgotten religious substratum of Russian culture. The omnipresent image of a white-haired Yeltsin

smiling with a raised fist atop a tank in the open air had some of the elements and effects of an icon, whose spiritual meaning was conveyed by the face and hands. He provided a stark contrast to the only picture the public ever saw of putsch leader Gennady Yanaev with dark glasses, shifty eyes, and trembling hands at an indoor press conference.

On the very first day of the coup, these two contrasting images suggested to the emerging audiovisual generation where good and evil were to be found in the struggle. And Yeltsin's legitimacy was emotionally sealed at the end of the crisis, when he publicly asked the parents of the three young men who died for forgiveness—as Russian Orthodox believers often do with each other before taking communion and as the tragic heroes do in the final lines of two of the greatest Russian historical operas, Mussorgsky's *Boris Godunov* and Tchaikovsky's *Mazepa*.

Key initial defenders of the Yeltsin White House came there directly from a liturgy in the Cathedral of the Assumption within the Kremlin, the opening event of a "Congress of Compatriots" held on the Feast of the Transfiguration. Old women church-goers (long dismissed as playing any but a forlorn and vestigial role in Russia) provided an alternate "motherland" chain of command for the young soldiers surrounding the White House, urging them not to shoot as they awaited "fatherland" commands that never came from their superior officers. Orthodox priests ministered to some in the ring of defenders as they awaited an attack; and, after the coup collapsed, everyone used one simple, half-forgotten word to describe it all—*chudo*, a miracle.

In those three days, the face of hope emerged from inside the outer face of fear. Fear—the great cement of Soviet power—had been steadily eroding in Russia as

Stalinist terror had been progressively diminished and rejected. Hope was discovered as Russia suddenly shed the withered outer layer of a corrupt system. But could Russians hope without exaggerating expectations? Would they find more of what they really hoped for in some new variant of their historically autocratic tradition? Or would they find hope in building their own version of the liberal democratic formula that Western Europe had adopted after World War II? These questions became the concern of far more people than ever before. The many polls, the proliferating polemics, and the semichaotic political and economic life of the new Russia reveal layers within layers that are difficult to fit into standard academic categories of analysis.

Reality is often more bizarre than fiction in Russian culture, and the serious examination of either the history or the literature of modern Russia does not lead to clear conclusions. The poet Viacheslav Ivanov once suggested that Dostoevsky and the best Russian literature achieved sympathetic penetration (*proniknovenie*) "from the real to the more real."[3] We may never be able to discern what is "more real" now, let alone "most real" for the future of Russia. But immersion in Russians' prolific self-analysis may expose us to deeper realities that bind this people together and provide some hints of where they might be heading.

3 | A New Nation in Search of Identity

With the breakup of the Soviet Union in 1991, Russia became, for the first time in its history, a nation rather than an empire. The Russian Soviet Federated Socialist Republic was renamed the Russian Federation. The fourteen other Soviet republics became independent, and some ethnic minorities and regional authorities in the fifteen smaller autonomous Soviet republics that remained within the Russian Federation hoped that they too might expand their autonomy.

The specter of a continuing devolution of central authority, even within Russia, intensified the desire of Russians to find an identity that could unify their still vast country and legitimize a postcommunist government. The rush to independence of Ukraine, Kazakhstan, the Baltic, and other Soviet republics had made 25 million ethnic Russians residents of foreign countries overnight. Russians in the new federation wanted to know what could still link them with their cousins now living in what they called the "near abroad." And they wanted to know what was distinctively Russian (*russkii*) about the new political entity that was formally designated to be simply a federation of all the citizens of Russia (*rossiiskii*).

Faced with such sudden, disorienting change, Russians had to rethink their politics, economics, history, and place in the world. In their new state of freedom, they have produced one of the most wide-ranging discussions of a nation's identity in modern history.

In the economic sphere, the new Russian state looked primarily to the West, and moved rapidly to institute private property and a market economy. In so doing, the Yeltsin government was following an old Russian tradition of suddenly instituting sweeping changes by adopting wholesale the model of their principal foreign adversary. Russians had taken their religion and art from a Byzantium they had previously raided, their first modern governmental structures (under Peter the Great) from a Sweden they had long been fighting, and their models for industrial organization from the Germans that they were about to fight in two world wars. In the 1990s, they basically adopted the model of the United States, their longtime Cold War adversary.

Habits of culture inclined Russians to exaggerate both their initial expectations of, and their subsequent disillusionment with, their rush into market reforms. Russians have repeatedly tended to adopt the end product of another civilization without replicating the processes of thought and institution building that made it possible. They took over Orthodox Christianity as a finished doctrine without any of the critical thinking that went into it. Now, they were setting up a privatized economy without any of the civic or judicial institutions that accompanied it in modern liberal states. They were trying to reach ends without means, to transplant flowers without roots.

The new Russian reformers were, in a way, victimized by the old Soviet legacy of utopian economic determinism. An increasingly urbanized and professional new generation had become disillusioned with communist ideology. But they clung to the underlying Marxist belief that an economic system controls everything important in society and will, by its own workings, produce a radiant future. They now believed that the magic of market mechanisms would deliver rapidly what central planning had failed to do. It was easier to embrace another variant of economic determinism than to reexamine this underlying assumption of so much modern secular thought, capitalist as well as socialist.

Much recent Russian criticism of market economics reflects a belated recognition that economic systems are not all-determining in human life. Even many liberal reformers now stress the noneconomic determinants in Russian history. Writers increasingly discuss distinctive spiritual, cultural, social, and psychological factors in Russian history that have operated independently of—and sometimes contrary to—economic self-interest. Efforts to define national identity have generally paid less attention to economic factors since the economy began improving after the near breakdown of the financial system in 1998.

Many young Russians see the search for a national identity as an anachronistic indulgence. Involved in practical activities that give scope to innovation and ambition, they often pay little attention to such speculative concerns. Those who have grown to adulthood in the postcommunist era often now call themselves "pragmatists." It has recently been shown that pragmatism was more widespread in early twentieth-century Russia than anyone had previously realized, and that Russian followers of William James originated the distinctive Russian tradition of the roundtable.[1]

The widespread Western belief that Russians are inherently nonentrepreneurial reflects ignorance both of the ingenious market networks of old Russia (the Novgorodian north, Old Believers in the deep interior, settlers in Siberia) and of the massive shadow economy of the Soviet period. Precisely because financial and administrative structures were so often dysfunctional at the national level in postcommunist Russia, people in the regions had to rapidly develop entrepreneurial skills simply to get things done. Although authoritarian methods often prevailed in the provinces, the predominant effect overall has been to put some limits on centralized power.

Russians continued to be interested in the U.S. model despite disillusionment with the way it has been applied economically. The Russian reform program sought to bring the benefits of a federal democracy, an open society, and a largely privatized economy into a continent-wide and multiethnic country rich in natural and human resources. For pragmatic reformers, the United States remains quite simply the most nearly relevant and successful example of how all of this has been done.

Political democracy gained a measure of popular legitimacy by successfully electing two presidents and parliaments at both the national and local levels. When Putin succeeded Yeltsin as president early in 2000, Russia, for the first time in its history, transferred supreme power peacefully and constitutionally from one elected official to another. President Putin followed Presidents Gorbachev and Yeltsin in initially developing a strong personal relationship with his U.S. counterpart. This lent symbolic legitimacy to adopting aspects of the American model. Putin had been a law student and later a political protégé of the most prominent and learned advocate of the rule of law in Russia: the late mayor of St. Petersburg, Anatoly Sobchak.

As president of Russia, Putin moved to correct the key initial failure of the Yeltsin government: rushing economic change ahead of political and legal reforms. Having achieved and held a popular approval rating far higher than that of his predecessor, Putin pushed legislation through the Russian parliament in 2002 to create a genuinely independent judiciary and to spread trial by jury to every political region of the Russian Federation.

But Putin's administrative training took place within the KGB, the archetypal instrument of Soviet totalitarianism. Half of the senior figures in his administration were thought to come from the security forces, and his rapid rise from obscurity to supreme power resulted almost entirely from championing war against Chechnya. His proclaimed objective of realizing a "dictatorship of law" dramatized the inherent conflict between the new idea of governance by law and the old tradition of arbitrary rule by a single leader.

Putin seemed to want to be something of a De Gaulle, using mildly authoritarian means to achieve democratic ends. But some feared that he might unwittingly become—or prepare the way for—an authoritarian nationalist resembling Serbia's Milosevic. The Soviet "dictatorship of the proletariat" became a dictatorship *over* the proletariat: many worried that a post-Soviet "dictatorship of law" might either drift or lurch into becoming a dictatorship *above* the law.

Worries about Russia's post-Soviet destiny impel those debating Russia's identity to try both to understand the process of development and to shape the ultimate outcome. The current debate draws in many more people from more varied places and backgrounds than in the past. And the discussants themselves can no longer enjoy either of the two forms of satisfaction open to them in the Soviet era: the material rewards for conformity or the moral gratification of dissidence.

The genuine Soviet accomplishment of near-universal basic education combined with post-Soviet freedom and openness, have broadened the range of subjects included in the debate over Russia's future. Politicians and intellectuals have often changed their minds on key issues as they put forward new thoughts not just about Russia but also about the meaning of history and of modern life in general.

Russians often characterize their current period of transition as a *smuta* or *smutnoe vremia* ("stormy time"). Their free-for-all talkathon about where they really want to go takes place in urban meetings, provincial journals, and, increasingly, everywhere online. Certain themes recur and seem likely to affect the eventual outcome of the broadened search for identity.

Russians tend to begin their quest for something new by attempting to recover something old. Their discussion has brought to the surface three very different aspects of Russia's legacy: a sanctified leader, spiritual renewal, and a balanced culture. Each was suppressed under communism but has been revived to suggest a new direction for Russia.

A Sanctified Leader

An idea that was initially seriously explored in post-Soviet Russia was that of a single leader who would restore moral order through a reestablished Russian Orthodox Church. The general idea of a strongman lifted above the day-to-day political process was given early momentum by Yeltsin's decision to adopt a constitution that gives even greater power to the president than the French—and not at all like the U.S. version with checks and balances that his original drafting commission had recommended.

Some called for a constitutional monarch like those in England, Scandinavia, and the Netherlands. Others studied the possibility of replicating the post-Franco Spanish experience of restoring a monarchy that could stabilize the transition from dictatorship to democracy. Still others spoke of a "people's monarchy" that would have broad popular legitimacy and would rule over a "unified civilized space" rather than an ethnic nation.[2]

Others argued for an absolute monarch, more on the model of a Byzantine emperor, allowing broad cultural autonomy, than of a late Romanov tsar promoting Russification.[3] An apocalyptical, anti-Semitic version of this ideal was advanced by Metropolitan Ioann of St. Petersburg in the early 1990s. The writings of this senior church official did not find many supporters in the Orthodox Church but were echoed politically in the early speeches of Vladimir Zhirinovsky and later—as discussed below—in the even more strident works of Alexander Dugin and Oleg Platonov.

The most original and widely admired version of this ideal was found in the writings of a long-neglected Russian émigré thinker, Ivan Il'in.[4] He argued that autocracy was compatible with a rigorous rule of law as long as both were supported by an established Russian Orthodox Church. His newly discovered, posthumously published writings seemed prophetic. He clearly predicted the downfall of the Soviet regime before his death in 1954. And he argued that autocracy, law, and Orthodoxy were all necessary to prevent the fragmentation and breakup of a post-Soviet Russia.

Il'in's ideal appealed to many who were fearful of interethnic violence and mindful that the pre-Soviet Russian empire had been united not by ethnicity but by religion. There was sympathy—and even some sentimental nostalgia—for the family of the last Tsar Nicholas II who had been murdered by the Bolsheviks in 1918. Most of their bones were finally discovered outside Ekaterinburg and reburied in the St.

Petersburg Cathedral of Sts. Peter and Paul. But post-Soviet monarchists tended to look beyond Nicholas and all the Romanov emperors for their models.

Medieval religious discipline was central to Il'in's neo-Byzantine ideal. The Orthodox Church hierarchy seemed to be endorsing social discipline over Christian evangelism in 1997, when it helped shape a new federal law on religion that recognized only Judaism, Islam, and Buddhism along with Orthodoxy as historic faiths of Russia. Protestant and Catholic Christianity were conspicuously omitted, presumably for threatening to dilute the central role of Orthodoxy within the predominantly Christian population. This hostility to most non-Orthodox Christian denominations was initially somewhat moderated, but was quietly reinforced and extended in the early years of the twenty-first century.[5] There seemed to be growing Orthodox interest in a closer link with Islam as a needed counterweight to the liberal permissiveness and decadence that were seen to be flowing in from the West.

Many ordinary people simply wanted a patriarchal autocrat subject to no controls at all. Nearly three-quarters of those surveyed in a nationwide poll in 1996 "completely agreed" that "power should be strong and strict," and two-thirds contended that "only the hard hands of a strong leader can bring order and put matters right in the country."[6] Similar sentiments were particularly strong in those regions of the "near abroad" where a predominantly Russian population found itself living under a non-Russian jurisdiction. In 1999, when I asked the newly elected Russian governor of Crimea (a province of Ukraine with a 70-percent ethnic Russian population) who would be the ideal leader for present-day Russia, he named Ivan the Terrible.

Spiritual Renewal

A second aspect of the pre-Soviet past that suggested new directions for the post-Soviet future was the rediscovered cultural heritage of Russia's "Silver Age" in the early twentieth century, one of its most creative periods of artistic innovation and religious revival. This unprecedented cultural flowering has been properly called the Russian Renaissance. It was a time of genuine rebirth. Russians became pioneers of modernism precisely by going back to their premodern cultural roots.

Restoration of old icons to their original glory inspired artists as varied as Vasily Kandinsky, Kazimir Malevich, and Marc Chagall to take painting into new directions by returning to the primal purity of deep colors, flowing lines, and semiabstract geometric shapes that were being rediscovered in Russia's half-forgotten, early Christian art. Music also leapt into modernism by turning back to an even older antiquity. Whether real or imagined, the sounds of Russia's pre-Christian, pagan heritage were summoned up in Stravinsky's *Rites of Spring* and Prokofiev's *Scythian Suite*. Nostalgia for the multisensory theatricality of the ancient Orthodox liturgy with its fusion of chant, image, and incense inspired Alexander Skriabin to produce a symphony of sounds, colors, and smells.

Russians were celebrating what Kandinsky called "the spiritual in art," liberating themselves from the realism and tendentiousness that had dominated Russian culture in the second half of the nineteenth century. Music, the most immaterial of the arts, was the dominant art medium. Alexander Blok, one of the many great poets of the age, saw the Russian Revolution itself rising out of the "spirit of music."[7] In his most famous, fevered, and musical poem, "The Twelve," Blok depicted a band of revolutionaries as a new version of the twelve apostles, swept by the wind into St. Petersburg with Christ leading the way.

A substantial part of the secular intelligentsia also rediscovered Orthodox Christianity during this period. Many key thinkers such as Nicholas Berdiaev, Sergei Bulgakov, and Semion Frank migrated from Marxism to Orthodoxy. A religion that had been largely stripped of its intellectual respectability was suddenly fortified with an unprecedented infusion of indigenous, idealistic philosophy.

The spark of faith that Vladimir Solovev had struck in the late nineteenth century became a spreading fire in the early twentieth century. The death in 1902 of Constantine Pobedonostsev, the Overprocurator of the Holy Synod, removed the last government official strong enough to exercise repressive control over the Church. The repeal of censorship in 1907 opened the floodgates for an inundation of philosophical speculation and religious writing. A lively church council gathered amidst the revolutionary turmoil of 1917 and reestablished the position of Patriarch, briefly recreating the clerical independence from the state that Peter the Great had destroyed two centuries earlier.

One of the most remarkable polymaths of the era was the mathematician, aesthetician, philosopher, and priest, Pavel Florensky. With the Soviet crackdown on all forms of religious expression, he retreated in the 1920s to the Monastery of St. Sergius, which was able to publish only a few of his works in very small editions before he was sent to die in the gulag. His last dream was to create a "symbolarium," a universal compendium of symbols that would provide humanity with an encyclopedic dictionary of the sacred imagination.[8]

Florensky's was but one of many projects by Russian thinkers to inventory the philosophical dimensions of human experience and to suggest that preoccupation with the spiritual side of life was a central aspect of Russian identity. Dozens of attempts to codify or tell the history of Russian thought (seen as including both literature, *belletristika*, and polemics, *publitsistika*) were undertaken, although rarely completed, in the late imperial and early Soviet periods.

Florensky was typical in his belief that the distinctive features of Russian thought were striving for "transfiguring life" and seeking "truth not in abstraction but in action . . . created in the name of the ideal of the integrity of life."[9] Histories of indigenous Russian philosophy began to replace the study of Western philosophy in Russia. Writers tended to stress the ethical focus and intuitive nature of Russian thinking and to commend its unsystematic and nonutilitarian character. In 1918, Nicholas Rusov proposed to create an encyclopedic *Dictionary of Russian Thinkers* to honor his mentor, the writer Vasily Rozanov.[10] Despite the broadening participation of Jews in the cultural ferment, many of the most creative figures like Florensky and Rozanov contributed to the anti-Semitism of the period.

In 1920, Gustav Shpet founded "the first Russian office of ethnic psychology" in Moscow and throughout the 1920s taught that Russian identity was defined by Russian philosophy, which in turn was focused on the "most puzzling and dark fact of Russia's existence." He suggested that "Russian philosophy is primarily philosophizing (*filo-softsvovanie*) . . . pre-scientific, primitive . . . rarely original, but . . . with its own tone of voice and special psychological overtones [in posing and answering questions]."[11]

Shpet, like Florensky and so many others, was arrested and shot in the 1930s as Stalin sought to end all independent philosophizing in the USSR. But émigré thinkers continued the philosophical and religious enquiry that had begun in the Silver Age. Georgy Fedotov in Paris argued for the recovery of Orthodox piety, stressing the tradition of *kenosis*, the Christ-like practice of self-emptying love. He saw a compatibility—indeed, an interdependence—between recovering the Orthodox faith and building a responsible democracy. Father Georges Florovsky wrote (in Belgrade and Paris) two magisterial works that recovered for modern readers (1) the full patristic heritage of the early Church fathers, and (2) the complex and absorbent nature of Russia's Orthodox culture.[12]

The works of Fedotov, Florovsky, and other émigré thinkers were recovered and published for the first time inside Russia after the fall of communism. Printings were often large, feeding a rising tide of curiosity and conversion that followed the collapse of the world's first atheist state. The revival of Russian religious thought was often enriched by the imagination of natural scientists. Nicholas Fedorov, the visionary head of the library of the Rumiantsev Museum (later Lenin Library, now Russian State Library), had taught Russia's pioneering nineteenth-century rocket scientist, Constantine Tsiolkovsky. Fedorov believed that other planets would soon be colonized and our dead forefathers resurrected, with modern science, in effect, vindicating biblical prophecy.

Vladimir Vernadsky, the founder of the new sciences of geochemistry and biogeochemistry, continued to prosper in the Soviet era despite his increasingly visionary idea that man was not only an organic part of the biosphere but also an immaterial force in the "noosphere," where everything is determined by the interaction between the human mind and the material world.[13] Multiple conferences and even special institutes have arisen in post-Soviet Russia to discuss the moral and spiritual implications of living in the noosphere. The discussion has involved more people more deeply in Russia than did the earlier consideration of the similar ideas of Teilhard de Chardin in the West.

Cosmic speculation reached megalomaniacal proportions in two monumental works of fiction in the late twentieth century: Daniel Andreev's *Rose of the World* and Leonid Leonov's *The Pyramid*. Each of these was, in effect, the life's work of a major literary figure (the long-imprisoned son of the great writer Leonid Andreev and the last work after long silence of the author of one of the best novels of the Soviet era, *The Russian Forest*).[14] Each of these fantasies combined occult and pagan imagery with Christian apocalyptical ideas in order to provide a new cosmology for the vague spirituality of postcommunist Russia.

Russian Orthodox writers revived the efforts of the Silver Age to link art with religion. Florensky had argued that icons inspired believers with both perfection of form and depth of meaning, and Evgeny Trubetskoi called them "meditations in color." The idea that Orthodox Christianity was best expressed in visual rather than verbal form was richly developed in Paris by Leonid Uspensky.[15]

Within the USSR in the 1980s, the venerable physicist Boris Raushenbakh began to see mathematical harmonies embedded in the composition of icons; in Pskov, the young monk Zinon revived the tradition of icon painting as a devotional exercise. He painted frescoes in the ancient manner for the reconstructed Danilov Monastery in Moscow, after Leonid Brezhnev made a kind of deathbed concession and permitted the reopening of the first monastery in Moscow in more than sixty years.[16]

An important figure in the ferment of the late Soviet period was the linguist and polymath V. V. Ivanov. An active reformer in the liberalized Supreme Soviet of the late Soviet period, he was part of the negotiating team for the democratic forces with the coup leaders in the Kremlin during the crisis of August 1991. In the midst of the dangerous standoff, he still found time to deliver a scheduled lecture on the historic aspirations of the Russian intelligentsia.

Ivanov sees in the concept of the noosphere the key to global collaboration both in solving common problems and in restoring the imbalance in modern culture between the two hemispheres in the brain. "The current high status of the left side of the brain" results from the written, alphabetized means of communication that supplanted humanity's earlier oral and pictorial ways of communicating. The new audiovisual culture of the late twentieth century opens up the possibility of restoring the right side of the brain to a co-equal role. Harmony within the individual could facilitate harmony in the noosphere.[17]

As head of the Library of Foreign Literature in Moscow, Ivanov had organized in the 1980s a series of freewheeling, high-level philosophical discussions that welcomed religious perspectives. His successor, Ekaterina Genieva, opened an entire division of religious literature as a kind of memorial to Father Alexander Men, the brilliant and influential priest who was murdered in September 1990 as he was preparing to give the first set of lectures on religion at Moscow University in nearly seventy years. Ivanov and Genieva gave the democratic press a place in which to do their work at their library when the hard-line coup leaders shut down the free press in August 1991.

Ivanov had been active in the circle of thinkers who periodically met in the Moscow kitchen of Nadezhda Mandelshtam in the late 1960s and 1970s. As the widow of a great poet who had died in the gulag and a close friend of another, Anna Akhmatova, she was a last link with the spiritual legacy of the Silver Age. The other leading participant, Varlam Shalamov, had survived seventeen years in the harshest of all the gulags in the frozen wastes of Kolyma. Mandelshtam moved in the two volumes of her memoirs from *Hope against Hope* (1970) to *Hope Abandoned* (1974). She told me in 1967 that Ivanov exemplified the hope of Russia. Ivanov's father was the novelist Vsevolod Ivanov, and his stepmother was the widow of the great writer Isaac Babel. At the beginning of the twenty-first century, Ivanov was also planning to bring a "symbolarium" into being, Florensky's visionary idea of a universal encyclopedia of sacred symbols.

In the late Soviet era, Ivanov had helped pioneer the innovative movement of humanistic scholarship called semiotics (the science of signs). Seeking to apply the discipline of linguistics to other forms of human thought and expression, this informal school met in the relatively free atmosphere of Tartu, Estonia. Participants in the Tartu seminars developed a body of criticism that ranged from psychiatry to cybernetics and encouraged a deeper appreciation of the multimedia richness of the Russian heritage. Semiotics was seen as a means of unifying human knowledge, and of rendering the noosphere intelligible as a "semiosphere."[18] Yury Lotman, the cultural historian from Tartu at the heart of the movement, characterized Russian culture as one of "explosion"—born of a passion for polarized positions that precluded compromise.

Post-Soviet culture drew fresh perspectives from the long-suppressed literary criticism of Mikhail Bakhtin. He had seen the medieval carnival as a brief occasion when authentic freedom replaced authoritarian routine; and he seemed to have anticipated the carnivalesque atmosphere around the Russian White House in August 1991 when freedom prevailed against communism. Bakhtin praised the "dialogic" nature of Dostoevsky's novels in which widely different views interact authentically—in contrast to the deadening monologue of Soviet culture. Dostoevsky had been the most reviled of the great Russian writers in the Soviet era. He was being rediscovered as one who fit pluralistic dialogue into an overall framework that rooted Russia's identity more in its religious heritage than in its military might.[19]

New appreciation of Russian literature gave prominence to the religious and moral writings of Gogol and Tolstoy produced in their later years and to hitherto neglected religious poems and music. Nicholas Leskov was finally recognized as one of the truly great Russian prose writers for creating "righteous heroes," that is, ordinary people with an extraordinary willingness to sacrifice for others. Others revived Leskov's tradition of writing sympathetically about Old Believers, holy fools, and other historic manifestations of grassroots Christianity.

A Balanced Culture

A formula for post-Soviet culture seemed to be emerging that echoed the advice first given by M. O. Menshikov, the most popular journalist of the Silver Age: Breathe in "only the best air from the West," while "feeding ourselves only with the best milk from our own Mother Russia."[20] This suggestion, that one can simultaneously breathe the new and drink the old, was exemplified for post-Soviet Russia by Dmitry Likhachev.

Likhachev was the last (and least known) of the cultural figures widely admired for speaking truth to power in post-Stalinist Russia. Joseph Brodsky and other poets and human rights activists played this role after Khrushchev's brief cultural "thaw" gave way to renewed repression under Brezhnev. During that period, two men became the modern equivalent of the truth-telling holy fools of an earlier era. The great writer Alexander Solzhenitsyn acquired that mantle by exposing the all-permeating and unforgivable horror of the concentration camp empire that had been so central to the Stalinist system. The eminent scientist and human rights activist Andrei Sakharov also assumed this role. Particularly after Solzhenitsyn was forced to emigrate in 1974, Sakharov dominated the scene with a liberal, secular, Westernizing ideal that rivaled Solzhenitsyn's religious and Slavophile vision.

After Sakharov's death in 1989 and Solzhenitsyn's retreat from public life soon after his return to postcommunist Russia, it might have seemed that a free Russia no longer needed truth-tellers. But the thirst for truth remained strong in the corrupt, cynical, and impoverished Russia that the disintegrating Soviet system left behind. Searching for real truth had continued through the Soviet period. But as in a matryoshka, the face of a truth-seeker was often hidden inside the outer face of power that dispensed daily propaganda under the label of truth (*Pravda*).

The most influential, populist journalist of the late nineteenth century, Nicholas Mikhailovsky, had repeatedly argued that the Russian word for truth has the double meaning of both scientific verity (*pravda-istina*) and moral justice (*pravda-spravedlivost'*).[21] Menshikov, a popular journalist of the subsequent era, had suggested that Russians were still uniquely capable of producing the kind of righteous person (*pravednik*) who could exemplify normative, moral truth even while pursuing objective, scientific truths.

Likhachev emerged as such a pravednik in the mid-1980s, when he became, in effect, a part-time tutor on Russian cultural history to Gorbachev and particularly to his wife Raisa. In this capacity and as the leading spirit in a newly created, semiofficial Russian Cultural Foundation, Likhachev brought both wide-ranging knowledge and moral force into the Soviet power structure as it was beginning to change. Already in his mid-eighties, Likhachev became an energetic and persistent advocate for both a comprehensive recovery of the entire Russian cultural heritage and a full opening up of the Soviet Union to the outside world.

By the late 1980s, Likhachev was the world's leading academic expert on the religious culture of old Moscow. Likhachev saw characteristics in the incessantly persecuted Russian Old Believers that needed to be emulated in modern Russia: hard work, honesty, and a dedication to literacy and to a culture that harmonized and unified "singing, painting, architecture, and literature."[22] Likhachev inspired and helped mount the exhibition of Old Believer books and manuscripts at the Library of Congress at the time of the Bush–Gorbachev summit in June 1990. Likhachev personally explained the virtues of their culture to Raisa Gorbachev as she opened the exhibit.[23]

At the same time, Likhachev was lyrical in his lifelong love of Westward-looking St. Petersburg. He had become by the 1990s the last surviving embodiment of the cosmopolitan culture of prerevolutionary St. Petersburg. As a survivor of the first totalitarian death camp of the twentieth century—on Solovetsky Island in the Arctic north—Likhachev had the legendary aura of one who had suffered.[24] His lonely vote in the Presidium of the Soviet Academy of Sciences against the expulsion of Sakharov gave him added stature with younger Russians, who began writing to him from all over Russia. Having seen as a boy the Bolshevik takeover of the Winter Palace in 1917, Likhachev became the main speaker in front of the same building at the largest rally anywhere in Russia in August 1991 against the hard-line communist attempt to stage yet another coup against a democracy struggling to be born.

After the collapse of the Soviet Union, Likhachev used his moral authority to speak truth to power in a remarkable series of letters.[25] He wrote Yeltsin to oppose sending troops into Chechnya, urging him not to lose the moral authority he had gained by asking the parents of the three young men killed in resisting the coup attempt to forgive him for being "unable to protect and save your sons."

Likhachev also urged the Patriarch to acknowledge publicly the nature and extent of the Russian Orthodox hierarchy's complicity with Soviet organs of repression so that the Church could be freed from half-truths to reclaim moral authority and better promote reconciliation in the society. He was, in effect, suggesting something like the public acknowledgment and repentance involved in the "truth and reconciliation process" after the fall of the apartheid regime in South Africa. In Russian cultural terms, he was suggesting obtaining objective truth (pravda-istina) about Soviet history in order to rise above retribution for the past and to build justice (pravda-spravedlivost') for the future.

In other letters, Likhachev counseled Gorbachev not to reenter the political arena, and he persuaded Yeltsin to be present for the final reburial in St. Petersburg of the bones of the last tsar and most of his family. Likhachev stood behind Yeltsin—both literally and figuratively—during the reburial service at the Cathedral of Peter and Paul in St. Petersburg, when Russia's first elected president gave one of his best speeches. With Likhachev holding a candle behind him, Yeltsin both lamented the murder of the imperial family and brought to dignified closure—as Likhachev had long advocated—the nostalgic dream of a monarchist revival in Russia.[26]

Likhachev internalized and articulated all three of the positive forces that have given Russian culture its distinctiveness: its traditional religious base, its periodic wholesale borrowing from the West, and its special feeling for the land and nature. The interplay of these forces has driven Russian culture forward—but has often driven the Russian people into conflict with each other. In his last years, Likhachev celebrated not only Russia's old Christian culture but also its new opening to the West and the redemptive power of nature. His last major work, *The Poetry of Gardens,* celebrated his own lifelong experience of therapeutic, everyday interaction with the natural world.[27]

It was the parks, not the palaces, of his beloved St. Petersburg that inspired him, just as the natural beauty of Solovetsky Island had sustained him during his long ordeal in the gulag. His memoir of that traumatic experience inspired the documentary film *Solovetsk Power.* The title was a play on the ubiquitous and intimidating phrase "Soviet power" (*vlast' sovetskaia, vlast' solovetskaia*) and implied that the essence of the USSR was its prison camps. Likhachev's late-life writings suggest that Soviet power posed a threat not just to people but also to the entire natural world.

Parks and gardens—like the Orthodox liturgy—offered a multimedia experience. A walk through the manicured inner or "regular" park on to the less-tended or "wild" part that verges on the open forest was a procession through many-colored objects of visual beauty, enriched by sounds (singing birds, rustling wind, crackling leaves underfoot), the smell of flowers, and, finally, the taste of mushrooms or berries.

For Likhachev as for Pushkin, there was a special appeal to the great park stretching out from the imperial summer palace ("Catherine's Palace") at Tsarskoe Selo (now known as Pushkin) outside of St. Petersburg. Likhachev seemed to intimate that the late-blooming literary culture of modern Russia would somehow revive like foliage in springtime so long as gardens continue to be tended and visited. Some of Pushkin's earliest inspiration had come from his exposure to the natural expanses of the park as a schoolboy at the Tsarskoe Selo lycée:

Kuda by nas ni brosila sud'bina	Whatever fate may throw us into
I schastie kuda b ni povelo,	And wherever fortune leads us,
Vse te zhe my: nam tselyi mir chuzhbina;	For us the whole world's still a foreign land;
Otechestvo nam Tsarskoe Selo.[28]	Our fatherland is Tsarskoe Selo.

Tolstoy returned to the natural world around his country estate at Yasnaya Polyana for the last thirty-five years of his life. Even the Soviet system tried to provide links with nature even for those it uprooted from the countryside, often inserting ugly "parks of culture and rest" into new industrial cities. Ordinary people throughout the Soviet era quietly kept flowers blooming in historic rural graveyards and cultivated their own small gardens, which proved far more productive than collective farms.

At the end of *Dr. Zhivago*, Boris Pasternak reconnects the natural with the supernatural dimensions of the Russian heritage in a brief meditation over the dead body of Zhivago. He was lying alone, awaiting impersonal cremation rather than a traditional burial:

> Only the flowers compensated for the absence of the ritual and chant. They did more than blossom and smell sweet. Perhaps hastening the return to dust, they poured forth their scent as in a choir, and, steeping everything in their exhalation, seemed to take over the function of the Office of the Dead.

> The vegetable kingdom can easily be thought of as the nearest neighbor of the kingdom of death. Perhaps the mysteries of evolution and the riddles that so puzzle us are contained in the green of the earth, among the trees and flowers of graveyards. Mary Magdalene did not recognize Jesus risen from the grave, "supposing him to be the gardener."[29]

Likhachev argued that there should be both "a culture of ecology and an ecology of culture."[30] The diversity of both the species in nature and the cultures of humanity should be sustained and honored. He saw Russia itself as an amalgam of many cultures beginning with the multiplicity of steppe peoples who were assimilated into the culture of Kievan Rus, which was itself "Scando-Slavic."[31] In conversation, he speculated that the "aggressiveness" of humanity in the twentieth century was not only destroying variety in nature but also spreading predatory instincts even down into the insect world.

Toward the end of his long life, he urged Russian culture to link up more deeply with its own traditions and, at the same time, to open up more broadly to the outside world. He increasingly identified with the uncompromising Old Believer tradition within Russian Orthodoxy, but he also sought to create a new type of multinational university that would locate each of its departments in a different country.

Likhachev was a soft-spoken man who lived in modest circum-
stances despite his celebrity. He received a growing volume of letters
from young admirers in the provinces. In 1999, the last year of his life,
he agreed to be co-chairman with me of a new program, Open World,
created by the U.S. Congress to bring emerging young leaders from all
over Russia for brief but intensive immersion in the life of communities all over America. He died on September 30, 1999, the last day of
the first year of the program, having helped identify many of the early
participants in that new effort to link the Russia he loved with the West
that he admired.

Likhachev exemplified Menshikov's ideal of "breathing the best air
from the West" while "drinking the best milk of our own mother Russia." These were two parts of a single, balanced identity. Equally important for him were two other traits that he both exemplified and asked
his young admirers in the new Russia to exemplify: dedication to productive work and to personal moral responsibility.

During the purges of the 1930s, he narrowly escaped death when he
was forewarned that he was on the list that the Leningrad security
forces had drawn up to fulfill their quota of required executions. Forever thereafter, he felt an obligation to the unknown person who was
taken in his place. And this was expressed in both the immensity of his
scholarly productivity and the intensity of his insistence that new freedoms required the assumption of new responsibilities. Many of the
young Russian leaders who came to America from all eighty-nine political divisions of the Russian Federation under the Open World program that Likhachev helped pioneer seemed to share his feeling that
building a new balance of culture was more important than reviving
the old balance of power.

4 | The Authoritarian Alternative: Eurasianism

Although Russia was rightly recognized at the beginning of the new millennium as a federal republic and a largely market economy, it was still heavily burdened by its authoritarian past. Its new leader, Vladimir Putin, was democratically elected and professed his commitment to reforms, but he had risen to power on the strength of his hardline policies in Chechnya and was consolidating his control by imposing tighter limitations on both regional and media autonomy. He was using authoritarian means for his announced democratic ends of strengthening the rule of uniform laws and reducing corruption.

No effective, organized movement initially coalesced against him from the combined ranks of old Soviet bureaucrats and new authoritarian nationalists (the so-called red–brown coalition). But new, nationalistic views of Russian identity enjoyed rising popularity. They offered ideological cement for a new autocracy should Russia's fragile democratic institutions break down or social violence break out.

At the popular level, many Russians sought simply to make ethnic nationalism a de facto ideology. The population of the new Russian Federation was now more than four-fifths Great Russian (compared to only one-half Great Russian in the USSR).[1] It thus seemed justifiable to proclaim a common identity that was ethnically Russian (*russkii*) rather than a pluralistic mix of "all those within Russia" (*rossiiskii*). The temptation grew in the new Russian nation-state to adopt the kind of emotional, almost tribal nationalism that had previously galvanized relatively homogeneous ethnicities into powerful political movements elsewhere in Europe.

Such European nationalisms took virulent, antidemocratic forms after the sustained violence of World War I and the breakup of the multiethnic empires of the Ottomans, the Hapsburgs, and the Romanovs. Various fascist-type movements rose to power out of the ashes of failed democratic experiments in the traditionally authoritarian cultures of Eastern, Central, and Southern Europe. Initially dismissed as marginal extremisms, these movements unexpectedly produced dictatorships that helped bring on World War II. At the end of the Cold War, Russia and the world faced a similar danger that some unanticipated, ultranationalistic movement could rapidly arise to reverse the democratic direction in which Russia was attempting to move. Some Russians even suggested in the early 1990s the creation of a "genotype preservation ministry" to help preserve racial purity in the new Russian Federation.[2]

During Putin's tenure, Russia offered many uncomfortable parallels with Germany in the early 1930s when Hitler rose to power: economic deprivation, unhappy demobilized soldiers, and popular resentment of both weak government and widespread corruption. Least visible but perhaps most potentially explosive of all the similarities was the smoldering resentment toward the Western democracies that often seemed to treat a struggling new democracy as if it were still the old autocratic enemy.

There was, however, no early consensus on the shape of an authoritarian alternative for Russia—and little desire, even among most communists in the new Russia, to use the Soviet system as a model. There also seemed to be less popular appeal than demagogues had hoped for in their use of traditional anti-Semitism and hostility to other ethnic groups as a focus for nationalistic mobilization through hatred. The demonization and continued repression of the Chechens remained a major exception.

Geopolitics with Passion

Hovering darkly over Russia's post–Cold War democratic experiment, however, was a new version of "Eurasianism," an ideology born among Russian émigrés after World War I, but revived and rearmed with a sense of geopolitical urgency. Eurasianism may prove to be the most important train of thought that was hatched among émigrés and brought back into postcommunist Russia. In sharp contrast to Likhachev's religious yet ecumenically and ethnically inclusive ideal of "Russianness" (*russkost'*), the new Eurasianism is essentially secular and exclusive. Eurasianists saw neither the deep Orthodox faith nor broad Western influences as defining the identity of Russia. They argued that Russia was a unique bi-continental civilization that needed to turn inward with strong rule in order to protect itself from both Europe and Asia. Russia would ultimately reap benefits from its location between the two.

The basic idea that Russia is not a slow-learning Western country seeking late entry into a "common European home" has its roots in Nicholas Danilevsky's *Russia and Europe* of 1868. He argued that Europe itself was no more than "a western peninsula of Asia" and that Russia's vast Asian domains assured it of ultimate predominance over the "Romano-German" periphery of Eurasia.

Eurasianism as a concept and a movement was created by a group of about twenty Russian émigré scholars in Bulgaria in the early 1920s. Although opposed to communism, they held out some hopes for the new Soviet regime, since it had miraculously reconstituted the Russian empire after a long and fratricidal civil war. They speculated that "an idealistic materialism" might create a new type of "symphonic personality" within the "continent of Russia-Eurasia."

Eurasianism was at heart a geographic conception of Russian identity. P. N. Savitsky, its originator, saw Eurasianists in the 1920s as "representatives of a new beginning in thought and life," rooted in the physical realities of the "Eurasian continent."[3] Russia was a self-contained universe composed of four ribbon-like zones—tundra, forest, steppe, and desert—stretching across two continents. The frozen tundra to the north and the scorching desert to the south formed a closed encasement for the forest and steppe regions in which a unique Eurasian civilization was formed. The long Mongol rule over this region from the early thirteenth to the late fifteenth century gave an authoritarian, Asian cast to the political culture of the Russian empire that succeeded it. The new Soviet Union continued to impose autocratic rule over the same area.

The revival of Eurasianism in post-Soviet Russia results in large part from anger at the loss of empire and revulsion at the perceived "Russophobia" of the new Westward-looking liberal elites. It is more political and less philosophical than the earlier Eurasianism. It is basically an authoritarian nationalism rooted more in ethnicity than religion, and more in geography than in language or culture.

A leading mathematical physicist, Igor Shafarevich, described all of history as shaped by a series of "great peoples" who were perpetually harassed and impeded in their civilizing mission by jealous and conniving "little peoples." He saw Russia as a kind of Gulliver held down by the Lilliputian ethnic minorities of the former USSR. The Jews were a particular target of Shafarevich's polemics: the model of a small people keeping the great people of Russia from fulfilling their proper leadership role. Although not an Eurasianist, he clearly believed that Russia's historic greatness lay in the purity of its ethnicity and the extent of its empire.[4]

Nationalists often claimed that the Russians in the newly independent Baltic Republics were being treated like black Africans under apartheid in South Africa. Vladimir Zhirinovsky, the most prominent ultranationalist political figure of the early 1990s, sought to abolish all the ethnically based, semiautonomous regions that remained within the Russian Federation. He saw Russia's largely Islamic neighbors as an external enemy that must be made to respect Russia by "a last thrust to the South."[5]

Others argued that all political ideals that came from Europe—communism, socialism, and liberalism alike—were inherently Russophobic. Some even found redeeming qualities in the Great Russian nationalism of Stalin who was seen as the only one of Lenin's heirs free of "inbred Russophobia."

The nationalistic popularizer Vadim Kozhinov contended in his *Victories and Disasters of Russia* that both Russia's victory in World War II and its postwar scientific achievements resulted from Stalin's nationalistic turn away from Lenin. He insisted that Stalin had begun to reinstate the Orthodox Church well before he visited the Patriarch in 1943 to mobilize the population against the Nazi invaders. Post–Soviet Russia was the scene of an epic struggle of "Russia, a unique civilization and culture" with "the forced implementation of Western economic models [which] will inexorably lead the country into full-scale social catastrophe." Kozhinov argued elsewhere that the Russian empire and USSR were in no way "the prison of nations," contending instead that Europe with all its wars and conquests has itself been "the graveyard of nations."[6]

Savitsky praised the Mongol occupation both for unifying the quarreling principalities of medieval Rus and for building a land empire that Great Russia could grow to dominate. To him Russian "imperialism" was in reality a stabilizing and civilizing force for the hitherto fractious and nomadic people of Eurasia. By expanding overland, the Muscovite empire of the sixteenth and seventeenth centuries brought order and unity to disparate peoples just as the ancient Roman empire had done. Modern European empires followed the less virtuous British model of colonizing distant overseas regions that had ancient cultures of their own.[7] Whereas the Russian empire brought peace to Eurasia, the newer overseas empires of the Western European powers brought division and war to the entire world.

Eurasianists in post-Soviet Russia often saw themselves not so much blending the culture of two continents as isolating themselves from either. Hope for the future lay precisely in Russia's "islandness" (*ostrovi-*

tianstvo),[8] that is, its insulation from corrupting outside influences. Having been forced by the West to shrink its borders, Russia must now look to its own East in Siberia to recapture its greatness and build its future.

The new Eurasianism expresses bitterness over Russia's harsh geography and repeated experiences of invasion and interference from the West. The "common European home" of which Gorbachev had spoken seemed to offer no room in it for Russia. Eurasianism was seen as a needed response to "Atlanticism," which was extending NATO membership into former Soviet satellites and even into constituent parts of the traditional Russian empire. Eurasianism was also Russia's answer to economic globalization, which was seen as undermining the unspoiled, community-centered peoples of the Eurasian heartland with the vulgar consumerism, licentiousness, and selfish individualism of the West.

In the ingenious view of Vadim Tsymbursky, Russia is an "island civilization" surrounded by a "sea" of very diverse countries stretching from Finland to Korea. This belt of sovereign states is "the Great Limitrophe": a kind of buffer zone separating Russia from the true centers of both European and Asian civilization.[9] Russia must neutralize threats to peace and stability within the Limitrophe lest she get drawn into war with the civilizations that lie on the other side of it: Romano-German, Western Slavic, Arabo-Iranian, Indian, and Chinese.

Tsymbursky holds that the Great Limitrophe will be the major arena for the geopolitics of the twenty-first century. It will become a place either for mediation between the different "continental" civilizations or for further extending the power of the "sea-based" Euro-Atlantic civilization. By virtue of its location, Russia is the only country able to play a leadership role that can both preserve the peace and prevent Euro-Atlantic dominance of Eurasia. To do so, a strong central government must rein in any purely regional foreign policies, since— as Putin noted—half of Russia's eighty-nine political regions have external borders.

Despite Russia's depleted power and diminished territory, it can still play a central, if not controlling, role as the pivotal power in the world's major landmass. Both geopolitics and geoeconomics are opening up fissures in the Euro-Atlantic world. With no real stake in any Eurasian conflicts beyond the Limitrophe region, Russia can be infinitely flexible in its choice of tactics at any moment; and its authoritarian political culture can help insulate its island civilization from the pressure for short-term results felt by elected leaders in the Euro-Atlantic world. Russia can play not just geopolitics, but also "chronopolitics." Coming later might make it possible to do better than the headstrong West.

In order to realize this long-term opportunity while heading off the medium-term danger posed by radical Islam and China, Russia must move its capital east of the Urals and develop a new "counter-elite" to that of the liberals in Moscow and St. Petersburg. Russia should, in the view of some Eurasianists, reconceptualize itself as a geoeconomic extension of the Asia-Pacific region. Siberia and the Russian Far East must be rapidly developed; and Russia should begin extending economic, although not military, cooperation with China and Iran as "strategic fellow-travelers."[10]

For less-sophisticated Russians, Eurasianism was simply an emotional vehicle for expressing pent-up resentment at being rejected or ignored by the West as the new millennium dawned. The United States was investing massively in a still-Leninist China and very little in Russia. Timely support for the war against terrorism in Afghanistan after the tragic events of September 11, 2001, did not seem to bring Russia many benefits. And so Russia sided with the Eurasian powers of China, Germany, and France in opposing the "Atlanticist" United States and United Kingdom on the issue of war in Iraq against even the most odious of "Eurasian" regimes.

For most Russians, Eurasianism did not express any growing fondness for—let alone understanding of—Asia. It represented rather a form of protest against their perceived humiliation by something they still vaguely called "the West." Talk of a unique Eurasian identity, fortified by some kind of "continental thinking," suggested that there was a real alternative to the liberal democracy that was not satisfying their exaggerated expectations of tangible benefits. Eurasianism seemed to promise protection against the insidious force of "globalization" (or "mondialism"), which was responsible for all their problems.

The new Eurasianism was popularized and fortified with passion by the Orientalist Lev Gumilev. He brought with him an aura of anti-Soviet legitimacy as a survivor of imprisonment and the son of two great poets of the Silver Age in St. Petersburg. His father, Nicholas Gumilev, had been shot as a counter-revolutionary in 1921. His mother, Anna Akhmatova, had been denounced under Stalin and was able to publish only fragments of her work in Russia during the half-century she lived under Soviet rule.

Akhmatova was the last of the great ladies of old St. Petersburg. That city's greatest architectural monuments had been built in the eighteenth century by two women, the Empresses Elizabeth and Catherine. Akhmatova, a woman of royal bearing, created in the twentieth century a last towering monument of classical Russian poetry and one of the most stunning literary indictments of totalitarianism: *Requiem*. In the prose epigraph to this long-labored-upon and long-unpublished work, she described waiting in one of the interminable lines to get news of loved ones taken to the gulag. Overhearing an expressionless woman wondering if anyone could ever describe what they were all going through, Akhmatova said, "I can," and noted that "something like a smile passed over what in earlier times had been her face."

In the poem itself, she describes her own plight in words that broke the silence of those being led to slaughter. She plays on the title of the novel most praised by the Soviet establishment, Mikhail Sholokhov's *Quiet Flows the Don:*

Tikho l'etsia tikhii Don,	Quiet flows the quiet Don,
Zheltyi mesiats vkhodit v dom.	The yellow moon enters the house,
Vkhodit v shapke nabekren',	Enters with his cap askew.
Videt zheltyi mesiats ten'.	The yellow moon sees a shadow.
Eta zhenshchina bol'na,	This woman is sick,
Eta zhenshchina odna,	This woman is alone,
Muzh v mogile, syn v tiur'me.	Husband in a grave, son in a prison.
Pomolites' obo mne.[11]	Pray for me.

Joseph Brodsky, the great St. Petersburg poet who later joined the emigration, was in many ways Akhmatova's spiritual son, believing that Russia would ultimately find its identity in culture. But her biological son, Lev Gumilev, emerged from relative obscurity to become the troubadour-in-chief of Eurasianism, yet another form of the authoritarianism that had killed his father and persecuted his mother.

After being released from imprisonment in 1956, Gumilev quietly pursued academic research in the relatively apolitical fields of ethnography and Oriental studies for many years. Then he suddenly burst into public prominence with his new theory of Eurasianism. His *Science of Ethnos*, initially published in Hungary in 1980, found a widening readership in a Soviet Union that was losing faith in communism.[12] His key concept of "ethnogenesis" provided a new approach to the old problem of charting the rise and fall of civilizations. His theory fulfilled the happy function of suggesting that Russian civilization might be on the rise even when the USSR was on the decline.

Gumilev argued that the decisive factor in history was the generation and dissipation of the energy supply in ethnic groups. Neither race nor class determines the great changes in history; rather, an "increased charge of energy" enflames a previously disunited and passive ethnic group with the all-important quality of *passionarnost'* (emotional, ethnic passion as distinct from spiritual passion, *strast'*). The divided peoples of Russia had acquired such passion in the fourteenth and fifteenth centuries, when they rose to supplant the Mongols as the dominant power in Eurasia. The mystical *hesychast* movement had inspired Eastern Orthodox believers with the belief that ordinary people could be infused not with the essence but with the "energies" of God through disciplined and repetitive prayer and long periods of silence.[13] Gumilev seemed to suggest that ethnic groups could be similarly energized today without subjecting themselves to any particular faith or discipline at all. Passion alone will cause a hitherto sleeping "ethnos" to pursue idealistic, and even illusory, goals as Muslim Arabs did in the seventh century and Christian Slavs did in the fourteenth.

Gumilev excited many with the thought that Eurasianism could provide a fresh charge of such passion for present-day Russia. The new ethnos was not based on race, religion, or even ethnicity in any narrow sense. Eurasianism was a new "superethnos" that could bring together and provide new direction for the diverse peoples of the world's great-

est landmass. It also provided an identity without a program. Reener-
gized with passion, even a territorially diminished and ideologically
depleted Russia could find a transcendent, geopolitical trump card for
the ongoing great game of competition with the West. The new
Eurasian "ethnogenesis" came from a blending together of "the plowman" and "the horseman": the sedentary but virtuous Slavic peasantry
with nomadic but daring "Turanian" warriors. The Turanians were the
Mongolian and Turkic peoples who made Asian Russia such an ethnic
mosaic. The Slavs were the strong, silent, heroic cultivators of difficult
terrain. Fused together into a new superethnos, they could resist "the
globalist temptation" offered by the only remaining superpower. They
could build a new and better civilization in unspoiled Eurasia.

Gumilev contended that the charges of energy that transform history
have occurred only in the northern hemisphere and "correspond, nearly
literally, to the thermodynamic processes occurring in nature." Varia-
tions in cosmic radiation accompany—and may even produce—"the
cyclical processes of ethnogenesis" that cause the rise and fall of civilizations. This new "geo-bio-chemical energy" transforms a previously
amorphous people into an impassioned ethnos whose surplus energy is
usually expended in territorial expansion. In the case of the early Byzantine empire, however, this energy was directed into religious expansion—into the Middle East, North Africa, and Southern Europe—all at
the expense of the Western Roman empire. "All passionaries are overac-
tive" and are eventually overtaken by exhaustion and entropy. They
seem doomed to fight one another until humanity learns to understand
the laws of ethnogenesis more fully and agrees to send passionaries who
persist in troublemaking out "into space so that they would discharge
their surplus energy and we could live on peacefully."[14]

Here was a nationalist mythology that promised everything,
demanded nothing, and seemed designed for readers of science fiction
in the space age. Russian greatness would be sustained by its bi-continental geography and an infusion of passion unattached to purpose.
Passion itself comes randomly from the cosmos, into whose expanses
those with troublesome passions will be forcibly expelled by those
who better understand the dynamics of ethnogenesis.

Eurasianism in a less fantastic form presented an appealing new geopolitical perspective for many Russians, particularly in the deep interior. Alexis Gunsky, leader of a Buddhist group in Samara, argued in his "Historical Models of Russian Identity" that Eurasianism was the most suitable model for present-day Russia. The "classical" nineteenth-century models of both Slavophilism and Westernization as well as the "postclassical" twentieth-century communist model are irreversibly outmoded. The liberal democratic model of the 1990s has failed not just because it did not fit Russian reality but also because Western liberalism itself is exhausted, having lost all its passion.

Western democracies were able to sustain their dynamism in a stable way only as long as they drew on "pre-democratic values and institutions," Gunsky argued,[15] citing the most sophisticated of the Eurasianists, A.S. Panarin, the head of the Institute of Philosophy of the Russian Academy of Sciences. Denouncing the "information imperialism" of the West, Panarin began publicly arguing in 1995 that Russia after the Cold War should play a role in Eurasia similar to that which the United States played in the North Atlantic world after World War II.[16] The United States became a new Caesar for Western Europe, and Russia would play the even more exalted role of a new Alexander the Great for Eurasia.

In two lengthy publications of 1998,[17] Panarin launched a sustained criticism of the "pharisaical Westernization" of postcommunist Russia. And he provided an ambitious scenario for Russia to play a leading role in the coming "planetary reformation" of the twenty-first century. Russia was to counter the "barbarization of post-Soviet space" through its "secret weapon": continuing cultural links with the archaic, tribal perspectives that have survived in Eurasia. These have become newly relevant for the postindustrial world. Since Russia is "a special type of civilization" rather than "an ordinary national state," it has a unique capability to unify a variety of traditional societies against the "irresponsible consumer hedonism" and "comprador modernism" of the "Atlanticists."

Russia must work out an "alternative model for post-modern man" to the "technological nihilism" of the "neo-pagan" West bent on "the

Latin Americanization of Russia."[18] The "nomenklatura-mafioso alliance" currently controlling Russia has succeeded in Westernizing the large cities and largely destroying the peasantry as an empirical reality. But peasant values live on as "a cultural-ethical-spiritual phenomenon." Long suffering has given Russia the moral right to provide a better model for all the world. The Russian intelligentsia should rally to the cause and sustain its historic tradition of championing the weak against the strong. Russia can provide a model for the world because it is a one-of-a-kind "pre-post-modern society"—not yet irreversibly modernized nor paralyzed by postmodernist skepticism.[19] Panarin advocates a neo-Byzantine structure that would bring together different ethnicities under an unspecified "fundamentalist ideology" that will help overcome "the break between the social sphere and the cosmos" that the West has opened up.[20] Panarin's strategy for Eurasia was to combine a "monologic" political authoritarianism with a tolerant, "dialogic" relationship between different cultures and ethnicities.[21] Panarin sees this as the exact opposite of Western democracies, which combine dialogic governments mired in endless parliamentary chatter with a monologic culture of materialistic individualism.

The principal dialogue in Panarin's "United States of Eurasia" should be conducted between Orthodox Christianity and Islam. These "two great written traditions" must work together against their common enemy: Western secularism and individualism. Russian Orthodoxy is more compatible with Islam than with Western Christianity. Out of the Muslim–Orthodox dialogue will come a new type of "continental thinking" that will reintegrate the republics of the former USSR culturally and provide a better developmental model for the postmodern world.[22] Islam and Orthodoxy can work together because Orthodox Christianity is more ethically demanding and less individualistic than Western Christianity. Eastern Christianity can develop a common interest with Islam in exorcizing "the demons of nihilism" from a neopagan West that has "lost its capability for spiritual reforms."[23] Metropolitan Kirill, head of external relations for the Russian Orthodox Church, has also, on occasion, seen Islam as a traditionalist ally in the struggle against the secularism and individualism of the West.[24]

Viacheslav Polosin, an Orthodox priest who had promoted in the parliament "an Eurasian–Orthodox–Muslim Union to succeed the Soviet Union," converted to Islam. Under the new name of Ali Viacheslav, he became editor of the *Muslim Gazette*. Another Russian, formerly Vadim Medvedev, took the new name of Abdul-Wahed Niiazov and founded the opposition Eurasian Party of Russia.[25] The radical, authoritarian Alexander Dugin founded a Eurasia Party, arguing that "the objective laws of geopolitics" point toward a Russo-Islamic alliance.[26] Neither of these parties acquired much initial traction; and both were accused of being, in effect, trial balloons for authoritarian forces within the Putin government.

Panarin sees Russia as an agent of "the revenge of history" against the Western idea that democratization and a globalized economy heralded the "end of history." He plays with the idea of Russia linking up with India, Iran, and China to counter the G-7 alliance of North America, Europe, and Japan. At the same time, he worries that any further weakening of Russian power could lead to the "Chinafication" (*kitai-izatsiia*) of Eurasia rather than to a loose alliance in which Russia would play a pivotal role.[27]

In 2000, Panarin warned against the unelected international elite of "nomadic" investors, lawyers, and economists who destroy cultural diversity "behind the backs of their own people." They have replaced the ideal of a "pilgrim" (who seeks to know the values of others in order to strengthen those within himself) with that of a "tourist" (who seeks endless selfish diversions without any moral purpose). It is a rich image conjuring up the contrast between popular Russian pilgrimages to the Holy Lands and to holy places within Russia and the dilettantish tourism of the Russian upper classes to Western Europe. The intellectuals in whom Panarin had seen hope for the future in 1998 are now portrayed as awash in relativism. They have given up their last links with their Christian heritage by freeing themselves of any sense of obligation to the less fortunate.

Two hundred years of the intellectuals' polemics against the rich have
ended; we have entered the age of the intellectuals' assault on the poor.[28]

Panarin's vision of Eurasia builds imaginatively on the ideal of dialogue that the critic Mikhail Bakhtin had found in Dostoevsky's novels.[29] But Panarin never makes clear how an authoritarian political
structure could promote a pluralistic dialogue. He uses Gumilev's language of "passionality" and "social energy" but reflects sadly that such
passion and energy are largely lacking in contemporary Russia. He
rejects the more extreme Eurasianists' suggestion that Russian civilization must move closer to China or Japan. He places his emphasis on
the binding role of culture that could be enriched by a new spiritual
alliance with India.[30]

Eurasianism is important not because of the theories of men like
Gumilev and Panarin but because it feeds the disillusionment that
many ordinary Russians feel about their unrequited love affair with the
West. It reflects the beginnings not so much of a new love affair with
Asia as of a desire to retreat back into one's own shell in the face of
confusing change. And it benefits from the more positive assessment
that many young Russians now make of the cultures of hitherto neglected ethnic Asian minorities.

The milder and more philosophical variants of Eurasianism in post-
Soviet Russia could lead to the same moderate political views that
most of the original émigré Eurasians finally embraced. They advocated a "middle way" between centralized collectivism and unbridled
capitalism—and a moral commitment to the integrity of the individual human personality. They advocated a new openness to different
cultures that would provide a foretaste of "the symphony of light and
sound in the world to come."[31]

The more popular variant of Eurasianism inside Russia today
points, however, in the opposite, authoritarian direction. Many advocates of stronger central authority in the Yeltsin era spoke of the need
for restoring order through "a Pinochet interlude." But Russia, unlike
Chile, does not have a preexisting culture of democratic institutions
capable of reasserting itself. Any such "interlude" in Russia would risk

being both more repressive and longer lasting than that of General Pinochet.

Anti-democratic Prophecy

The worst-case scenario would be that which has long been advanced by Alexander Dugin, a prominent member first of the anti-Semitic Pamiat' society, then of Eduard Limonov's fascistic National Bolshevik Party from 1993 to 1998. Dugin's version of Eurasianism has many of the characteristics of Nazism. In his lengthy magnum opus, *The Bases of Geopolitics*, he advocates "the sacred ideal of a return to the Nordic sources of civilization." He insists that "the Russians' battle for world domination is not over." The essential prerequisite is that Russia think of itself as neither "a regional power" nor "a nation state," but as "a new Eurasian empire."[32]

This "new empire" must mobilize the Eurasian continent for a global struggle against "Atlanticism," which, through its ideology of "mondialism," is planning world domination. In the coming contest between "the mainland and the seas," an "alliance of Eurasian forces" will lead a planetary, supraracial, supranational, geopolitical revolution, based on the fundamental solidarity of the third world with that part of the second world that rejects the program of the "rich north."[33]

Russia is to be the leader not only in rejecting the schemes of the "rich north" of Europe and North America but also in forging new "axes" for anti-Atlantic agitation with Berlin, Tokyo, and Iran. The key to success will be a "Russo-Islamic pact." The reason for confidence is that "the objective logic of geopolitics" will unite all traditional societies against "the totalitarian ideology" of liberalism.[34]

Russians can use their unique upbringing in "the great space" of Eurasia to "think spatially" (i.e., *myslit' prostranstvom*, the title of the lengthy addition he made in 1999 to the third edition of his *Bases of Geopolitics*). Dugin proposed that Novosibirsk in Siberia become the new Russian capital, and he provided a bewildering array of geographic charts depicting various ways that a land-based "Aryan" coalition can be mobilized by Russia—essentially to revive the Cold War on a new and more rigorously geopolitical basis.

In the program he designed in March 2002 for his new Eurasia Party, Dugin no longer spoke of winning a global conflict with the United States, but of restoring parity and sustaining a nuclear deterrent.[35] But the imperial vision remains intact. Russia will become a "Eurasian Union," the lynchpin in a "continental bloc" that will prevail over the Atlanticists. Intensive scientific development in this Union will lead Eurasia both forward to economic modernization and back to traditional village values. And the Internet will permit economic activity to return from decadent cities to healthy rural locations.

All kinds of religion are welcome in the new union[36] along with various forms of government and economic organization. But all the "geopolitical elites" will work together to oppose the common enemy under Russian/Eurasian leaders, who will preferably be "charismatic theocrats." Russians must prepare for leadership by digesting the classical texts of German geopolitics as they once digested German philosophy.[37] The new party's slogan, "Eurasia above all," calls to mind the "Deutschland über alles" of Hitler's Germany.

Unintended psychological support for Eurasianism emerges, ironically, from the very passion of some young liberals to free the writing of Russian history from all of its past mythological baggage and self-righteousness. The reform-minded group seeking to create a historically based, liberal study of politics in Afanasiev's new Russian State Humanistic University in Moscow has been attempting to break Russia free from the perverse continuity they see between the Mongol, Russian, and Soviet empires. Russian political culture, they contend, remains all too closely connected to its autocratic Asian progenitor.[38]

Far from rejecting this heritage, a group of scientists and mathematicians at the older Moscow State University led by Gleb Nosovsky and Anatoly Fomenko seem to have embraced it. Using dating techniques and probability theory, they conclude that the Russian and Mongol empires were, in fact, one and the same entity during the 250 years wrongly referred to as the period of the "Mongol yoke." Accordingly, "Russia and Turkey are parts of a previously single empire."[39] This astonishing conclusion is part of Nosovsky and Fomenko's "new chronology" of world history that uses equations and graphs to cast in doubt the accepted views on much of premodern times. They contend that Troy was located in Italy, that the encyclopedic *Almagest* attributed to Ptolemy was written by others a millennium after his death, and that the entire saga of Russians struggling with the Mongols/Tatars is a retrospective fabrication of the Romanov dynasty. They argue that almost nothing in the traditional view of Russian history prior to the fourteenth century can be factually verified.[40]

The radical revisionism of Nosovsky and Fomenko's *New Chronology of Rus* has its origins in the attempt by Nicholas Morozov to synthesize science and history during twenty-five years in prison. Morozov had been the first systematic theorist of modern terrorism and a leader of the revolutionary group that assassinated Alexander II in 1881. During his long subsequent incarceration, he produced a massive seven-volume work entitled simply *Khristos* (Christ). The discovery of the manuscript for Morozov's never-published eighth volume (*On Russian History*) provided Nosovsky and Fomenko with fresh philological and scientific arguments for concluding that Western influences created a false picture of hostility between Russians and Mongols.[41]

All of this might have been quietly blown away in the wind tunnels of academia had not the popular chess hero Gary Kasparov lustily taken up the cause of the new chronology in the mass circulation journal *Ogonek*. Insisting that "whoever controls the past, controls the future," Kasparov accused the Germanophile Romanov dynasty of destroying the records of Russia's harmonious links with its Eastern neighbors and inventing insulting names for all their enemies. For example, the ill-fated Tsar Dmitry who preceded the first Romanov was called Otrep'ev (from *otrep'e*, meaning scum); the rebel leader against Catherine the Great was named Pugachev (from *pugach*, screech owl).[42]

Russia's greatest living archaeologist, V.L. Yanin, ends his devastating critique of the New Chronology School with an attempt to explain its popularity:

> We live in an epoch of total non-professionalism, which spreads through the entire society from the power structures to the lowest levels of the

educational system. The ordinary school produces dilettantes who assume that their miserable and faulty knowledge is adequate for judging professionals. A society brought up on scandals craves negativity and shock effects. It loves the sleight of hand trickery of a David Copperfield or an Anatoly Timofeevich Fomenko.[43]

Gennady Zyuganov, leader of the post-Soviet Communist Party, has used Eurasianism to provide new legitimacy for a return to authoritarian government. In a volume of essays, he urged Russia to recover its "national governmental self-awareness" and become "the principal supporter of the Eurasian bloc against the hegemonic tendencies of the U.S.A. and the great Atlantic space." According to Zyuganov, Russia is an "autonomous economic organism" with an "all-planetary significance" and "vectors of a worldview" that radiate out from the Russian "ethnos." Russia must reassert its "ethnic commonality" with its "mononational core of Great Russia, Little Russia, and Belarus," which, in turn, has "Eurasia as a superethnos." "Gorbachev destroyed the citadel of Eurasia," which was the USSR and its East European satellites. But Zyuganov suggests that an even broader Eurasian power bloc might someday be formed by working toward an alliance among Russia, China, and India. Alexis Podberezkin, his collaborator in the same volume, suggests forming yet another "axis"—with Turkey, Ukraine, Georgia, and Azerbaijan.[44]

While awaiting such geopolitically desirable outcomes, Russia must pursue "de-Americanization" and an active "defense of the interests of the Russian-speaking population." Zyuganov issued some of his presidential campaign literature from the monastic village of Sergiev Posad. He claims a Christian past as well as a geopolitical future for ethnic Russia, which must reassert its right to leadership as

the principal bearer of the Slavic "cultural-historical type," the lawful heir of the bi-millennial civilization of the first apostolic Christian communities, of Kievan Rus, of Muscovite tsardom, of the Russian empire, and of the USSR.[45]

The seemingly implausible idea that Orthodox Christianity and atheistic communism can join forces to revive Russian patriotism and reestablish strong government had been made in July 1990 by the new head of the Russian Communist Party, Ivan Polozkov. It was made again in February 2003 by the newly dismissed head of the Russian history department of St. Petersburg University, Igor Froianov. In an interview for the project "Leaders of Patriotic Russia Speak," Froianov said that there were only

> two organized forces that can provide the foundation for the patriotic movement . . . the Russian Orthodox Church and the Communist Party of the Russian Federation.[46]

Eurasianism as an ideology is almost certainly too arcane and too full of questionable history and inner contradictions to withstand scholarly cross-examination, let alone command broad popular support. A relatively well-educated population is not inclined to respond to Gumilev's appeal for a new outburst of passion based on cosmic rays, or to Dugin's call to activate a bloody new geopolitical pseudo-science, or to Zyuganov's placing apostolic Christianity and Soviet totalitarianism in the same lineage of legitimacy. The fatal weakness that even the more moderate Eurasianist Panarin shares with Gumilev and Dugin is a near-total dependence on hostility to the West and a near-total absence of any positive program for Russia. This weakness is often camouflaged by the attribution of saintly qualities to all the contradictory elements of an idealized Russian past.

An extreme, but not atypical example is *Holy Rus'*, the magnum opus written over a quarter of a century ago by the most prolific of reactionary nationalists, Oleg Platonov. He begins by asserting that Russian civilization began in the second millennium B.C. with a distinctive "spiritual-moral" paganism onto which Christianity and a rugged rural life added an array of supplementary moral virtues, all of which comprise "Holy Rus."[47] This civilization began to be undermined in the seventeenth century by a variety of "foreign devils" (*chuzhebesiia*) from the "damnable non-Rus" (*okaiannaia ne rus'*) of the West.[48] These were the forerunners of a rival "Jewish-Masonic civilization" that led Russia to revolution. Since then, Russia has been unsteadily "on the paths of return to Holy Rus."[49]

The surprising hero of this great return turns out to be Joseph Stalin. Although Platonov accuses the Soviet leadership of killing 87 million people in the 1918–1955 period, he hails the murderer-in-chief for taking "the first step toward the salvation of Russia from Jewish Bolshevism."[50] Stalin destroyed "not less than 800,000 Jewish Bolsheviks" who were counting on superimposing a Jewish government on Russia.[51] By turning from communism to nationalism in the 1930s, Stalin changed from "an instrument for the destruction of Russia" into an instrument for the advancement of Holy Rus itself. Stalin was "outwardly atheistic but, in fact, a believing man."[52]

Platonov cites the late Metropolitan Ioann of St. Petersburg as the inspiration for his *Holy Rus* and claims that the authoritarian cleric gave him a kind of last testament, *Overcoming the Time of Troubles,* ten days before his death, suggesting that

> the national question was primarily only an external form beneath which was hidden the striving of Russians to preserve their faith.[53]

Platonov presents an implausible set of matryoshka images—a believing Stalin nested inside an antireligious leader, and a spiritual people advancing their faith inside an atheistic ideology that was destroying it. He sees the conspiratorial, Jewish-Masonic face of "non-Rus" covering over an idealized image of Holy Rus. His longest book is devoted to tracing how the notorious "protocols of the elders of Zion" have allegedly been used to build the "behind-the-scenes world empire" of the Jews. Other full-length books are equally obsessed with unveiling hidden foes within and without Russia: *Russia Under the Power of the Masons* and *The Illicit Secret: Judaism and Masons against Christian Civilization.*[54]

Platonov embellishes Shafarevich's image of parasitic "small peoples" destroying heroic "great peoples." Jews are seen as undermining the Russian empire the way that Spanish conquistadors did the empire of the Incas. In his *Why America Will Perish: The Secret World Government,* he ascribed to the United States the very attributes previously attached to the Soviet Union. The United States is the true "evil empire," bent on world domination with the aid of a concealed worldwide "nomenklatura and its servants." America is an agglomeration of detested "little peoples," "the crystallization of the Jewish-Masonic spirit," and "the embodiment of the evil of Jewish-Masonic civilization."[55]

> America is not a government, not a nation. It is simply a large territory on which immigrants from different countries live . . . an artificial conglomerate of people foreign to each other, united . . . by instinctive fear of their common responsibility for crimes against humanity.[56]

Like other disciples of Metropolitan Ioann, Platonov lifts the conflict with Western values to the metaphysical level. Satanism, sodomy, and all the other sins of rootless cosmopolitanism are signs that the reign of the Antichrist may be at hand and the second coming of Christ about to occur. Present sufferings are "Russia's crown of thorns." Alexis Moroz, a priest in St. Petersburg, sees the vague talk of "spirituality" as a crime against the Holy Spirit and "the new jargon about all-humanity" as a "spiritual Chernobyl" for Russia.[57]

Platonov suggests that Russians will be vindicated at the Last Judgment only if they accept the universal mission that Metropolitan Ioann defined for them: "reconstructing Holy Russian power." Russians must simultaneously show reverence both for the Christian "new martyrs" who died in the Soviet era and for the man who killed them. For Platonov, as for most other protofascist forces in Russia, Stalin was

> one of the greatest figures of world history, who played the decisive role in the salvation of Russia from the genocide of the Jewish Bolsheviks, and humanity from the tyranny of the new Western order.[58]

Nothing better indicates the convergence of the extreme positions of "right" and "left" than the way Platonov's view parallels that of Zyuganov. In his manifesto "The Coming Rus," the communist leader, like Ioann and Platonov, compares Russia's present condition to the Time of Troubles of the early seventeenth century and believes that Stalin pointed the way out for contemporary Russians.

Reverence for power (derzhavnost') and collectivism are the heart of "the people's consciousness of government."[59] What Russia needs now is an authoritarian version of "people power" (narodovlastie) chosen by a militant, popular assembly like the *zemsky sobor* (Council of the Land) that ended the Time of Troubles and brought in a new tsar. Russia will then replace its corrupt new version of the "Rule of the Seven Boyars" (*semiboiarshchina*), the last stage of weak governance (1610–1612) under the Polish occupation of Russia at the end of the original Time of Troubles. The task for Russians—now as then—is to rally the Russian people to drive out the Westernized "elites" and form a new government that strongly imposes a "natural hierarchy of power functions" on a dispirited population. All that Russia needs is "a creative synthesis of the cadre policies of Stalin and the ideological searching of Il'in."[60]

The popular appeal of xenophobic nationalism has probably not yet crested. Nor has authoritarian Eurasianism yet found either its most sophisticated spokesmen or its most appealing political demagogue. There are many potential disaster scenarios inherent in any return to autocracy in a country with Russia's geopolitical location and so many weapons of mass destruction. However, if Russia were to succumb to negative nationalism and take a sharp autocratic turn, it would probably not last for long. Repression would be difficult to sustain in a vast country that has been so dramatically opened up to political freedoms and to the outside world in the information age. Nor does Russia have a large enough population or the military resources to sustain the kind of aggressive foreign policy that hypernationalistic states generally need to maintain their legitimacy.

Eurasianism has spread autocratic seeds onto harrowed soil. But they have not yet taken deep root, and they look more like the autumnal scatterings of a withered plant than fresh growth with the promise of harvest. Eurasianism may well be the last gasp of a depleted intelligentsia seeking to cobble together an ideology that could revive Russian power and give themselves a central role in its exercise. It expresses a vague longing to see Russia as an empire rather than just a nation and to re-cement its inhabitants together with an Orthodoxy largely emptied of Christian content.

Autocratic Russian nationalists have often played with the idea of forging an anti-Western alliance with authoritarian forces in Islam. The terrorist wave that began on September 11, 2001, continued late in 2002 with the bloody Chechen siege in a Moscow theater and escalated with suicide bombings in Moscow in 2003. All of this convinced some to look on Muslims as many had once looked on Jews—as the presumptive enemies of Russia.[61] The Russian government dissented with America over the war with Iraq in the spring of 2003 but did not satisfy the Eurasianist desire to strengthen ties with neighboring authoritarian Islamic powers.

Dugin saw the Iraq war as a kind of wake-up call for Russia to become "the core of a Eurasian imperium" composed of those "who live by traditional values: Hindu, Islamic, Slavic, Chinese civilizations." Dugin called from the "right" for what Zyuganov had advocated from the "left": "a powerful Eurasian geopolitical bloc" to resist the alleged American assault. The danger from the United States, he argued, comes not only from the old "imperialism" (based on material interests and championed by the Republican Party), but also from the new kind of cultural "empire" (based on universalizing the American way of life and advanced by the Democratic Party).[62] The different traditional cultures of Eurasia must stand together against the forced imposition of both American power and liberal values.

Franco-German resistance to the Anglo-American coalition against Iraq even provided a glimmer of hope that continental Europe might join the Eurasianist resistance to the Atlanticists. However, said Dugin, for this "bloc" to succeed,

> Russia must become something more than it is—a super-Russia (*sverkh-Rossiia*). . . . Russia must not only preserve, but even grow its atomic might. It is necessary for Russia to include in the process the distribution of weapons and export of technology to Iraq, India, the Arab world, Europe.[63]

At its core, Eurasianism is classical negative nationalism. In the Russia of today, it essentially represents a grasping for more linkage with non-European powers even though these may themselves be seeking greater liberalization and integration with the "rich north." The practical result of Russia forging any serious anti-Western alliance with either China or radical Islam would more likely be the increasing vassalization and/or destabilization of Russia than the building of any Rus-socentric "new Eurasian empire." Any major move of the Russian Federation toward authoritarian nationalism based on Russian Orthodoxy or ethnicity would deepen conflict with Russia's own substantial Muslim minority and with the rapidly growing Muslim populations in the newly independent Central Asian states of the former Soviet Union.

Dugin, like many troubadours of autocracy, summons up a wide range of pseudoscholarly resources to sustain negative nationalism. The inside cover of one of his most bizarre works advertises it as a collection of texts that reaches

> from politics and sociology to theology, alchemy and astrology which are united along a common axis—endless hatred toward the contemporary world with its antitraditional, profane "values" and endless love of the ideal, spiritual native land . . . our Great Rus.[64]

Faced with their inability to establish an authoritarian nationalist regime in post-Soviet Russia, proponents like Dugin tended to lurch into apocalyptical prophecy rather than return to practicalities. He juxtaposed Eastern "eschatological gnosis" with Western futurology in his *End of the World* (*Eschatology and Tradition*) of 1997.[65] And he was said to have described the planes that destroyed the World Trade Towers as "swallows of the Apocalypse."

Platonov and other followers of Metropolitan Ioann continue to amplify Ioann's own apocalypticism. The introduction of computerized accounting numbers on Russian products was resisted by some leading clerics as concealing the number of the beast identified in the Book of Revelations (13:17–18). The introduction of a tax identification number for all citizens in 2001 was considered a signal that the reign of the Antichrist had begun and that the end of the world was near. A Russian journalist explained the reasoning of those who refused to accept a government-issued number:

> [The] Antichrist will come in the form of global computerized control of individuals, who will have computer chips implanted in their hands. Tax IDs, which "replace" the name given at baptism with a number, are the first step toward such a satanic goal.[66]

In brief, authoritarian nationalism continued to have popular appeal despite its failure to produce either a major political movement or a convincing ideology. There were recurrent visions of a Eurasian counter to Western liberalism. Eurasianism as an ideology had been philosophically deflated at birth by two lengthy analyses in the first serious public discussion of its ideas in 1995. One critic pointed out that it was simply a muddled and retrograde recycling of discredited European ideas.[67] Another saw it as a case of "therapeutic politics" designed to "legitimize a restorationist ideology" that would make Russia "first among equals" in an anti-American bloc. It was described as "compensation" for no longer being a superpower, "a dangerous ideological myth," and "a counterfeit interpretation of Russian history that leads to a counterfeit political program."[68]

Overall improvement in the economy in the early twenty-first century might have been expected to collapse this ideological house of cards. But reforming regimes tend to be most vulnerable to upheaval not when economic conditions are at their worst, but when things begin to improve and expectations outstrip the capacity for satisfying them. Popular discontent continued to smolder about Russia's diminished standard of living and place in the world. The post-Soviet collaborator with the Communist Party faction in the Duma, Sergei Glazev, fortified apocalyptical nationalism with statistics that lent fresh credence to his argument for central governmental control over the economy.[69] He argued that Russia was "a dying country" that had already fallen "to the level of Mongolia and Guatemala" and would have only half of its already reduced population by the middle of the twenty-first century.[70]

Many among the educated professional class were sympathetic to Glazev's insistence that the government must resume massively subsidizing scientific research to ensure Russia's future power and prosperity. Glazev's advocacy of renationalizing natural resources was disturbing to Russian democrats, but his nationalist–leftist alliance was a success in the 1903 Duma elections.[71]

Many strange new institutes and publications with pretentious names (Platonov's *Encyclopedia of Russian Civilization* and Dugin's Center of Special Metaphysical Studies) sprang up to provide seeming scholarly authority for the political mobilization of anti-Western feelings in the general population.[72] Unless and until democracy and free markets are better legitimized in Russia, the danger will continue to exist of a corrosive—and perhaps explosive—descent into authoritarian nationalism. It could ride on the train of thought expressed by Sergei Kurginian, the maverick founder and director of a self-styled "Experimental Creative Center" in Moscow.

Kurginian, a relatively recent adherent to the Communist Party, combines old Marxist terminology with verbal flourishes suggesting that he is forever offering new analyses of "neo" phenomena. The "criminal-bourgeois revolution" that overturned the USSR has led to the "neofeudal disintegration" of Russia. But now "we are entering into the space of neoabsolutism" which will be created by a new "alliance of a neomonarch and the neoaristocracy against the neofeudalists." This veiled call for a new compact between a dictator and the intelligentsia will "depend on heroic deeds (*podvizhnichestvo*) by the workers," but the new alliance will receive popular support because the "neoaristocracy" (unlike the old intelligentsia) will be activists creating a new postindustrial economy and society.

Russia is suffering, in Kurginian's view, from "self-narcoticization" (*samonarkotizatsii*), "the desire to drift for awhile in virtual reality" with a government that "is not a muscular system. It is lazy, cowardly, lax" and unable to mobilize its own people. As a result, Russia is shamefully content with being just one actor among many in a multipolar world. But the fact is that

> There will not be a multipolar world. . . . Either you return to your superpower existence and its world-projects or you are nothing at all. And a government is needed that can realize this social task.[73]

Kurginian faults not only the feeble Russian government but also its pusillanimous political opposition that challenges it only with a "cardboard sword." The very institutions of democratic rule are "managed chaos." The problem "is not that democracy is disappearing [but] that it is *not* disappearing." Democracy itself is "the main danger."[74]

Kurginian was a geological engineer from 1972 to 1986 and since then has been artistic director of a new studio "theatre on the boards" (*na doskakh*). His 1986 version of *Boris Godunov* seemed to portray that tsar's ill-fated reign as prefiguring the failure of *perestroika*. Kurginian joined the Communist Party in 1988, has remained a member, and in 2001 answered the classic question, "What is to be done?" by citing Lenin's famous rephrasing of Archimedes: "Give me a revolutionary organization, and we will overturn Russia."

While venting his aesthetic distaste for democracy and its practices, Kurginian expresses despair over the lack of "forces" to supplant it at present. He ends up calling for a "national discussion" to prepare a "nationalistic agenda."[75] This procedure would seem unlikely to do more than feed back into the intellectual talkathon that he deplores. But he has stated more bluntly than most the persistent demand of many Russians for an authoritarian alternative to maintain unity and restore pride in Russia.

Kurginian supported the hard-line communist putsch of August 1991, and reaffirmed in November 2000 that he is "an ideologist of an emergency rule."[76] He added in January 2003 that "the integration of Russia into the international community and the preservation of Russia's integrity as a state are mutually exclusive goals."[77]

In the last days of the USSR, Kurginian had attempted to convert the Communist Party into an authoritarian nationalist organization that would suppress independence movements in non-Russian republics and repudiate the Gorbachev reforms. His ninety-page manifesto of late 1990, *Postperestroika*, and his draft proposal for a new Communist Party platform in July 1991 called for the resistance of "collectivist" societies everywhere against the "individualistic" West. A copy of *Postperestroika* was found a month later on the desk of Vladimir Kryuchkov, the head of the KGB and a key organizer of the attempted communist putsch against the Gorbachev government.[78] Had the coup succeeded, Kurginian's ideas might well have become central to a more explicitly nationalistic ideology for the Soviet Union.

Kurginian now argues that Russia can be saved only "by a counter-elite (but not at all a restorationist [i.e., Communist] one)." He indicates that he remains "a Communist Party member only because things are bad." And he suggests that the new elite may be fascist. Fascism is rising "precisely in the international sphere" and is "not to be confused with the banal nationalism that everyone fears."[79] Kurginian—like many Russians—seems to want his country and its leaders to be feared—as under Ivan the Terrible and Stalin, as it can never be under the "banal nationalism" of present-day politicians. He professes opposition to fascism, but his call for some new "counter-elite" to deliver Russia from its democratic morass raises the question of whether redemption will be obtained by developing a Russian version of fascism, by mobilizing Russian resistance to fascism elsewhere, or by some grotesque combination of both.[80]

5 | The Travails of a Democratic Identity

Almost all of the wide range of thinkers that I convened in three roundtables in Russia at the end of the 1990s were hostile to ideologies and anxious to move Russia from authoritarian to democratic rule. Yet, they also generally believed that some kind of answer to the question of Russia's identity had to be found if they were ever to gain the popular support needed for this transition.

Advocates of participatory and accountable governance seemed, at times, painfully aware that most Russians did not yet share their own commitment to reform. In popular speech during the early 1990s, the very word *demokrat* had often been rendered as *dermokrat* (shit-ocrat), and *privatizatsiia* (privatization) as *prikhvatizatsiia* (confiscation). And many ordinary Russians remained bewildered by the seeming permissiveness of a pluralistic society and angered by the widening gap between rich and poor.

The Russian people had come together in their initial determination to dismantle Soviet totalitarianism. But new leaders committed to democratic reform found themselves hemmed in by the continuing power of a sprawling and self-perpetuating state bureaucracy. Communism had produced the most extensive and intrusive variant of this omnipresent governmental phenomenon. The Soviet state bureaucracy was the culmination of a long Russian tradition of a petty officialdom that did nothing well except protect privilege and prevent change. Far from driving out the crime and corruption that grew with freedom, the bureaucrats tended to incorporate these sordid practices into their own way of life. Having rejected the communist myth of a "Great October Revolution," many felt themselves victimized by the "Great Criminal Revolution" of the capitalists.[1]

Alexander Yakovlev, a key initiator in the Gorbachev era of the attempt to break the power of the encrusted party bureaucracy, characterizes *chinovnichestvo* (the rule of the clerks) as the main obstacle to progress in post-Soviet Russia. The *chinovniki* were and are, in his view, keeping Russia from moving beyond fitful assertions of willful freedom (*volia*) on to the institutionalization of civic freedoms guaranteed by law (*svoboda*).[2]

An important recent study of Russian officialdom from the eighteenth to the early twentieth century concludes that although higher authorities determined how bureaucracies would function, "chinovnichestvo had the possibility of influencing the interpretation of the function and, in the end, using it for self-interested objectives (including embezzlement and bribery)."[3] This description seems equally valid for the prior Muscovite era and for the subsequent Soviet and post-Soviet periods. The Russian word for embezzlement, *kaznokradstvo*, literally means "robbing the public treasury," which is often seen as what basically happened during the rapid privatization of state-owned property after the collapse of communism.

The term *sovok* was coined and used briefly in the early 1990s to describe someone who continued to think and act in Soviet ways in the new era. And the persistence of "Sovietness" (*sovkost'*) continued to be recognized even among many of those who helped bring down the Soviet Union. The liberal writer Alexis Kara-Murza suggested that real reform may always be doomed in a Russia where liberalism has historically been only "a by-product of strengthening the state." Another reformer, Igor Kliamkin, extended this line of thought by suggesting that

> liberalization can only be the by-product of bureaucratization. But this leaves aside what is well nigh the main question: Can a corrupt Russian bureaucracy become the subject of liberalization?
>
> In our conditions, the by-product of bureaucratization will be not liberalization, but dictatorship.

Lilia Shevtsova argued that the basic struggle between the old bureaucracy and the new wealth was more important than all the petty conflicts and shifting political alliances in postcommunist Russia.

> Ironically, the most devastating wars are waged between the two most interconnected elites: the business and bureaucratic elites. . . . The lack of developed institutions makes these classes vicious and the results unpredictable. . . . Bureaucracy continues to be the dominant force within the Russian system of government, as it has been through the ages.[4]

The Descent into Indifference

The possibility of dictatorship by a few has been sustained and, in some respects, enhanced by the disillusionment of the many. At the dawn of the new millennium, the immediate danger to democracy in Russia seemed to be less an overthrow from above by a dictator, than an undermining from below by the populace—or from within the nominally democratic government itself.

A scholar close to Yeltsin, Georgy Satarov, stressed "the need to demythologize history" and to bring out for a public washing all the "dirty underclothes" of the Soviet era.

> The twentieth century was the century of totalitarianism, and there might be more ahead. . . . We need to find a vaccine against it; we must make a serious study of how the bacilli enter and infect the organism.[5]

Alexander Yakovlev undertook this very task in the 1990s by launching what was originally projected to be an eighty-eight–volume publication program of previously secret documents of Soviet rule.[6] He was joined in this effort by Rudolf Pikhoya, a historian from Ekaterinburg whom President Yeltsin had chosen to serve briefly as the first post-Soviet head of the Russian state archives.

On the eve of his 1996 reelection campaign, Yeltsin commissioned a group headed by Satarov to seek out and define the proper content for an "all-Russian, common-national idea" (*rossiiskaia, obshchenatsional'naia ideia*).[7] Satarov's group had to evaluate a questionnaire in which 1,521 respondents were asked to rate thirty propositions on a scale with five levels ranging from "entirely agree" to "entirely disagree." The propositions covered the full range of values and slogans then circulating in Russia. There was a sharp split in the values affirmed. The top four propositions with which most respondents completely agreed (by 78.8 percent to 87.2 percent) stressed democracy and individual responsibility (rule of law, human rights, taking care of home and family). But four of the next six propositions with which most respondents also completely agreed (by 65.6 percent to 72.5 percent) called for authoritarian rule ("the firm hands of a strong leader," "strong and strict power," "a leader who can make people follow him"). In analyzing the range of opinion expressed in his poll, Satarov divided popular attitudes into the six categories shown below.

Democrats	17.2%
Partisans of a strong hand	12.6%
Communist revanchists	17.0%
Disillusioned apoliticals	17.1%
Nihilists	22.8%
Romantics	13.3%

These and other polls point to the contradictory nature of public opinion. Again we confront a *matryoshka*—a democratic face on the outside but an authoritarian one on the layer just inside. Still further inside, there seems to be a doll expressing near total indifference, if not hostility, to ideas in general and politics in particular. The final three categories in Satarov's inventory of attitudes subscribe to no political ideas at all. Yet, these three together command more allegiance than the sum of the other three categories that do express political beliefs.

A poll of young Russians two years later revealed a similar dichotomy. On the one hand, they preferred developing their country economically rather than building it into a great military power (80 percent to 15 percent). But, on the other hand, twice as many were sorry rather than glad that the Soviet Union no longer existed (57 percent to 28 percent).[8] From the suffocating controls of the Soviet "ideocracy," a free Russia developed what Satarov calls "ideaphobia." "Nihilist" was the most popular of Satarov's categories. The analysts of the subsequent poll of young people concluded that they were, in fact, "the no generation."

Neither Satarov's semiofficial poll nor a related state-sponsored essay contest succeeded in defining a unifying national idea for the Russian Federation. The prize-winning entry came from Gury Sudakov, a scholar-politician in the northern city of Vologda, who advocated a blend of Russian traditions and democratic reforms.[9] "Communal existence in our difficult climate was the key to our survival," wrote Sudakov. Russians instinctively seek "harmony in the soul" rather than material things and thus "are not market-oriented." "The stormy and emotional in Russian human nature" has over time been held in check by a conscience that has been strengthened by suffering. "If a Russian could not sigh, he would suffocate from the overflow of emotion."

According to Sudakov, in the nineteenth century radical extremists in little circles (*kruzhkovtsy*) "threw out ethics from socialism and went for the axe," rejecting the creative and moderate tradition of Pushkin and Russian culture generally. But there can be no more revolutions because "only evolution is capable of saving civilization and culture."

Russia must resist the "global nihilism" of the individualistic West that is "sucking out the soul of the people" with its "Gospel according to Sales." Nevertheless, the Russian task is not to reject but to "bring a sense of balance to a market economy." And this can be done

> only through democracy and a civil society. We need citizen self-govern-
> ment to unleash the people's initiative and to protect them from the ego-
> tism of those in power.

The subtitle of Sudakov's essay cited above is, "When Will the Holiday of the Danish Kingdom Appear in Russia?" The author is citing the practice in Copenhagen of permitting any child to come to Tivoli Park on his or her birthday and use all the amusements free of charge for the entire day. Russia needs something like this to inculcate both "lightness of being" in adults and citizenship in children. "If the state respects its small citizen, then, when he grows up, he will definitely be concerned about his state."

Satarov also summoned up an image of childhood when I pressed him in 1999 for his own view of where Russia should be heading. He pointed to a brief animated cartoon from the popular television series, "Tales of the New Russia." A little boy is trying to build a toy house with blocks, but wind and rain are pouring in on him through open windows. His loudly quarreling parents have knocked his house down. The child looks up and simply asks them to shut the windows and stop the fighting so that he can start building his house all over again.

Can young Russians acquire the "passion" to overcome the inertia of bureaucratic chinovnichestvo? Can they develop the horizontal relationships necessary to overcome their long authoritarian tradition of vertical control from the top down? And will the boy who just wants to build his own little house become indifferent to the broader concerns of his homeland? Would a free day in the amusement park really make any difference?

The Yeltsin entourage gave up all visible efforts to continue the search for a unifying national idea as his popularity eroded. Many Russians seemed eager simply to forget about ideas altogether and concentrate on the accumulation and enjoyment of material things. Those who succeeded, the wealthy "New Russians," tended to retreat from society, surrounding themselves with security guards and taking their children and money abroad. Many who stayed in Russia withdrew from public life just at the time when opportunities to participate were expanding. Withdrawal sometimes took a religious form. More often it took the form of a deliberate indifference to all ideals expressed by two new slang terms of the late 1990s: *stiob* and *pofigizm*. [10]

Stiob describes an approach to life that takes no person and no words seriously. The popular late-night television show *Vremechko* (A Little Time) popularized this attitude with an endless flow of satire featuring senseless crimes, idiotic phone calls, preposterous examples of irrational behavior, and condescending reports on everyday life. The show originated on the popular NTV network, which was the most sympathetic to, and inclusive of, national minorities. After NTV was muffled by two successive government-supported changes of management, the program's "heroes" became almost exclusively ethnic Russians—suggesting to some a new kind of appealingly mindless national identity.

Some critics saw stiob as an example of "postmodern irony." Others saw *Vremechko* and *Kukly* (Dolls), the popular satirical television puppet show, as perpetuating the old Russian tradition of attempting to cleanse corruption with comedy. (The producer of *Kukly* told me, however, that he had been inspired by puppetry that he saw in France.)

For many Russians, stiob expressed a distinctive new Russian attitude toward life that they also characterized as pofigizm. The term is derived from the slang term *po figu*, roughly meaning, "I don't care about anything." This was described as "the Russian national philosophy" by Viktor Yerofeev, one of the most popular post-Soviet writers and talking heads on television. He saw total indifference as a natural reaction both to the material irritants of everyday Russian life and to the abstract ideas like democracy and human rights that are piped in from the West to camouflage Russia's national humiliation. Yerofeev describes pofigizm as "the philosophy of someone who has been knocked senseless," "an organic Russian state of mind," and a distinctive Russian synthesis of Western self-doubt and Slavic laziness.

Pofigizm differs from Western cynicism, since it is indifferent to personal success and to any and all ideals of oneself or others. This attitude is, in some ways, the spiritual descendant of an attitude in the late Soviet era known as *nibonicho* (neither God nor the devil). This sense of total apathy helped weaken Soviet ideology, but is now seen by some as foredooming post-Soviet freedoms. Yerofeev argued in the late Yeltsin years that "pofigizm has killed reforms and democracy." That fear continued into the Putin era.

In 2002, a popular, independent Duma deputy from Vladivostok described Russia as having returned to the "stagnation" of the Brezhnev era.[11] The reformist Alexis Kara-Murza saw Russia not as an active power in Eurasia ("Evraziia") but as a land of powerless passivity, combining European decadence with Asian authoritarianism into "Aziopa."[12] A sociologist saw "Russia as a society where everyone is at risk" and where regions can get federal subsidies only by vying with one another to win official status as a "zone of environmental disaster." With narcotics more available than medicine, "the production of risks" tends to replace the production of goods. In the face of all this, the legendary "patience of Russians" has become

> not a resource for peaceful reforms, but rather a symptom of the exhaustion of vitality, and, therefore, a threat to their existence as a nation.[13]

A major summary of the proliferating literature on post-Soviet society concluded that "success and well-being are associated either with good luck or with immorality."[14] Another survey reported that the predominant negative feeling in Russia was simply "exhaustion and indifference."[15] Another study reported that 84 percent of those polled in December 2000 believed that they were unable to influence in any way decisions taken by higher authorities. The populace was able to survive only by "passive adaptation" to ever-lowering expectations. The study saw Russia becoming "a nation of spectators." A full one-third of the growing number of television viewers never turned off their television sets in the course of the entire day. The number of newspapers declined by one third, and that of magazines by 87 percent from 1990 to 1998.[16]

With state educational subsidies drastically reduced, Russia was seen as close to producing not only an underclass of the perpetually poor but also a fundamentally new and potentially explosive phenomenon: a culture of poverty among highly educated people.[17] In the face of all this, some intelligent young Russians saw the continuing discussion of Russian identity as the final talkathon of a dying intelligentsia, the terminal buzzing of autumn flies repetitively banging up against a closed window.

In the postmodern imagination of the post-Soviet generation, Russia no longer seemed to be Gogol's open-air troika hurtling across, and soaring above, the endless steppe on a spiritual quest with bells ringing. It was seen, rather, in terms of Pelevin's image of a closed train conveying unwitting passengers toward a ruined bridge. Yury Boldyrev, a founder of the Audit Chamber and popular hero of the anticorruption campaign of the early 1990s, retired from public life altogether at a young age to live in the provincial countryside, declaring that "a society incapable of acting may deny itself a future."[18]

Nor was hope to be kindled by lighting candles in front of icons. In post-Soviet Russia, there seemed to be only a *Black Candle* and *Dark at the End of the Tunnel*—to cite the titles of two of the most important novels of the 1990s. *Black Candle* was the joint work of the great dissident balladeer of the late Soviet era, Vladimir Vysotsky, and the Irkutsk writer, Leonid Monchinsky. The book grew out of their joint journey in 1976 to live with ex-prisoners still working in the remote gold mines of the frozen north. Their bleak report is written in the language of the camps and could not be published until 1992, after the fall of communism. Monchinsky, who did most of the writing after Vysotsky died, explains that

> We did not set out to write a book of horrors; we simply lived (and live) in a world where nothing needs to be contrived, because reality exceeds our fantasies. One time we were talking to a man who was eating people. He said, "it was repugnant only at the very beginning; since then, I even like it."[19]

Dark at the End of the Tunnel by Yury Nagibin bemoans "the suffocating vulgarity of the world's province," and contends that

> the greatest guilt of the Russian people is their perpetual guiltlessness in their own eyes. . . . Everything that has been done in Russia was done with Russian hands and with Russian consent.[20]

Nagibin thought that his father was Jewish and concealed this knowledge all his life, only to discover that his father was an ethnic Russian—and to realize that he could never live "without complexes."[21] The last line of his novel is, "It is hard to be a Jew in Russia, but even harder to be a Russian."[22]

Russian literature spiraled even further downward in the prize-winning, best-selling novel of 2002: Alexander Prokhanov's *Mr. Hexagen*. The title bears the name of the explosive that blew up apartment buildings in Moscow, and the cover depicts the skull of Lenin. Its publisher calls its author a "necrophiliac," and its plot has been likened to a nested doll of conspiracies within conspiracies.[23] An alcoholic "Little God" is dominated by his nymphomaniac daughter (thought to suggest the Yeltsins) who is controlled by evil Jewish oligarchs working with former KGB agents. They, in turn, are working for the New World Order. "The Chosen One" (Putin) then comes to power to avenge the apartment bombings which have, however, been staged by the corrupt secret services, probably at the behest of the same Jewish oligarchs whose ultimate aim is to take power and ship Russians to the Arctic and the organs of the healthy to Israel. This merciless, anti-Semitic, surrealistic gloss on Moscow politics in the 1990s is the work of a "red–brown" extremist who sees his nation adrift in "ruins full of demons" and Putin's policies as nothing more than "makeup that is put on a corpse in a morgue."

Things do not seem much brighter to believers at the other end of Russia. An Orthodox Christian writer from the Russian Far East suggests that resignation to failure in this life lies deep in the Russian consciousness. The saying *sud'ba-zlodeika* (fate is an evildoer) suggests that the gap between God's love and man's misbehavior will never be overcome and that the Russian people need "preparedness for a future that will be worse than the present."[24]

The Return of Moral Vision

Despite periodic nightmares of despair (and fitful Eurasian dreams of glory), post-Soviet Russians have slowly developed a guardedly optimistic middle position. They have moved out of indifference and cynicism through a characteristic Russian mood swing—not so much to belief as to hope.

Data from the All Russian Center of Public Opinion Studies at the beginning of the new millennium showed a radical upturn in optimism about the future after thirteen years of unmitigated gloom. The number of pessimists about the future was cut in half from 1999 to 2001. At the end of 2001, only 5 percent of those polled believed that the year 2002 would be worse than 2001; and by the spring of 2003, polls showed that "half of Russians are happy for some reason."[25]

This surprising return of hopefulness cannot be attributed just to the continued popularity of President Putin and the slight turnaround of the economy after a near-meltdown in August 1998. It may be explained in part by a genuine insight contained in Gumilev's often-mythic writings. He attributed Russia's periodic great accomplishments—like those that unified Russia in the fourteenth and fifteenth centuries—to sudden outbursts of passion and energy.

But the driving force then was not, as Gumilev suggested, cosmic rays leading to military conquest. It was rather the spiritual power of monks who believed that asceticism and prayer linked them with the "energies" of God. They created a pictorial Christian culture that unified Western Eurasia, and they were at the forefront of the colonization that led North and East to North America.[26] Similarly, the great writers of the nineteenth century channeled a new burst of energy into a vernacular literature infused with moral passion that gave a sense of common identity to a newly literate Russian populace.

Even under atheistic communist rule, official Russians continued to speak of their "spiritual culture." In the early years of the new century, authentic aspects of this Russian tradition seemed to be returning after a decade of chaos and depression. Cynicism remained widespread, but the characteristic Russian cynic became not so much a postmodern man mocking everything as a premodern Diogenes lighting his small lamp in a dark world in search of an honest person. The sense of a once and future community of moral responsibility is rooted in the moral awakening that swept away communist power. It sprouted elections offering real choices in hard times, survived a terrible blight of crime and corruption, and is beginning to flower into institutions with some chance of surviving even the harsh winters that are sure to come.

In contrast to the Eurasian view that Russia must protect its people from Western decadence by closer alliance with authoritarian Asian neighbors, Igor Chubais suggests that Russia will serve Asia better by helping to regenerate, rather than by rejecting, Europe.

> Russia, thrust out onto the climatic outskirts of Europe can be considered its moral core.[27]

Chubais, brother of Anatoly Chubais, the often-maligned chief architect of economic privatization, sees Russia's long-delayed market and democratic development being gradually grafted onto a moral culture still embedded in the religion and rural folklore of a people not yet as self-indulgent as their Western neighbors.

> The formula for a new Russia will look like this: support for collectivism and mutual help in matters of ordinary daily living; but step-by-step affirmation of individualism in the productive and professional sphere.[28]

What is needed to secure a democratic identity for postcommunist Russia is a "spiritual cleansing (*ochishchenie*) . . . not in meetings or on barricades, but in the souls and conscience of people." This has not yet happened in Russia, which "goes on rehabilitating people . . . [but] never fixes guilt on anyone . . . [or provides] judicial recognition of the illegality of the total system." Once the moral slate is cleaned, Russia will be free to develop an accountable and participatory government of laws that will make possible accelerated internal development of the country. Then, "the expansion of our ideas, culture, and technology should forever exclude [any renewed preoccupation with] the expansion of power."[29]

A new generation of scholars is studying Russia's historic "archetypes of power" and practices of worship to help explain why such a process of cleansing has not yet taken place. Every time major reforms were introduced in modern Russia (1861, 1917, 1991), they were presented as a total break with the past along with a complete denial of any responsibility for that past. Power (*vlast'*) is seen as a superhuman force operating above history and society. Peter the Great was hailed as a sculptor creating a new country from clay, giving Russia a "second baptism."[30]

The populace in all these cases of allegedly progressive change was patronized as an inert, "archaic" object devoid of will, let alone the responsible citizenship that democracy requires. This archetype continues to be supported by a compliant television, which has only one real hero: "the exhibitionist power" of a "noncompetitive and authoritarian" government.[31]

Polls in 2002–2003 reveal guardedly hopeful views about the future. One poll showed that belief in strong central rule was accompanied by an almost equally strong faith in democracy.[32] In another, designed to assess attitudes toward the first decade of reform, respondents expressed a clear preference for group equality over individual freedom; yet 83.6 percent singled out the proverb "Whatever is done is for the better" from among forty-two offered to describe their basic feelings. The analyst of the polling data comments that

> These words are the quintessence of the typical Russian optimistic fatalism coexisting with passivity and non-interference with life that goes on as if "all by itself". . . . This position is the polar opposite of the basic reliance on individual initiative typical for the Protestant ethic according to which one must make oneself and one's life.[33]

The underdevelopment of individual responsibility in Russia is traced to the persistence of collective rituals of public penance in both the Orthodox Church and the Communist Party. A young St. Petersburg scholar contends that individual, private confession did not play the same role in Russian as in Western Christianity. Instead, rituals of public penance developed. Privacy in confession was downgraded by Peter the Great, who increased surveillance of priests. The communists after 1917 intensified and secularized this tradition by requiring self-revelation before a collective (*proiavlenie lichnosti*) and obligatory denunciation of others (*oblichenie*).[34]

One reformist politician of the early post-Soviet era, Sergei Baburin, argued that Russian Orthodoxy must, nevertheless, be central to Russian identity. The Church in the past helped integrate a multiethnic society—and now can use its communitarian teachings to counterbalance the excessive individualism and human dislocations of the new market economy. A former deputy speaker of the Duma, Baburin juxtaposed the Russian ideal of *narodovlastie* (popular rule) to the "nihilistic liberalism" of the West—and his own "enlightened traditionalism" to a purely nationalistic concept of Orthodoxy.[35]

The new vision of an essentially moral identity for Russia builds on Dmitry Likhachev's distinction between patriotism and nationalism. He saw patriotism as a natural, positive sentiment, extending familial bonds to one's native land. Nationalism, by contrast, is an artificial, negative ideology driven by fear of external enemies and sustained by witch-hunts for internal scapegoats. Baburin contrasted a benign "nationalism" with a "perverse chauvinism" to describe the same dichotomy.[36] Baburin found Russia's distinct identity in its unique fusion of a soaring, spiritual culture with an earthy attachment to the land. The breakup of the USSR was an historic tragedy—not so much because Russia lost its outlying republics, but because it perpetuated Stalin's original reorganization of a multiethnic empire into a series of ethnic compounds.

Baburin participated in the democratic opposition to Yeltsin in the immediate aftermath of Yeltsin's shelling of the parliament in October 1993. He subsequently became interested in the "Japanese way" of developing consensus without either social violence or excessive legal wrangling. In 2003, he moved into ethnocentric and authoritarian nationalism. He named his marginal new party The People's Will (Narodnaia Volia) after the nineteenth-century populist revolutionary group that assassinated the reformist Tsar Alexander II; and he joined Sergei Glazev's bloc of left-nationalists.

Many Russian democrats express sympathy for some eventual, peaceful modification of Russia's borders. Most Russians favor unification with Belarus. Many share Alexander Solzhenitsyn's hope that reintegration might someday also be worked out with Ukraine. Like Solzhenitsyn, the liberal scholar Igor Zevelev adds to the list Northern Kazakhstan, which, like parts of Ukraine, is heavily populated with ethnic Russians. But Zevelev cautions against following the often-cited model of Kemal Ataturk in breaking up the Ottoman empire:

> Kemalist Turkey started its experiment with a nation-state by subjecting its Iranian, Greek, and Kurdish minorities to genocide and expulsion . . .
>
> A Russia without clear-cut frontiers may be the only peaceful solution to the "Russian question". . . . Eurasia's blurred political map [may make it possible] for Russia and other Eurasian peoples not to repeat all the steps and mistakes made by Western Europe. The "German question," for one, was firmly resolved within the framework of European integration once the borders that the Germans had fought over for a century became obsolete.[37]

Igor Chubais sees grounds for such hope in the Russian people's general absence of deep hatred for foreigners and in their predisposition toward "soft co-existence" with neighbors in outlying regions.

Some advocates of a democratic rather than an authoritarian future for Russia buttress their case with new theories about the "noosphere." The prolific economist Yury Yakovets argues that all past theories about inevitable conflicts and the rise and fall of civilizations are now obsolete. The broad cycles in human affairs (the sociosphere) and in the natural world (the biosphere) are being superseded by the interaction of the human mind with the cosmos (the noosphere). All of humankind is now reaching "through the storms to the stars."[38]

The ecological crisis has become global and cannot be resolved by either arrogant central planners or "the uncontrollable randomness of the market." Nor can one rely on the naive "eco-centrism" of those who see science and technology as part of the problem rather than part of the solution. Questions must now be resolved collaboratively between nations and disciplines in the noosphere, "the sphere that determines the influence of human thought and activity on biospheric processes."

The "positive variant of the noosphere for the twenty-first century" has been foreshadowed by the "stable development" achieved already in compact, homogenous countries like Norway, Sweden, Finland, Switzerland, and Japan. Russia has the resources and talent to replicate this model on a larger scale and validate it for multiethnic countries— and perhaps even for the world as a whole.

Yakovets rejects the Eurasianist idea of closer alignment with China, which, unlike Russia, has not kept alive its "spiritual core" and its capacity to think not just globally but also cosmically. He describes two possible future scenarios for Russia:

(1) *The pessimistic:* A new authoritarianism in which the worst case would be a Pol Pot; the best, a Pinochet. In either case, Russia would be "Albanianized" into an isolated, autarchic state.

(2) *The optimistic:* A new and larger-scale South Korea or Singapore in which a new generation would create with surprising speed a booming new nation that amalgamates Westernizing political reforms with the economic dynamism of the early Soviet New Economic Program and the first stage of the Chinese Communist economic reforms.

Yakovets then sets forth a third, preferred scenario, which he calls *the realistic* but never describes as precisely as the others. As set forth throughout his writings, it seems to involve adopting American and Swiss models for federal democracy, and German and Scandinavian models for relating to the global market economy, reviving pre-1917 Russian culture, and adding the subsequent "synthesis of art, high technology, and the market" in the United States and Japan.[39]

Under this scenario, Russia could provide a model for other developing countries by becoming not just another traditional nation but a new type of community in which every individual's development is linked with the commonalities of the globe and the imperatives of the noosphere. Whatever the scenario for the future, Russians will play a central role in shaping it. "Russia will be at the forefront—either of the revival or of the collapse of civilization."[40]

The Rise of the Regions

The horizons of Russian democrats have been widened by the political rise of the provinces. Polling data show that surprisingly large numbers of Russian citizens identify a city or region as their primary locus of allegiance.[41] The breakup of the Soviet Union was followed by a "heraldic rush" in provincial Russia to adopt or invent symbols, seals, and banners of their own.[42] By the spring of 2003, it was clear that "Russians prefer to read the press published in the regions, not that published in the capital."[43]

Ethnic Russians in regions of the federation that have non-Russian majorities often now identify themselves with their region rather than their ethnicity. A poll of 1,000 in the far northern and ethnically Russian district (*oblast*) of Archangel showed that 46.9 percent identified their locality as their native land (*rodina*) and only 43.3 percent defined themselves as Russians.[44] Forty-eight percent of ethnic Russians living in Tatarstan in 1997–1998 referred to themselves as Tatarstanians.[45]

President Shaimeyev of Tatarstan made gestures to neutralize potential ethnic tension between Russians and Tatars by simultaneously restoring the cathedral and building a mosque within the Kremlin in Kazan. He also set up a new Islamic university to reduce the temptation to study radical Islam abroad.

Ethnic Russians themselves often take the lead in trying to revive the tradition of regional autonomy (*oblastnichestvo*) that was gathering strength in the late years of the prerevolutionary Russian empire. Emil Pain, an upbeat reformer, warned that civic indifference in the provinces could be "no less dangerous than social upheaval." He noted that in nominally Jewish autonomous Birobidzhan in the Russian Far East, "it is the Russian population that speaks out for the preservation of the Jewish autonomous oblast, where almost no Jews remain."[46] Since ethnic Russians are now the overwhelming majority of the population in the Russian Federation, provincial political leaders generally promote regional rather than ethnic identity in order to strengthen their power vis-à-vis the central government. Ethnic Russians in Siberia and the Far East have even hinted at suggesting secession from the Russian Federation.

The development of regional perspectives even among ethnic Russians is particularly evident in the resource-rich but impoverished regions in the north and east. The hardy souls who live in these "territories of discomfort"[47] fear that they are in danger of becoming nothing more than "a raw material appendage" of the Russian Federation and Europe generally.[48] In an age devoid of heroes, northerners and Siberians are often seen as the courageous bearers of the rustic values needed to revive Russia: closeness to nature and historic freedom from the servile legacy of either serfdom or bureaucracy.

The Eurasianists who advocate moving the Russian capital east of the Ural Mountains argue variously that "a new democracy" needs "a renewing center" and that Russian power and influence can be more securely established in Central Asia than was ever possible in Eastern Europe.[49] Many more insist that Moscow has to be marginalized, since it has preserved the old bureaucracy and, at the same time, become hopelessly Westernized. Moscow has gained a vested interest in reducing Russia to a dependent province of the Euro-Atlantic world.

Whereas Moscow has become Westernized, St. Petersburg, the erstwhile "window to the West," has become a sometime defender of Russian traditionalism. This defense of Old Russia can be authoritarian and centralizing as it was with Metropolitan Ioann of St. Petersburg. Or it can take a federal form as it did with Governor Vladimir Yakovlev. He recommended consolidating all the northern territories into a single political unit with St. Petersburg as its capital city. Putin's successful candidate to succeed Yakovlev, Valentina Matvienko, featured in her electoral campaign a far-reaching proposal to make St. Petersburg a model city for the new Russia.[50] Liberals hoped that St. Petersburg might recapture the special authority in the north and the freedoms that medieval Novgorod had enjoyed—just as autocratic nationalists idolized Ivan the Terrible, who destroyed those freedoms.

The Northern Territories are a legally defined entity extending from Murmansk and Archangel all the way to the Pacific. This was the scene of slave labor camps and forced repopulation in Soviet times but also a region where workers received higher wages than elsewhere. It has subsequently suffered from neglect and depopulation. Sensing that energy resources might soon be exhausted everywhere else, some feared that this vast, resource-rich domain might become the source of "the major wars of the twenty-first century."[51]

The north is sometimes seen as the epicenter not just of Russia's past suffering but also of its future salvation. The village writers and a growing number of journalists have invested the region with all manner of redemptive attributes. Economists have described it as a bottomless cornucopia of natural resources, and ecologists assert that the north is the lungs of the world, the last virgin forest still breathing on—and for—the planet. The Siberian-born writer Sergei Zalygin turned *Novy Mir* into the most influential "thick journal" of the late Soviet period, largely through his powerful environmental advocacy and his publication of two long-proscribed Russian literary masterpieces: Boris Pasternak's *Dr. Zhivago* and Alexander Solzhenitsyn's *Gulag Archipelago*.

In post-Soviet Russia, the frigid north and east have grown in imaginative appeal even as they have shrunk in population. Northerners have been credited with developing a unique style of "landscape architecture." Wooden buildings were organically linked with unembellished natural surroundings; frescoes and icons in their churches mimicked the colors of northern vegetation; and compositions featured their beloved horses.[52] At the same time, northerners preserved pre-Christian values—sometimes characterized as "aryan" (despite the opprobrium attached to the term),[53] sometimes described as a return to the pagan Sun God represented as a white horse. A nuclear physicist in the academic city of Novosibirsk has set up a "Museum of the Sun" and sees Russia leading the rest of the world back to a solar religion that will unify all existing creeds.[54] An economist from Yakutsk, the Siberian city built on permafrost, sunnily suggests that global warming will make his own region increasingly hospitable to agriculture.[55]

A number of literary figures and local officials see a relatively unspoiled and underpopulated Siberia playing a special role in the regeneration of Russia. Some reformers suggest that freedom will be increasingly secured in the vast spaces of Siberia. The population is more cosmopolitan and intelligent than is often realized. Stalin tended to send to prison or exile ethnic groups with international connections and thinkers and entrepreneurs with independent ideas.

The Library of Congress has found particularly receptive collaborators in Siberia for its online digital library of documentary images tracing the parallel stories of the westward movement of the United States and the eastward expansion of Russia. On October 12, 2002, Lyudmila Putin, spouse of President Putin, was at the Library of Congress witnessing the placing on the Internet for this "Meeting of the Frontiers" project of rare materials from seven Siberian archives. Bi-national teams worked together at conferences in Alaska and Moscow on how to use this project for teaching purposes. Some Siberian participants suggested that a Russian adaptation of the U.S. Homestead Act might help populate its still largely empty spaces.

Siberians, often the sons and daughters of the gulag, played an important role in the democratic resistance to the communist coup attempt of August 1991. Many had been brought by the Yeltsin government from east of the Urals to Moscow to welcome back Russian émigrés for a Congress of Compatriots that opened on the very day of the coup. Siberians were at the forefront of those who went on the morning of August 19, 1991, from the opening liturgy in the Cathedral of the Assumption in the Kremlin directly to the Russian White House to stand by the barricades.

In the post-Soviet era, the long-suppressed writings of nineteenth-century Siberians like Nicholas Yadrintsev and Grigory Potanin have been rediscovered. They were imprisoned for advocating greater Siberian autonomy and an American-type federalism for Russia at the time of the sale of Alaska to the United States. In 1908, Potanin described how Russians themselves discover freedom and the urge to innovate:

> [Siberia is] a milieu where the creative Russian spirit can freely unfold its wings, unbound by the traditions with which they were bound in the mother country.[56]

Eleanora L'vova, a veteran ethnologist from Tomsk, laments that the historic focus on "the great idea" of Russia and its vastness has "made us forget about our smaller homelands and . . . covered up and obscured the idea of everyday life (*ideia povsednevnogo*)." She sees new relevance in Potanin's never-realized ideal of writing a new kind of historical textbook that would

> begin with the home and radiate out to the land surrounding it, the village, and the oblast, moving out to the furthest borders of our native land.[57]

Practical, economic reasons are now advanced for attaching particular importance to Siberia. It is seen not just as a great repository of natural resources but also as an emerging transportation bridge between Europe and Asia. Academic and government officials suggest that Siberia has the potential to provide (1) an expedited European land link with East Asia by improving the Trans-Siberian Railway and building a parallel East–West highway for trucking, and (2) shorter air routes between South Asia and North America by opening new channels and airports for transpolar flights.

The growth of regional consciousness has had more immediate impact on the culture and psychology of the Russian Federation than on its politics and economics. The federal treaties and new laws of March 1992 and the new constitution of December 1993 established legal equality among all eighty-nine political subdivisions of the Federation and varying degrees of autonomy for each. But the widely differing interests and resources of the regions and local conflicts between newly constituted legislatures and regional executives prevented the development of effective common stands against the power of the Kremlin.

Particularly after Yeltsin's conflict with the Duma in October 1993 and the subsequent repudiation of reform parties in the December Duma elections, Yeltsin basically governed by presidential decrees. A chill descended on any region pressing for greater autonomy after war began against Chechnya in 1994 and was renewed in 1999. Putin sought to further rein in the subdivisions of the Federation by dividing them into seven groupings—each with a Putin-appointed supergovernor to watch over them. He also weakened the power of the upper house of the Russian Parliament, the Federative Council, by excluding provincial governors from their initial right to be members.

Although frustrated politically, the regions often made remarkable cultural and economic progress through their own independent initiatives. Film festivals, which often featured locally made documentaries, were held in 2003 in Rostov on the Don, Saratov, Perm, and Vladivostok. The film *Saratovskie Stradaniia* (The Sufferings of Saratov) chronicled ordinary daily life in a provincial city and focused attention on the fate of the individual in society. The Perm festival, "Flahertiana," was entirely devoted to the pioneering American silent film director Robert Flaherty, whose epic eskimo documentary, *Nanook of the North*, apparently appealed to the Siberians. Young people in the regions seemed to find renewed hope in the popular phrase that Likhachev associated with Siberia and the deep interior of Russia: "freedom (*svoboda*) is will (*volia*) plus space."

The Motherland and the Role of Women

The middle name of every Russian is still a patronymic based on the name of his or her father. The tsar was popularly legitimized as everyone's beloved "papa" (*batiushka*). The word "fatherland" (*otechestvo*) was historically used to promote filial-type obedience to central authority in Russia. The term helped relegitimize Stalin's Russia after a decade of horrific purges: Russians came back together to fight World War II under the sanctified name of "The Great Fatherland War."

Subsequently, however, the term fatherland acquired imperial overtones and lost much of its luster after the collapse of the Soviet Union. The new Russian Federation was rarely spoken of as "the fatherland." In the last days of the USSR, an authoritarian nationalist group under General Boris Tarasov tried to combat democratization with a group that used one term for fatherland: *otchizna*. The ambitious mayor of Moscow, Yury Luzhkov, later sought to vault from local to national leadership by making the more familiar term for Fatherland, Otechestvo, the name of his new political movement. It failed badly in the election of 2000, and the song "Arise, Fatherland" was banned from broadcasts during the campaign without much protest.

The vacuum created by the erosion of the fatherland ideal has been filled in part by increased attachment to the more intimate concept of a motherland (*rodina*). Stalin had attempted to co-opt this ideal by making "for the Motherland, for Stalin" (*za rodinu, za Stalinu*) the battle cry of World War II and by erecting grotesquely huge feminine statues called Rodina in large cities as war memorials. But, since then, this ideal has been increasingly associated with folk songs, language, and the life of the spirit rather than with the panoply of power and enforcement of authority. "Motherland" suggests the more nurturing and communal side of Russian life—an identity that had been suppressed in Soviet times but kept alive at the local level. The new democratic government of Russia was no longer popularly represented as speaking for the fatherland so much as the motherland.

President Putin, as he began the new millennium, invoked the term "motherland" in a speech at an unprecedented Kremlin ceremony awarding state decorations to Christian clergymen. He especially praised the historic role the Orthodox Church played for the scattered Russian diaspora. "Living far away from their motherland, the Church is the only island of Russia that helps preserve the national culture and language." A subsequent major article on how to develop a better global image for the President and his government was entitled "How to Promote the Motherland." And Sergei Glazev gave the name "Motherland" to his left-nationalist bloc that fared so well in the 2003 Duma elections.[58]

Those attempting to put a human face on central authority often wrapped themselves in the words and symbols of warmth, spontaneity, and devotion associated with the motherland ideal. In so doing, writers in Moscow "rediscovered" and idealized the simple values of the Russian provinces in the 1990s much as populist intellectuals had done in St. Petersburg in the 1870s.[59]

Russian history has often seemed to alternate between long periods of passivity before power and sudden outbursts of revolutionary violence. Some have seen in the legendary long suffering (*dolgoterpenie*) of the Russian people the expression of a female principle, and, in their periodic upheavals, the expression of a masculine principle. Georgy Fedotov argued in the emigration that this tension was embodied in the rival ideals of fatherland and motherland. The latter was identified with both the omnipresent icons of the all-protecting Mother of God and the persistent popular belief in Mat' syra zemlya (literally, Damp Mother Earth). Motherhood ruled both the Christian heaven and the pagan earth in the so-called duality of belief (*dvoeverie*) of many ordinary Russians.

Writers and intellectuals in the nineteenth century idealized "Mother Russia" (*Matushka Rus'*) even as they berated the patriarchal rule of the tsar. The original Westernizer Peter Chaadaev saw her as a kind of peaceful, feminine buffer between the aggressive masculinity of two threatening powers:

> Between Germany and China lies Mother Russia [Rus'-Matushka). If this link between these two powers disappears, people will face great catastrophes.[60]

Somewhat later, an incantation by the poet of populism, Nicholas Nekrasov, invested her with a mystical mix of paradoxical qualities—the kind of "coincidence of opposites" that theologians had often used to describe God:

Ty i ubogaia,	Thou art wretched,
Ty i obil'naia,	Thou art abundant,
Ty i zabitaia,	Thou art cowering,
Ty i vsesil'naia,	Thou art all-powerful,
Matushka-Rus'!	Mother Russia![61]

Writers took this idea to excess in the early twentieth century. Vasily Rozanov insisted on loving the motherland "precisely when she is weak, small, humiliated, stupid, finally even depraved. Precisely, precisely when our 'mother' is drunk, is telling lies and entangled in sin, we must not distance ourselves from her."[62] In the aftermath of the Bolshevik Revolution, Boris Pilniak wrote, "Poverty-ridden, naked, barefoot, hungry, full of lice, savage—yes, it is my mother country, my mother."[63]

One recent writer in Samara (on the great river popularly known as "Mother Volga") has argued that the Soviet emphasis on the fatherland over the motherland prevented the notions of the state and of the nation from ever converging in Russia.[64] With the collapse of a militaristic fatherland, the Russian state may now have the opportunity to be well thought of as a nation by developing its motherland identity. Another writer from Samara stresses the "feminine" qualities of compassion, humility, and lack of vindictiveness as key characteristics of Russian national identity.[65] And a Western scholar has suggested that, "Russian patriots, deep down, are really *matriots.*"[66]

The Russian media in the late Yeltsin years tended to promote local, familial, and household values rather than those of an increasingly unpopular central power. National themes and central authority were reemphasized under Putin, a practitioner of martial arts who rose to power through "masculine" aggressiveness in Chechnya. But his perceived "feminine" qualities of modesty, simplicity, and familial and religious values were also played up to help sustain his popularity.[67]

Some of the leading religious thinkers in the Russian interwar emigration had suggested that Russia might someday build democracy on the moral base of Orthodox Christianity. Georgy Fedotov acknowledged that there had never yet been "an Orthodox democratic government," but he saw in "the striving of contemporary European democracy to link itself with the defense of the person . . . a secular reflection of the Christian ideal of society."[68]

Long before the human rights movement, Fedotov seemed to suggest that a similar process might transform Russia, where the Christian ideal was still deeply rooted. Nicholas Lossky contended that, while Russia had always had an authoritarian central government, ordinary life at the local level was largely regulated by "a practical democracy . . . freer than in Western Europe."[69]

Such an everyday (*bytovaia*) democracy seems to have developed at the grassroots level in post-Soviet Russia—in part out of the sheer necessity to get simple things done in the face of a corrupt bureaucracy and a dysfunctional central state. For the first time in Russian history, institutions were beginning to emerge from the bottom up and the periphery in rather than just from the top down and the center out.

Also for the first time, large numbers of women were beginning to play a significant role in Russian political life. Forty-four percent of the emerging young leaders who came to the United States in the Library of Congress's Open World program between 1999 and 2003 were women. They were chosen competitively on the basis of merit and promise—not to satisfy any quota for gender equality. The average age of participants in the program was 38, and the women, like the men, came from every part of Russia, bringing with them not just the classic "feminine" traits of endurance and compassion, but also the "passion" and "energy" previously equated with the heroic, "masculine" side of Russia. These young women seemed overwhelmingly committed to change—whether following the political model of the pioneering Passionaria of pluralism and postcommunist architect of a liberal nationalities policy, Galina Starovoitova of St. Petersburg, or the social service model of Sister Maria Borisova of Kazan, the Orthodox nun who founded a series of Orthodox youth movements.[70]

The nature of generational change in Russia has traditionally been described in masculine terms of the tension between liberal fathers and radical children in Turgenev's famous novel of the 1860s and the youthful stirrings against the Stalinist generation during the Khrushchevian "thaw." The new generation of youth in the 1980s rejected their parents' "era of stagnation," but, in the process, rediscovered the forgotten legacy of their grandparents and great-grandparents.

A particularly important linkage of the young with the old involved grandmothers and babushkas during the attempted putsch on August 20, 1991. Everyone was then expecting a military attack on the Russian White House. Young tank troops were awaiting an order from the coup leaders to crash through the ring of young people defending the fledgling democratic government inside. But it was the older women who went on the attack. They moved out to scold the crew-cut troops for even thinking of attacking their pony-tailed brothers on the barricade.

The young soldiers, lacking written commands from their superiors, were taking orders from their mothers, grandmothers, aunts, and the selfless babushkas who had brought them up and had kept alive memories of Russia as a motherland. The fearsome Red Army seemed to dissolve into a band of nineteen-year-olds being cautioned against misbehavior. The older women of Russia had become for a moment "world historical figures" in a way that the Russian intelligentsia had never expected—and that Western historians have not yet recognized.[71]

Struggling toward Optimism

Cautious optimism about the future of democracy in Russia is expressed in the writings on Russian identity by the young Olga Volko-gonova[72] and her colleague at Moscow State University, V. V. Serbinenko. They see the task of postcommunist Russia as resuming the creativity in all spheres that occurred between the Revolution of 1905 and Russia's involvement in World War I. The general breakdown of European civilization during that conflict brought communism to Russia. Russia's flowering culture was then repudiated by a form of repression without precedent even in the most unenlightened periods of tsarist rule.

Serbinenko points out that Russian émigrés who espoused democracy in the interwar period (the theologian Fedotov and the jurist P. I. Novgorodtsev) were critical of many practices of Western democracies and realized that democracy was "only a process" and not a panacea. Unfortunately, postcommunist democracy builders in Russia sometimes seemed to succumb once again to the fatal illusion of the Russian intelligentsia: that an ideal society can be created by an elite fixated on the inevitability of history rather than on the reality of their own country.

This utopianism prepared the way for communist totalitarianism; and, in post-Soviet Russia, "no less utopian seemed the efforts to construct a 'free society' with the help of some kind of universal democratic recipes." Serbinenko cites the chastening observations of the émigré Novgorodtsev about the actual workings of democracy and elections when superimposed suddenly in Europe after World War I. The result tended to be "either oligarchy or anarchy—with the next stage of political development being the strongest and severest forms of demagogic despotism."[73] Serbinenko sees hope for Russia's future democratic development in the growing realization among the young that real change comes from evolution rather than revolution. Improvement depends on accepting individual responsibility rather than anyone's arguments for the inevitability of anything.

The main obstacle to anything approaching democracy in Russia from early modern times to the present is the persistence of an amoral privileged elite. From the aristocracy to the nomenklatura to the superrich "new Russians" of today, the controlling force is a parasite that perpetually patronizes ordinary people. The hope for Russia lies in the parallel persistence of democratic practices in everyday life (*bytovaia demokratiia*)—and in the spread of education, which has made democratic development realizable as well as desirable for Russia.

Time and again, in different ways, Russians explain their postcommunist unhappiness in terms of the gap between the pretensions and the reality of democracy. In so doing, of course, they are almost always implicitly accepting democracy as the norm for Russia. Even critics of democracy often see it as a potential vehicle for lifting their country out of its lamentable current condition. Most writers on Russian identity end on a hopeful note—finding democratic qualities in some largely overlooked part of Russia's history, psychology, or social structure.

In a particularly bleak assessment of contemporary Russia, *Why Russia Is Not America*, Andrei Parshev argues that Russia will never play a successful role in the emerging global marketplace because of its harsh climate and continued dependence on the export of raw materials. By bringing in the vaunted "rule of law" from the West, Russians are merely adding Parkinson's and Murphy's Laws to an already overbureaucratized and underproductive country. Russia is already a colony of the West and may end up being nothing more than "Upper Volta with rockets."

Rolling on with his mixture of irony, black humor, and overextended metaphor, Parshev hints that there might be a lesson for Russia precisely in the recent history of Upper Volta. Though poor and living in harsh natural conditions like the Russians, the people of Upper Volta had the good sense to rise up against a king who was living abroad and to change the name that the French had given their country to Burkina Faso, which literally means "the land of honorable people."[74]

Parshev recounts the chaotic subsequent political history of one coup after another in the Burkina Faso capital of Ouagadougou. But despite it all, they (unlike Russia) sustained their independence from Europe. Russia might begin its revival by thinking of itself at least as "a land of honorable people with rockets." The inherent honor of the Russian people will make it possible for them to craft an original form of democracy out of their own historic traditions. In order to develop their own internal market, they must throw out external predators and those remnants of Russia's own foreign-oriented elites who have not already taken their wealth and their families out of the country.

Parshev characterizes his book as a handbook "for those who have decided to remain in Russia." He offers as the epigraph to his concluding section "an expansion of Murphy's law": "There is no situation so bad that it cannot become worse."[75] Yet, he also clearly implies that things can get much better if Russians learn to appreciate and build on their own largely forgotten traditions of democratic behavior at the local level.

Precisely because Russian peasants were less productive than those in Western Europe, they learned to work cooperatively and to regulate themselves freely without written laws or formalized political institutions. Parshev's argument for the enduring importance of "the democracy of everyday life" is not a mere reiteration of past Slavophile or populist beliefs about the redemptive potential of peasant communal institutions. Parshev draws instead on the latest research by the head of the section on medieval Russian history at Moscow State University, L. V. Milov, *The Great Russian Plowman and the Distinctiveness of the Russian Historical Process* (1998).[76] Great Russian plowmen allegedly drew their plows with horses rather than with oxen as in the West. As a result, the Russian peasant, unlike his Western counterpart, was neither intimidated by, nor dependent on, mounted feudal magnates—and did not live in fear of the armed highway robbery that was common even in England.

Serfdom came later to Great Russia than to Western and Central Europe. Most civil and military administration remained in patriarchal peasant hands throughout the eighteenth and nineteenth centuries. The Russian army did not have all the intermediate layers of commissioned and noncommissioned officers that Western armies inserted between top commanders and ordinary soldiers. As a result, the Russian military preserved more democratic forms of communication between seemingly unbridgeable social classes than did the more stratified chains of command in a superficially more democratic England and France.

Parshev draws on numerous firsthand accounts of eighteenth- and nineteenth-century wars to support his contention that the Russian army often fought as well or better without its commanding officers. He implies that the enduring peasant structures of consultation and cooperative action may be as valid for civil administration today as they were for military battles in the past. He echoes Likhachev's contention that "aggressiveness" (*aggresivnost'*) is not inherently characteristic of Russians. He delights in pointing out that once, when Moscow and Tver sent forth armies to fight each other for dominance in medieval Russia, both armies got lost in the forest, never met in battle, and eventually settled down to clear and cultivate the land.

Parshev insists that Russia must (1) cut itself off from a Europe that turned itself in the twentieth century into "one continuous cemetery," and (2) create a new kind of semianarchistic civilization that will be built on the morality of peasants rather than the amorality of lawyers. He argues that capital punishment has not been, and need not be, characteristic of Russian (as distinct from U.S.) civilization. But he recognizes that cruelty will always be part of any peasant package in a poor, self-isolated country like Russia.

> Since our spice cake will always be less sweet, our whip will have to be thicker [*potolshche*]. And since we have little hope of getting a successful tsar, our whip will have to be embroidered not from the top down, but from the bottom up.[77]

It is a characteristically ambiguous, but somewhat disturbing prescription. Parshev may simply be suggesting that Russia should be better prepared to defend itself and that power should be devolved from federal to local authorities to deal with guerrilla or terrorist campaigns. But he seems also to be providing a new justification for the old Russian tradition of summary "people's justice" (*narodnaia rasprava*). As expressed in seventeenth- and eighteenth-century peasant uprisings (*bunty*), in nineteenth-century Russian revolutionary theory, and in twentieth-century Stalinist practice, this kind of public "justice" by local mobs has amounted to little more than large-scale lynching.

Likhachev in his last years expressed relief that the Yeltsin government did not succeed in its effort to define a new national ideology for Russia. The same sentiment has generally been voiced by the rising young generation in which Likhachev placed his hope for the future. Professional people and provincial entrepreneurs were more inclined to talk about realistic "future scenarios" for their country than about the ultimate nature of the "Russian idea."

The most ambitious effort to spell out such scenarios came just before the election of President Putin early in 2000. "Up to 100 of the country's decision makers" weighed more than 380 "key factors" and consulted many other experts. The sponsoring "members of Club 2015" reached no clear consensus or prognosis. But their discursive and colorful summary report suggested the following three basic paths that Russia might take to reach the year 2015[78]:

- A bad scenario "of Lost Time," in which basic decisions are deferred, Russia falls further behind in the world economy. But the country remains somewhat livable, thanks to a "Minister of Provisions" called "Sandpiper" (since "every sandpiper praises his own swamp") and a government of "Ecological Salvation."
- An even worse scenario (variously described as "The Poisoned Rake" and "Megaserbia") in which Russia becomes authoritarian, lunges into foreign adventures in a fit of nationalistic bravado, allies itself with dictatorial Asian regimes, verges toward breaking up, and becomes impossible to live in.
- A good scenario in which a new "social contract" has evolved between the private sector and a restructured and accountable system of government. It is variously described as "The Renais-

sance Hippopotamus," "The Grass Breaking through the Pave-
ment," "Eurorussia," and "The White Crane" (the latter suggesting a "technological series of miracles that should [put Russia]
on the path of a developing society as a united country").

These scenarios were sketched out in the wake of the near economic
collapse of August 1998. Their combination of insight and imagination with irony and irreverence represents the exact stylistic opposite of
the didactic and portentous antidemocratic doomsaying that also
poured forth after the crisis.

In his book *Genocide: October 1993–August 1998*, Glazev indicts the
Yeltsin leadership for committing "a policy of genocide against our
own people" for the benefit of "'new Russians,' most of whom are not
ethnically Russian." The only way of avoiding "the annihilation of the
Russian cultural genotype" is to "develop a modern edition of the Russian national idea," renationalize key institutions, create a "mobilization economic policy" that will suppress popular consumption, and,
finally, "'close' the country and keep order by force."[79]

The English edition of Glazev's treatise has an introduction by Lyn-
don H. Larouche, Jr., and Glazev's career path suggests a danger that
could lie ahead for Russian reform: turning to autocratic nationalism
out of disillusionment with democracy. Glazev was minister of foreign
economic relations in Yeltsin's first cabinet but resigned after the abo-
lition of the Duma in October 1993. He was subsequently elected to
the Duma, where he served in the Communist faction and developed
a new nationalistic-collectivist philosophy. He has since been working
to bring together old communists and new nationalists. Although he
seemed to see himself building a social democratic opposition to the
Putin government, he could be preparing the way for an authoritarian
"red–brown" opposition to liberal democracy.

Fascism, in the many forms it took between the two world wars,
generally emerged from the ruins of failed democratic experiments in
traditionally authoritarian cultures. Nationalistic dictators on their various paths to power often attracted substantial support from intelligent
people in the throes of repudiating what they had previously idealized.

Particularly in the early stages of its original Italian version (*fascismo della prima ora*), fascism on the "right" used the rhetoric of the "left" about realizing some new kind of "people's democracy" from below.

Totalitarianism was always a blend of allegedly democratic socialist ideals with illusions about a heroically self-reliant national identity. Even in its most virulent racial form under Hitler, "Nazi" was an acronym for "National *Socialist.*" And even during Stalin's most genocidal period of class warfare, his official rallying cry was for "Socialism *in one country.*" It seems grotesquely appropriate that the only man Stalin apparently trusted by the end of his bloodletting in the 1930s was Hitler—judging by his disastrous failure to heed ample warnings in 1941 of Hitler's impending attack on Russia.

There have been many unexpected ways in history that *les extrèmes se touchent*[80]; and the terms "left" and "right" seem increasingly inadequate, if not irrelevant, for describing either the thinking that is taking place or the coalition that could rapidly form inside Russia. There is no presently visible coherent popular ideology or large-scale movement dedicated to overthrowing democratic institutions.[81] But the soil has been harrowed and the seeds have been scattered for a potential rapid growth of authoritarianism.

Yury Afanasiev was a key leader of the pioneering Inter-regional Group (*Mezhregionaly*) that in the late Soviet period mobilized leaders from different localities to press Gorbachev for far-reaching democratic reforms. He has since expressed deep disappointment with the failure of post-Soviet political leaders to press reform more vigorously.[82] He has poured his undiminished energies into founding and developing an altogether new Russian State University for the Humanities, which may be the most vibrant, new large institution of higher learning in postcommunist Russia. Shortly after the democratic defeat of the hard-line communist coup in August 1991, I asked him if he feared a second putsch attempt. The danger that he saw lying ahead was "not putsch two, but uprising one."

The risk remains that some sudden outburst of violence could trigger a chaotic uprising and lead to an authoritarian reaction. "Times of trouble" in Russia have historically ended by creating even more autocratic governments than had existed previously. Whether the violence were to spill into Russia from across vulnerable borders or to flare up from smoldering internal grievances, the West would not be insulated from the destabilizing consequences of a return to autocracy in the Eurasian heartland.

There are many possible doomsday scenarios for Russian democracy. A small spark dropped into a seemingly peaceful but humiliated and inflammable populace could produce fires that would be easier to spread than to extinguish. No one can confidently predict either the likelihood of an outbreak or the extent and direction of the conflagration that might follow. But there is continuing danger in the psychological/cultural condition of a once-proud people inclined to feel that no one respects them—or even credits them with being, like Burkina Faso, "a land of honorable people." Many ask if only their rockets can bring them the respect they need from others to secure their self-respect as a people.

One of the most original views of Russian identity and destiny comes from a group of young reformers and historians connected with Afanasiev's new university. They build on Afanasiev's basic argument that Russia has been given its enduring sociopolitical identity by a "Russo-Mongolian synthesis" that overconcentrated power and property in the hands of a single ruler.[83] Far from "freeing themselves from the Mongol yoke," the Russians, in Afanasiev's view, adopted the extreme Mongol concentration of power as their own heritage. As a result,

> In Russia, relationships had a coercive, not a contractual character and gave birth to a pyramid of power where both dominance and dependence were defined vertically.[84]

This basic condition lasted even into the nominally democratic Russia of Yeltsin and Putin. Reviewing the future scenarios of the 2015 project, Afanasiev predicts a combination of the bad and the worst: "lost time," in which real reforms come too late, and "Megaserbia," in which Russia takes a last "imperial lunge" before falling apart.[85]

Taking off from Afanasiev's view that "our type of society has no equivalent in world history,"[86] a pair of historians has developed a new discipline they call "Russiology" (*rossievedenie*) to explain how their unique society came into being—and to suggest how it might finally begin to shake off its autocratic heritage. According to Yu. S. Pivovarov and A. I. Fursov, an utterly unique "Russian system" was set up in the Mongol period and consolidated by "the great autocratic revolution" that concentrated unlimited power in an "Orthodox khan" garbed as a Byzantine emperor. Great Russia produced a military-patriarchal realm in the north that was ruled by coercion rather than contract.[87]

Power was more important than law or even territory. "Power first, population second," was the watchword of the thirteenth-century warrior-saint, Alexander Nevsky. For fighting Western rather than Mongol foes, he should have been called Alexander Ordynsky (Alexander of the Horde). The heir to the contractual, feudal traditions of Kievan Rus was Lithuania to the West. The key to the development of Muscovy to the East lay in a series of attempts by Russian leaders to sustain the absolute power of the Mongol/Tatar khan by creating some militant new security force fiercely loyal to the autocrat. Each of these new militias appeared in a time of chaos and produced a convulsion that led to terror: the hooded *oprichnina* of Ivan the Terrible, the guards regiments of Peter the Great, and the Cheka of Vladimir Lenin (the abbreviation for "the All-Russian Extraordinary Commission for Combating Counter-revolution, Speculation, and Delinquency in Office"—the progenitor of the massive Soviet security apparatus).

Popular resentment was deflected from the autocrat and his militia to the privileged social group most dependent on central power: the boyars in Muscovy, the aristocracy in eighteenth-century St. Petersburg, the bureaucracy in the nineteenth century, and the Communist Party nomenklatura in the twentieth. When some functions of power were extended to the aristocracy in the eighteenth century, the vast peasant majority was rendered even more powerless. When the bureaucracy ballooned in the nineteenth century, it became more difficult to realize in practice reforms that even aristocrats backed in theory.

The dynamism in this "Russian system" came from the periodic decision of the autocrat to break up the very group that he had previously created for his own protection. Preventive purges were needed to keep the once-favored group from becoming a power in itself. As a result, reforms inevitably ended up protecting, if not strengthening, central power.[88] The Soviet system prior to Gorbachev left a particularly pernicious legacy by sharing small measures of central power with a much larger and more intrusive support group (the Communist Party elite), producing thereby even greater despair in the already largely paralyzed population (*populiatsiia*).

Pivovarov and Fursov depict communism as a by-product of capitalism and characterize the collapse of communism not as a victory for capitalism but as a manifestation of the broader crisis of capitalism itself. They reject both the "Westernizing-liberal-market" and the "religion-and-soil modernizing" prescriptions for Russia. Both are "utopian" answers not based on any real analysis of "the Russian system." The only hope for real change in Russia lies in the emergence of people and organizations that can accumulate property and authority independent of central power—and create thereby "a political sphere" that has never before existed in Russia. Within this sphere different interests can compete and the government can become a referee rather than the sole all-dominating player.

The authors end up calling, in effect, for an academic remedy. Russia needs a modern political science if it is ever to understand politics, let alone begin dismantling the enduring bureaucratic structures that sustain overcentralized power.[89] The beginnings of such a science can be found in the independent analysis of the 1996 poll of popular feeling about Russia made by two scholars from a newly founded Institute of Sociological Analysis. By probing deeply into the attitudes expressed on the relationship between the strength of government and the well-being of the people, Pivovarov and Fursov come up with different categories and more optimistic conclusions about the prospects for democracy in Russia than did the original analysis by Satarov.

Even those Russians who seek, above all, "a strong and authoritative" government want it to be based on, and not at the expense of, "the well-being of its citizens." Post-Soviet men and women are more individualists than collectivists.[90] Only a participatory and accountable government can overcome the "alienation from government that began already in the Brezhnev era." Neither nationalists nor proponents of central power (*derzhavniki*) favor a return to communism. Westernizing democrats share with Orthodox traditionalists a surprising number of common attitudes despite enormous differences in social background and educational level between the two groups.[91] The Orthodox Church and the family have had enduring meaning for Russians and are essential for the effective functioning of any Russian democracy.

Russia "must move on from declarations of general principles to decode and clarify their content." There is a profusion of ideas, but "there is, strictly speaking, no competition of ideas in Russia today"— and thus no real movement toward practical reform. Cowardly thinkers hide behind abstractions and are reluctant to say publicly that, "Westernization today does not contradict but corresponds with the national interests of Russia and is compatible with order and stability in our country."[92] Reformers too often feel that the people "would not understand" Western ideas without a protective coating of anti-Western demagoguery. But, in fact, ordinary people are moving beyond the intellectuals who continue to view them too condescendingly. Russia is now producing, for the first time in its history, "Westernizers from the people" (*zapadniki iz naroda*).[93]

Pivovarov and Fursov suggest that the new spirit of tolerance among the population is also rooted in "the tendencies that arose in the entrails of the Soviet system in the last decade of its existence in opposition to its own nature." To achieve a democratic future, Russia should "destroy only a little from the past, but surmount it . . . with a new well-ordered form of everyday life that is better than the old."[94]

Two works produced at the turn of the millennium illustrate, respectively, the retrospective and the prophetic power of the upheaval of thought that freedom has brought to Russia. Regarding the first, a group of historians led by Afanasiev produced an integrated program for making a fresh review of the Russian experience in the twentieth century. They call for a new type of "total history" that gives priority to using primary sources in all media within an "open system" that requires both "situational analysis" of specific human episodes and broad consideration of the global context. The project is a practical outline for use in Afanasiev's new university in Moscow: it rejects not only the obligatory *Short Course* used in the Soviet period but also the use of textbooks altogether. Making heavy use of online materials, the program encourages pluralism, cooperative projects, and lifelong learning in remote locations.[95]

Regarding the prophetic, looking ahead in 1999 to the twenty-first century, Afanasiev's younger colleague, Fursov, saw humanity "on the threshold of a pointillist world" moving "from world war to universal war . . . which can go on everywhere in the world, at many points between many agents . . . and not between two agents or blocs." He foresaw long before September 11, 2001, an epidemic of terrorist attacks and small group wars (*miatezhevoiny*) against central authorities. This violence will represent humanity's lashing back against the poisonous "triad" of a globalized economy, postmodernism in culture, and the depletion of natural resources.[96]

Afanasiev himself sees Russia as a continuing danger to its own and other peoples until it definitively exorcises "the demiurge of power" and breaks its historic fusion of power and property. Russia must "overcome" its unfortunate history in which central power did not emerge as a result of the interplay of various social forces and is not limited by any institution with independent integrity. Power in Russia has always been monolithic (*monosubektna*), supported by people who do not work for institutions with authority so much as exercise functions for an authoritarian leader.[97]

The only way of shedding "the heritage of the Horde in our genes" (*nasha ordynskaia genetika*) is to develop political institutions and economic interests independent from central power. But pure market economics is not a true antidote to totalitarian autocracy. Liberalism, like communism, sees human society only as "the mechanical sum total of many me's." Following the émigré philosopher Semion Frank, Afanasiev characterizes this as "singularism."[98] He sees post-Soviet Russia in danger of lurching from its "continuation of ancient universalism" to an "atomic" individualism in which "even the money is fleeing from Russia." He estimates that $37 billion left Russia in the decade 1991 to 2001.[99]

Afanasiev seems to advocate a communitarian approach that will create a civil society independent of the government, rebuild Russia from the bottom up, and severely limit central power. He sees Russia creating many independent centers of innovation and productivity. He wants to achieve the kind of society that emerged in Western Europe in its "golden thirty years" between 1945 and 1975.[100]

Afanasiev is Russia's leading disciple of the Annales school, which helped liberate the postwar writing of history in Paris from its Marxist shackles by emphasizing structural developments over the long term (*longue durée*). Afanasiev is investing for the future by pouring his energy into educating the young in the responsible use of freedom. His entirely new, post-Soviet university may be the first to be formally named "humanistic." It is an institution that has been growing steadily both intellectually and physically. It has taken over real estate once occupied by the Communist Higher Party School; it is a place where pluralism seems to coexist with enthusiasm and where pofigizm seems relatively rare.

In the midst of all the dangers that Afanasiev sees lying ahead for Russia, he finds grounds for hope in a poll taken on the eve of the new millennium. It shows that the most important changes in their lives that Russians could identify from the wreckage of the twentieth century were, in order of importance: literacy, access to education, access to information, and access to health care.[101]

The identity of Russia in the new century seems likely to emerge less from the current logotherapy of those who grew up under communism than from the fresh perspectives of the post-Soviet generation in Afanasiev's university, and in many other new and renewed institutions of learning yet to be discovered or invented in Russia's great interior space.

Conclusion

What is one to make of this churning potpourri of ideas about the nature and destiny of Russia? Does it reflect the disintegration of a once-coherent culture, or the creative progression toward a more open and pluralistic society?

The wide variety of approaches and aspirations among Russians today represents an affirmative exercise of their new freedoms. But, at the same time, a nationwide poll in May 2002 indicated that 57 percent of Russians favor the imposition of censorship on the Russian media.[1] Does this reflect some basic, deep desire to return to autocracy, or simply the normal tendency in maturing democracies both to use and to abuse the media?

The beginning of an answer, if there is one, would seem to lie in the fact that the tensions and contradictions in Russian thinking today do not seem to lie *between* groups so much as *within* individuals and their ever-shifting subgroups. That is why polling data consistently reveal so many contradictory opinions within the same cohort of people. That is why so many advocacy organizations and programmatic pronouncements are short-lived, and so many labels are misleading. One of the most intelligent Russian political figures to ally himself with the Communist Party after the collapse of the Soviet Union, Sergei Glazev, professed to have done so because "the real liberals today are in the Communist Party of the Russian Federation."[2] The most reactionary and authoritarian major political organization of the 1990s called itself the Liberal Democratic Party. But this creation by Zhirinovsky—like almost all Russian political parties—was a small organization containing conflicting elements within its leadership.

Parties were often little more than ambition seeking a platform, placards in search of a crowd. In registering a year later for the Duma elections of December 2003, none of the five leading parties recorded as many as 20,000 adherents. Later website listings attributed just over half a million members for Putin's United Russia Party and for the Communists[3]; but none of the other parties claimed anywhere near that number. The parties, in any case, tended to dissolve themselves into voting blocs that often featured celebrities as well as politicians on their electoral lists.

The parliamentary elections of December 7, 2003, represented a clear victory for the authoritarian nationalist over the liberal democratic impulses in the new Russia. The Communist vote was cut in half; the vote for Zhirinovsky's party was doubled; and a new anti-Western party urging renationalization of property received almost as many votes as Zhirinovsky. Led by Sergei Glazev and the ethnic nationalist Dmitry Rogozin, this party was created by Putin and given the appealing name of Motherland (Rodina) in order to split the Communist left.

Putin's political dominance of the Duma was assured by gaining more seats for his Unity Party than for the combined total of the three leading runners-up (the abovementioned parties). All three of these parties, moreover, were even more aggressively authoritarian than Putin. The two genuinely democratic parties were virtually eliminated from the

Duma. (Neither Yabloko nor the Union of Right Forces attained the 5 percent needed to gain party representation. The combined vote of these two well-established parties was a little less than that of the newly and artificially created Rodina group. The number of seats for the two liberal parties in the Duma fell from forty-eight to seven.)

Putin persisted in describing elections themselves as proof of his continued commitment to democratization—and his pre-election imprisonment of Russia's wealthiest man, Mikhail Khodorkovsky, as a sign of his commitment to enforcing laws uniformly. But his suppression of criticism in the mass media and politically selective enforcement of laws seemed to suggest that Russia would find its true identity only by reasserting top-down central authority—what Russians called the "power vertical"—against the democratic trends that had been developing from the bottom up.

The best that the shattered liberal democratic politicians seemed able to hope for was that the Communists were also diminished and the voters had finally given expression to a long-awaited "national centrist . . . consensus" that would ultimately prove to be "national reformist."[4] But the resurgence of Zhirinovsky's party and the blending of confiscatory socialist and ethnic nationalist slogans under the tranquilizing label of "motherland" raise anew the possibility of a Nazi-type movement developing within a facade of democratic institutions. More likely would be the unintended evolution into some original Russian variant of a corporatist state ruled by a dictator, adorned with Slavophile rhetoric, and representing, in effect, fascism with a friendly face.

This study has sought to probe beneath the ever-shifting sands of elite politics—and to focus on thinkers and trains of thought that seem to reflect moods in the broader society. There is a need for supplementary study of what is being expressed in the stories, songs, and symbols of popular culture. Beginning with the decision to revive the Soviet national anthem and the red flag for the armed forces, there seems to be a drift toward nationalistic solutions. The debate continues over which statues to keep standing in public places[5] and over what to emphasize in teaching about the Soviet period.

There is also a need for deeper understanding of both the present pathos and the future possibilities of the intellectual enterprise in Russia. The new Russia no longer accords special moral authority to an alienated intelligentsia. Nor does it provide adequate public funding for its scientific establishment. Nor is there yet enough of a prosperous or philanthropic business class to provide sustaining private support for Russia's great intellectual and artistic talent. Yet many people with higher education or a profession now call themselves "middle class" even when they have lower-class incomes.[6]

If Russia is to prosper internally and to compete internationally, it will have to support and utilize better its still extraordinary intellectual resources. Continuing to depend on exporting fuel and manufacturing weapons perpetuates monopolistic bureaucracies. The Russian polymath Viacheslav Ivanov argues that the present material deprivation of young Russians in the information age could lead them to become more inventive—which, in the long run, "makes possible a new industrial upsurge."

> The shortage of good computers for many years did not stop them [young Russians], and in fact promoted the development of efficient ways to use imperfect technology.[7]

There are similar developments in the artistic field. The decline of the once heavily subsidized Bolshoi Theatre has been accompanied by a flowering of low-budget opera companies in Moscow, with young artists in innovative performances.

Ivanov believes that "the task of the intelligentsia is to be the country's guide through the 'noosphere'" and to articulate "basic spiritual values . . . in the language of our own times." Like Likhachev, he sees the hope of Russia lying largely in the regions. Out of the harmony existing among the ethnic cultural associations newly created by the reformist governor of Novgorod, Mikhail Prusak, "quietly are born the trends of the future, so different from the nationalist-socialist madness of the past." This can provide a model for preserving "cultural and linguistic diversity" within a democratic Russia.[8]

The variety and vitality of public debate about the nature and destiny of Russia suggest some conclusions that offer hope but no assurance. The very existence of such a discussion suggests that democratic government is already largely legitimized in Russia. Many of those who reject the label affirm the values of democracy. All but a few ultraextremists criticize their opponents not for their democratic ideals but for failing to live up to them.[9] Those who argue for a non-Western path often do so in the name of alleged grassroots democratic traditions within Russia. The near universal call for a "civilized" and "normal" society in Russia assumes that Western democracy is the desired standard.

Almost all discussants also assume that future change in Russia will be evolutionary rather than revolutionary. Postcommunist Russia has been remarkably free of either the utopian illusions or the internal social violence of the Soviet era.

There has, of course, been a tragic exception in the continuing Russian war against Chechnya, which has imposed immense suffering on the Chechens. There have also been grotesque terrorist strikes against Russians. The appalling loss of life in Chechnya has left wounds that will not heal easily, and there is a continuing possibility of broader violence spreading on or across Russia's borders with the volatile Caucasus or perhaps in Central Asia. If new conflict or even regional chaos resulted, a fresh wave of authoritarian nationalism could well sweep away much of Russia's fledgling democracy.

Young Russians today generally see their journey ahead neither in terms of Gogol's troika flying across the open steppe into the heavens nor in terms of current novelist Victor Pelevin's closed train headed for a ruined bridge. They accept uncertainty, float in and out of politics, and are less concerned with their ultimate destination than with finding reliable directions for getting to the next city.

The search for Russia's identity has in recent years opened up a broader discussion about the meaning of history as a whole that may be the wordiest in the world. Biblical authority is invoked on all sides; it is woven together with modern environmental science to suggest scenarios and timetables for impending catastrophes. But the Bible is also invoked to legitimize constitutional rule.[10]

Entire institutes have been formed to apply the teachings of the economist Nicholas Kondrat'ev and the émigré sociologist Pitirim Sorokin to the study of history. Almost every Russian writer dealing with the identity problem has included lengthy discussions of Western philosophers of history who were not much discussed in the West during the same period (along with long-forgotten Russian counterparts such as Nicholas Danilevsky and Constantine Leontiev). More recent Western treatises such as Samuel Huntington's *Clash of Civilizations* and Francis Fukuyama's *End of History* have been subjected to exhaustive (largely negative) criticism by many of the Russian writers cited in this study.

Implicit in this preoccupation is the assumption that Russia still has an important role to play in human history. Only a few believe that it can play such a role militarily. Some argue that Russia can, nevertheless, exercise new leadership through its unique location in Eurasia— as a transportation bridge, a political pivot, and/or a mediating force between Europe and Asia. But many more seem to think that Russia's unique role in history lies in the spiritual, cultural, and scientific arenas more than in traditional measures of economic and political power. A democratic version of Eurasianism foresees Russia helping create a Eurasian Union like the European Union—in effect, sustaining independence and rooting democratic institutions in the former Asian republics of the USSR[11]—and perhaps also helping reinvigorate the spiritual life of a fatigued and decadent Europe.

The West has never followed the Russians' achievements and aspirations in "spiritual culture" (a term officially used even in Soviet times) as closely as their material accomplishments in politics and economics. Media coverage in recent years has tended to focus on material failures, dangers, and problems; and Russians themselves do not always articulate their hopes as well as their fears. So it might be useful—if presumptuous—to attempt to draw out the consensus of hope bordering on expectation that I have found implicit in the materials surveyed for this book and explicit in conversations with many of the emerging young leaders taking part in the Open World program, which I chair.

Russians hope both to gain respect in the outside world and to regain self-respect at home.[12] They generally believe that they, like the United States, are part of European civilization. As they become better acquainted with the real state of that civilization, some are beginning to sense that they may have something to give to, as well as gain from, that linkage.

Many see that their unique Eurasian location can enable Russia to bring the best of Europe to Asia rather than the worst of Asia to Europe. And many young Russians tend to be open to the best in Asia and hostile to the worst in Europe. Russia's most popular novelist (Pelevin) and rock singer (Boris Grebenshchikov) have both become Buddhists; and historic anti-Semitism seems to have lost most of its resonance in Russia with any but marginalized fringe groups.

Thinking in Russia is dominated no longer by the utopian ideas of an intelligentsia—and not yet by the practical interests of an entrepreneurial middle class. There is, nonetheless, a widely shared desire to make some sense of the great suffering that has been characteristic of Russian, and particularly Soviet, history—and which many people are still enduring. Russians are seeking to find not so much a happy ending to a largely sad history as some promise of redemption or renewal within that history. That desire seems to have penetrated into a population that is, at the same time, becoming more tolerant of ethnic and religious variety and more inclined to experiment with new and more responsible ways of doing things.

There is almost no desire to return to the social or political models of either the communist or the tsarist past. Yet there is, at the same time, intense nostalgia for key features from the last years of both periods—for the spiritual culture of the late tsarist era and for the material orderliness of the late Soviet period.

It would be a mistake, however, to assume that when Russians look back they are not moving forward. The innovative civic and social reforms under Alexander II followed upon an intense period of historical enquiry and nostalgia about the Russian past. The Silver Age recovery and restoration of the oldest icons inspired Russia's pioneering breakthrough to abstract modernism in painting; and the search for Russia's pre-Christian antiquity propelled Stravinsky and Prokofiev forward into modern music. The churning reexamination of Russia's entire autocratic history may well be both a prerequisite to and a harbinger of further dramatic innovations in its political system.

Outside observers have often tended to assume that Russians have no desire—perhaps not even any capacity—for innovation based on foreign models. Yet few nations have shown anything like the Russians' capacity for unanticipated, new creativity in their periodic, sudden encounters with foreign art media. If building a constitutional rule of law is more an art than a science, Russia's explosive past history with the arts may suggest a wider range of future possibilities than could be expected from linear projections based on past Russian political history.

Whenever Russians have confronted a new and unfamiliar art medium, they have repeatedly first slavishly imitated the foreign model and then innovatively lifted the art form to an entirely new level. The very fact that they had no previous experience with a new type of human expression made its belated discovery a deeply traumatic rather than a mildly adjustive event.

The first and most important cultural explosion in Russia was its sudden, wholesale adoption of high-Byzantine pictorial art. There is no significant evidence of prior cave drawings or pre-Christian, classical or pagan painting in Russia. The rapid spread of a new and deeply religious art throughout Rus in the eleventh century provided Russians with their first and most enduring emblem of cultural identity. Icons were windows into the next world. The pictorial theology of Russian Orthodoxy created a subliminal bias in Russian culture for seeking salvation rather than just satisfaction in works of art.

Russians subsequently moved from imitation to innovation in the eighteenth century, adopting and transforming Baroque architecture from Italy in order to sanctify secular power in the new capital of St. Petersburg. They moved with equal suddenness in literature and music during the nineteenth and early twentieth centuries, infusing Western European models of the novel and the opera with stunning originality despite little prior indigenous achievement in either area. And in the early Soviet period, Russians transposed the entertaining new Western art form of the cinema into a medium for sanctifying the message of revolution.

In many cases, however, this process of imitating and then transforming a foreign model led to a breakdown in the culture and a breakup of the art media themselves. Russian religious painting, after developing its own originality in Muscovy, broke down altogether in the decade of the 1660s. Russian imperial architecture became irretrievably confused and eclectic in the early nineteenth century. The sudden explosion of originality in Russian music and literature in the late tsarist era was impelled by a search for meaning outside of power; but its very intensity helped delegitimize a mellowing autocracy and left people susceptible to the utopian fantasy that legitimized totalitarianism. The new medium of the movies, which initially played a key role in supporting Soviet power, ultimately helped undermine it.[13]

Will Russia's current effort to master the art of democracy lead to a breakthrough or to a breakdown? Can Russia, on the exposed eastern frontier of European civilization, produce and sustain its own indigenous form of democracy, as it has with so many other imported forms of creativity in the past?

The many conflicts and contradictions in the way today's Russians view Russia's yesterdays make resolving the question of identity central in shaping the Russia of tomorrow. Russians are simultaneously facing both a slow *breakdown* of inherited Soviet structures and a halting *buildup* of more participatory and accountable ones. This condition produces a certain neurosis in the culture, but releases new energies in society. And it opens up possibilities for more sudden and far-reaching changes than are possible in normal times.

Russia's current situation is rather like that at the end of Frank Stockton's famous short story, "The Lady or the Tiger?" The imprisoned hero is preparing to open one of two doors that will release him from bondage. He knows that one will lead to a beautiful lady with whom he can live happily ever after; the other, to a hungry tiger that will consume him. We are not given the answer.

Russia is opening its door into the new millennium. Will it ultimately seek to ride once again the Siberian tiger of autocracy? Or will it be able, finally, to give Lady Liberty a hearth and home in the Eurasian heartland?

In terms of the *matryoshka* image, it may not be important what expression we see on the face of the outer doll at any given moment (the answer to the poll of the day). Each doll is only a thin veneer concealing different inner layers. According to some folk beliefs about a matryoshka, what matters ultimately is the identity of the face that finally appears on the solid wood of the innermost doll.

No clear identity has yet been imprinted on the solid wood. The cover of a millennial anthology of pro-democracy essays called *In Russia Something Is Going On. . .* depicts a little boy surrounded by matryoshka dolls showing the faces of Russian leaders of past decades. The boy smiles as he holds up the only solid doll. It is labeled 2000, but it has no face.[14]

Many Russians no longer seek their identity in the face of any politician. Having long acquiesced in professing total allegiance to their leaders' policy and politics (both meanings are contained in the words *politika* and *politburo*), many now look for meaning outside political systems altogether. Politicians of all stripes assert a reverence to "spiritual values" that is as insistent and incessant as it is vague. But it seems doubtful that the realm of practical politics in which they work will ever satisfy the groping for some kind of transcendence that can take Russians beyond what they have known in the past and are experiencing in the present.

Many Russians seem to see their future in terms of the motherland that they feel inside themselves—not yet having found in the outside world either a fatherland that they can respect or foreigners who respect them. Motherland (*rodina*) suggests family linkage (*rod*) rather than national identity. The universally preferred word for nation is still *narod* rather than *natsiia*.

"Narod" means people rather than nation to most Russians, and they are inclined to think that it was their *people's* ability to sustain integrity and cooperate sacrificially at the local level that enabled them to survive their nation's mistaken purges, concentration camps, and corruption. Family, close friends, small circles, and community projects have become more important to more people precisely as the leaders of central power ministries (*siloviki*), the fabulously rich oligarchs, and the omnipresent government bureaucracies seem to have become more remote from the people.

Small-scale business and barter communities have grown along with local chapters of transnational fraternal organizations (Rotary, Junior Achievement). The rapid growth of non-Orthodox Christianity (particularly Baptist and Pentecostal) in many parts of Russia is often attributable to the close sense of community that they generate. And much of the dynamism of the Orthodox Church itself comes from the unprecedented development of new parishes and parish-based activities. Having grown up beyond the borders of the Roman empire, the Russian Church, unlike almost all others in Europe, could not build on preexisting Roman diocesan and parish administrative structures. The restoration of churches and the assumption of previously forbidden educational and pastoral activities have opened up a broader scope for parish work in postcommunist Russia.

The ability to work together at the local level contributed significantly to the Russian military effort in both world wars. The *zemgor* (country–city) committees in World War I were particularly exemplary. In the wake of the Soviet collapse, Russians are beginning to improvise the kind of nongovernmental, nonprofit organizations at the local level that Alexis de Tocqueville found so important for the success of democracy in America. The workings of U.S. civil society were almost universally hailed as the most important discovery made by young Russians who came to America for the first time under the Open World/Russian Leadership program.

The spirit of togetherness engendered by local, cooperative activity was seen by many Russians as the expression of an indigenous tradition that they call *sobornost'*. This is a Slavophile-originated term derived from *sobor*, a word with the multiple meanings of cathedral, council, and the simple gathering in of people or of things that had previously been scattered. It expresses a desire to find a measure of common purpose for a people and a culture long rent with splits and schisms. It provides the post-Soviet generation with a social ideal that is different from either Eastern collectivism or Western individualism. And it suggests that there is a spiritual dimension to nonpolitical, small-scale human community.

The basic human embodiment of the sobornost' ideal is the family. Family happiness was the ideal of much nineteenth-century Russian literature. The persistent integrity of the family throughout the twentieth century protected the Russian people from some of the intrusive inhumanity of the Soviet system. But sobornost' is thought to be exemplified in a wide variety of communal undertakings ranging from the camaraderie of pioneering construction work in harsh climates to the intense discussion of proscribed ideals in small urban circles.

Semion Frank, one of the most important and neglected thinkers of the late imperial period, argued in the emigration that sobornost', "the choral principle in Russian life," was not just an ideal from the past but a force for the future. Sobornost' overcame the potential hostility between I and thou with a kind of organic, spiritual unity that differed from "sociality" (obshchestvennost') in which isolated individuals are aggregated into materialistic interest groups.[15]

Some post-Soviet writers see sobornost' as a—if not the—defining element in giving distinctiveness to Russian civilization. Already in Metropolitan Ilarion of Kiev's eleventh-century "Sermon on Law and Grace," God is seen as bestowing grace not just on individual people but on the people as a whole. Law regulated unfree people in the desert, but grace is the water that brings life into dry places and is the "source of sobornost'."[16] "This word alone contains in itself a complete profession of faith"[17]; it is expressed in the liturgy (literally "common work" in Greek) of Orthodox worship, which is sung chorally. Bible passages are listened to collectively in an Orthodox Church, rather than read silently at home.[18]

For those rediscovering their Orthodox Christian heritage, sobornost' describes the kind of communion with others that is open to an individual seeking to discover what St. Augustine described as that which is within me which is deeper than myself. For others seeking a "third way" between socialism and capitalism, sobornost' represents an indigenous communitarian ideal on which to base a humane, social democratic future.

But is there any real commonality, togetherness, or unifying force within the Russia of today? Some would say that the face of Russia is now surreal and its expression cynical. Cynicism, however, is morality in search of a home.[19] The most famous cynic, Diogenes, was in search of an honest man; and the number of such men—and women—is growing rapidly in Russia. For the first time in Russian history, the uniform rule of law is widely recognized as a necessary condition for a healthy future. If Yeltsin ruled largely by administrative decrees in the 1990s, Putin was governing mainly through legislated laws, even if he often applied them selectively.

But what is necessary may not be sufficient for Russians who have historically been more responsive to moral entreaties than to legal rulings. Russians have had a deep and unique historic relationship with the Christian religion. They were among the last European peoples to be converted; they chose Orthodoxy, one of the oldest and least changing branches of the faith; and they kept it central to their culture far longer into the modern age than did the creative people of any other large European Christian nation.

Soviet Russia summarily rejected Christianity and all other religions to create the first government in human history dedicated to the elimination of religion as such. Despite the checkered record of their hierarchy in collaborating with their communist persecutors, Russian Orthodox believers suffered one of the largest-scale martyrdoms in Christian history. Then, after communism imploded, Russia produced—disproportionately among the young and educated—perhaps the twentieth century's largest wave of new converts in a single country in a short space of time.[20]

The great majority of Russians now identify themselves as Christians. But only a slight majority of Christians identify themselves as Orthodox, and only a small number of the Orthodox regularly attend services.[21] President Putin has endorsed the growing religious pluralism, but he wears a cross and has said (on Solovetsky Island at the site of Russia's first gulag) that "without Christianity, Russia could hardly exist."[22]

I suggested in my *Face of Russia* that the three core elements shaping Russian culture have been Orthodox Christianity, a special feeling for nature, and a periodic passion for innovations from outside. This study suggests that the Russian people's current search for identity is, in many ways, a renewal of the interrupted creative ferment of the Russian Silver Age under the last tsar.

Central to that great autumnal explosion of Russian culture prior to World War I was the search in a long-divided country for philosophic harmony and a synthesis of the arts. A major center for this quest was the artistic colony in the countryside at Abramtsevo, outside Moscow, sponsored by the pioneering merchant philanthropist Savva Mamontov. In his private theater, the great Fedor Chaliapin first sang the title role in *Boris Godunov*. Several Rimsky-Korsakov operas had their world premieres there with the soprano Nadezhda Zabela singing in front of sets designed by the painter Victor Vasnetsov. Zabela's husband, Mikhail Vrubel, was the greatest painter of the age. He branched out there into ceramics and majolica, using colors that he believed corresponded to the themes in Rimsky-Korsakov's music.[23]

The matryoshka, which I have used to suggest the different layers of belief inside the Russian psyche, is itself an artifact created at this time and in this place. Mamontov's brother Anatoly was in charge of "Children's Education" (Detskoe Vospitanie), a workshop-museum-store at Abramtsevo designed to gather in, refine, and replicate the best children's toys from rural Russia.

But outside influences were once again flowing into Russia then. Two Russian artist-craftsmen were fascinated by a nesting doll recently imported from Honshu Island in Japan. They substituted the figure of a Russian peasant mother for the bald old man on the Japanese original and created the first matryoshka. It contained eight wooden dolls, each different from the preceding one. The total ensemble represented the members of a united and happy family—the basic unit of Russian sobornost'. The outermost doll was a mother; the innermost doll, an infant in swaddling clothes.[24]

Could the secret of Russian identity lie in the simple representation of mother and child on wood on that first matryoshka at the end of the nineteenth century? From the revered, two-dimensional medieval icon of the Vladimir Mother of God to this first three-dimensional modern matryoshka, the image of mother and child depicts the core of sobornost', the first and most basic human relationship on which all others depend.

In my *Face of Russia* I dwelt on Andrei Rublev's haunting icon of Christ, which was rescued by a priest from a firewood shed in the early Soviet period. The face was elongated as if to follow the grain of the wood—as earlier pagans had done when carving the sculptured figure that was to protect a family dwelling (*domovoi*). The survival of this single, simple icon (known simply as Spas, meaning the Savior) by Russia's greatest painter seemed to symbolize (more appropriately than the recent reconstruction of the gigantic Church of Christ the Savior) the Russians' recovery of their "spiritual culture" in the midst of material deprivation.

Rublev created his art during the time that Gumilev cited as showing the greatest "passionality" and release of "energies" in Russian history. And the imaginative recreation of the monastic painter's life in Andrei Tarkovsky's film, *Andrei Rublev*, presented a lingering artistic rebuke to the "age of stagnation" that preceded the fall of communism. Rublev's last and greatest painting depicts the sobornost' that exists even within the Christian God: the three persons of the Holy Trinity. The icon is the ultimate "meditation in colors" designed to lead the viewer into both a higher realm and her or his deeper self. The same beatific vision of three intersecting circles that Rublev provided for Eastern Christianity, Dante described for Western Christendom in words in the last canto of his *Divine Comedy*.

Most Russians do not take part in active worship, but many are still searching for a transcendence to take them beyond what they have known in the past and are experiencing in the present. Cults and narcotics provide illusory escape for some, and the rate of suicides has grown alarmingly.[25] But many persevere in the search for a God who can give encouragement and direction to two basic impulses in modern Russia that have now spread to the population as a whole: conscience and curiosity.

In his essay, "Who Are We?," the writer Fazil Iskander said,

> Conscience makes life difficult in order to make the meeting with God easier. . . . The workings of conscience are an endless rehearsal for that meeting.

If justice depends on the workings of conscience as well as the crafting of laws, truth is advanced by the driving force of curiosity as well as by the discipline of science. Curiosity requires both openness and focus—in Iskander's words, "changing our slovenly universality to an honest particularity" that can overcome the indifference of *styob* and restore "the enthusiasm of creation" to everyday life.

> We are a people who have lost our appetite for creation—the appetite for a precisely executed drawing, for earth neatly sliced by a plow . . . for a passionately written page.[26]

A native of Muslim Abkhazia in the Caucasus, Iskander sees the key to both intellectual creativity and social justice in the stubborn perseverance of love, which "was the main thing in Christ's teaching." "Inspiration is being in love with unfolding truth."[27] For him and for others in the Russia of today, the truth that must unfold is both normative and scientific—the two imperatives implied in the classic double meaning of the Russian word *pravda*.

In contrast to earlier times, truth is now pursued and construed in more practical, localized, and small-scale ways. Some have contrasted Russia's "catastrophic" past identity based on utopian illusions with its new and more down-to-earth identity based simply on "home-building."[28] Russian development has been impeded by its tendency to go from one extreme to another. In *Culture and Explosion*, his last book written as the Soviet Union was imploding, the great Russian humanist Yury Lotman saw Russia at last beginning to value "step-by-step people" (*postepenovtsy*) capable of gradually building a new and unique set of institutions worthy of its culture.

> In the real world, explosions cannot be made to disappear. The point is only to overcome the fatal choice between stagnation and catastrophe. . . . If the movement is forward . . . the emerging order will hardly be a simple copy of the West. History knows no repetition. It loves new, unforeseen paths.[29]

In order to find their own path, Russians will have to work out a balanced understanding of their own history that glorifies neither catastrophe nor stagnation. Historically, Russia has been, for the most part, neither a "family of peoples" nor a "prison of peoples." For all the repression and stagnation during the thirty-year reign of Nicholas I, he is now found to have executed only five people.[30] Yet, the cruelties of his rule were so dwelt upon by the Russian intelligentsia that Soviet propagandists were able to exaggerate them wildly to help divert attention from the genocidal policies of the Stalin era.

At the other extreme, the near universal fascination and praise of Peter the Great even in the Soviet era has tended to mask both the physical and psychological devastation that his top-down forced Westernization created in Russian society. It is particularly grotesque to see the Soviet-style giant Tseretelli statue of Peter built in Moscow after the fall of communism, as if to suggest that one of Stalin's favorite tsars should be the model for democratic reforms.[31]

It is encouraging that both Gorbachev and Putin regard the genuinely reformist Alexander II as their main model among past leaders of Russia. And there is further hope to be found in the new generation's fascination with the culture of the Silver Age, the decade of relative freedom under the last tsar, Nicholas II, between the Revolution of 1905 and the outbreak of World War I. But Nicholas like Alexander was murdered by revolutionaries. Their tragic fates raise the deeper question of whether senseless deaths can have any meaning—or expanding freedom, any real future—in Russia.

Can Russians banish old myths about their history without creating new ones? The current obsession with the nature and meaning of the

Mongol era for Russia is a crucial test case. The long-accepted popular view was that modern Russia came into being through a series of crusading struggles against their former occupiers: pagan and later Islamic foes to the East. The new Eurasian myth-in-the-making suggests that Mongol rule was the progenitor rather than the foe of modern Russia. The long era of Mongol overlordship both preserved Russian Orthodox Christian culture (by shielding it from corrupting secular influences from the West) and provided a realistic model for a continental empire (by combining absolute central power with a tolerance for ethnic diversity).

Beneath the often clumsy current debate about what the documentary record really tells us lies the deeper, normative concern about what kind of society is right for present-day Russia. Out of the current intellectual free-for-all, the outlines of fairly clear answers are beginning to emerge for both the scientific and the moral questions. Mongol rule did not impede the spiritual culture but did transform the political culture that Moscow inherited from Kiev.[32] However, the balance between good and bad that the Eastern Slavs found in their extended encounter with the Mongol–Tatar world is determined by one's own values as much as by knowable facts.

So what, if any, are the shared values of the Russian people? Popular participation in national life is expanding, however haltingly and unevenly. As a result, the core values of ordinary people are becoming increasingly important in determining the choices that will eventually shape the future of Russia. As the culture increasingly defines itself from the bottom up and the periphery in, it may be better understood through its rich folklore, neglected regional perspectives, and great ethnographic diversity than through any attempt to reach conclusions about its complex past political history. Along with freedom and a pluralism of ideas, there seems to be a new willingness to assume that there are many different ways that history could have developed and still can proceed.

The Jewish philosopher Franz Rosenzweig once said that truth is a noun only for God; for people, it is always a verb. For the younger generation in Russia today, it has become a surprisingly active verb. They may not be able to replicate the incandescent genius of Russian art and culture in the Silver Age. But they give every indication of keeping the flame of liberty burning in so many ways and places that it is hard to imagine Russia ever again being frozen in glacial repression.

The outside world may have some things to learn from this internal discourse among Russians. Having lost most of their power to make history, Russians may have been freed to rediscover certain basic truths about history. As they decompress from a culture that once pretended to offer total explanations of everything, they are holding almost everything up to question. There are traces of self-indulgence in the lamentations exemplified by such titles as *To Be or Not to Be . . . for Humanity?*, *How Is Russia Possible?*, and *Russia Does Have a Future!*[33] And there is something faintly masochistic in their solemn efforts to depict Russia as a "caldera," a spreading volcanic crater,[34] or to determine whether Russia is in a "catastrophic" or only a "precatastrophic" phase of modernization.[35]

Beneath their frequent posturing and agonizing, however, most Russian thinkers explicitly or implicitly affirm two basic beliefs about human history. Neither of these convictions is widely proclaimed—and the simultaneous affirmation of both is a great rarity—in the modern Western world.

The first belief is that progress is not built into human history. No Russian version has emerged of the American dream that whatever the problems of today, tomorrow will somehow always be better than yesterday.[36] Most Russians see faith in human progress as, at best, a noble illusion; at worst, a willful, tragic, and perhaps terminal mistake of the human race. Pervasive pessimism about the future may, in part, be the Russians' rationalization for both the failure of utopian Soviet futurism and their subsequent disillusionment with the liberal optimism that initially accompanied democracy building. But there is almost always a deeper undercurrent of authentic anxiety about the entire human future. This is evident in Mikhail Gorbachev's late-life conversion to a passionate environmentalism,[37] in the popular fascination with biblical prophecies, and in the tendency to read Western treatises like *The Clash of Civilizations* and *The End of History* as apocalyptical rather than analytical texts.

A second belief underlying the entire Russian discussion might seem to contradict the first. It is the conviction that, however bleak the historical outlook, individual Russians in their new conditions of freedom are now deeply responsible for the conduct of their lives. This belief derives strength from the writings of a special group of thinkers from the Russian past that the new generation especially admires: the leading philosophical minds of the Silver Age who went on writing about Russia's identity in the "first wave" of emigration.

Many young Russians now believe that personal moral responsibility freely assumed by individuals provides the only sure foundation for avoiding some new version of the inhumanity produced by collectivism in the Soviet era. They see the secret of totalitarianism lying in its denial not just of freedom, but also of its Siamese twin, responsibility. While rejecting historical inevitability, they also reject that favorite mantra of the Soviet system: *Eto ot menia ne zavisit* (It doesn't depend on me). The growing civil society has even brought into being a nationwide newspaper by and for the homeless.[38]

Russians had already been inspired by the testimony in the late Soviet years by writers like Varlam Shalamov, Evgeniia Ginzburg, and Alexander Solzhenitsyn, who had suffered in gulags within the country. In the post-Soviet period, the young have been re-energized by discovering the ideas of surrogate grandparents who endured the special pain of forced exile, yet continued to care and write about their mother country. The Russian word for compassion, *sostradanie*, literally means shared suffering; and post-Soviet thinking has been not only influenced by the ideas but also affected by the sufferings of those who went before. Even a conformist novelist of the Stalin era called it a "procession through suffering"[39]; and there has been a small but steady stream of truth-tellers who have been martyred in unsolved assassinations since the fall of communism.

There remains a question—not about the identity of Russia, but about the search for identity itself. What, if anything, lies behind the

Russians' intensive focus on, and extensive discussion of, this subject? One cannot explain this fixation in purely political, economic, or social terms, if—as I have contended—the debate rages within individuals more than between groups. Nor can this quest be understood in the psychological terms used to analyze individuals. The Russians' capacity for suffering should not be equated with masochism or their inner schisms with schizophrenia. Still less does the appearance of extreme positions indicate social paranoia. The most remarkable fact about the many ultranationalist organizations and action groups has been their failure so far to attract broad popular support.

As we probe deeper in search of solid wood within the matryoshka, we may find that a more universal search for personal truths-to-live-by lies hidden inside the layered faces of alternative identities for the nation. The depth—and the confusion—of the Russians' search for identity may come from their two-sided understanding of the word truth itself. As we have seen, the word "pravda" suggests both normative, moral truth and descriptive, scientific truth. The Russian debate hopelessly intertwines the two and makes it difficult to paint a "true" picture either of what their nation is or of what it should become.

This confusion in the discussion of Russian identity becomes less vexing if it is seen as the outer form of the Russians' attempt to activate both types of truth within themselves. When cross-examined for their core views about each of these two distinct forms of truth, even political antagonists tend to reach agreement: *factually* on the continuing unproductiveness of the economy, the unaccountability of the government, and the ecological, demographic, and geopolitical vulnerability of the nation; and, *normatively,* on the need to sustain basic freedoms, expand personal responsibility, improve social services, and deepen their "spiritual culture."

Something like a minimal political consensus seemed to have been reached by the spring of 2003. The establishmentarian democrat Georgy Satarov all but adopted the main positions of the authoritarian oppositionist Glazev: that there was no accountability in government, inadequate acceptance of responsibility in the society, too much reliance on foreign models, and too little foreign assistance.[40]

Even political extremists seemed to concede that Russia's future must be shaped by evolution rather than revolution, by elections rather than insurrections. On the "left," the communist leader Zyuganov defined the "people power" (*narodovlastie*) that he would like to see in Russia as a combination of moderate Slavophile and liberal Westernizing ideals: sobornost' (the traditional religious principle of togetherness) and *vybornost'* (the democratic practice of elections).[41] On the "right," the authoritarian Eurasianist Dugin even paid grudging tribute to the democratic development of post-Soviet Russia. "The shape of the new 'democratic' Russia remains rather stormy (*dovol'no smutnym*)." But

> The initial radical liberal-democratic idea gradually had to give way to a Westernizing conservatism. . . . The straightforward Russophobia in the eyes of the young reformers has given way to an "enlightened conservatism" and "moderate" Europeanism.[42]

He still puts xenophobic Eurasianist glosses on Russian history. He outdoes even the "new chronology" school by characterizing the three centuries of rule by the Romanov tsars in St. Petersburg as the "Romano-Germanic yoke."[43] And he harbors the hope that "the internal, substantive, 'Muscovite' content of sovietism" will be realized someday by an "Eurasian version of the National Idea." He argues that "the struggle for a National Idea . . . is far from over." But he concludes—more with a sigh than with a call to arms—that "power in contemporary Russia as it searches for a National Idea still remains within the framework of Westernization." The best he can offer his authoritarian allies for the future is, in effect, more treatises: "a detailed exposition of the Eurasian Project."[44] Dugin has transformed the apolitical, quasi-religious "Russian idea" into an authoritarian and geopolitical "National Idea." But he implicitly seems to recognize that practical policy and real power can be contested only within broad areas of agreement in an evolving democracy.

Most Russians continue to be cynical about national politics and policies. It will be difficult, if not impossible, to legitimize democracy and the rule of law in Russia unless something can be done to bridge the continuing socioeconomic and psychological abyss between the ruling elites and almost everyone else. The power exercised by both the bureaucratic central government and the wealthy new oligarchs is morally offensive to most Russians—and often makes their own attempts to recover personal responsibility seem irrelevant to the broader public arena.

Intelligent Russians may pour so much energy into the debate about identity because they see so little room for effective action to help shape it. Ordinary Russians are more concerned with understanding what is actually happening day to day around them (their version of *pravda-istina*) and with how to live decently in their local communities (their form of *pravda-spravedlivost'*).

And that leads to a final question about the search: Why and to what end are so many Russians pursuing a basically personal, philosophical search for truth by discussing the nature of an impersonal, geopolitical entity? It may be because most citizens of the Russian Federation (and many in the "near abroad") have shared something that they have not yet otherwise fully talked out and moved beyond: immense deprivation and many-sided suffering. The only part that has been fully acknowledged and honored by public monuments is the suffering caused by foreign foes. Yet just as much suffering was inflicted on them by themselves, and over a longer period of time.

This condition of denial impacts on a society in ways that can never be understood, let alone remedied, by roundtable discussions—even those that may someday be convened after all the mass graves and buried documents have been unearthed. Words alone will never provide a road map into a happy future for those who once thought they stood on a mountain. They now know that there is no easy way out of their valley—and that the shadow of massive, innocent death still hangs over it.

An intelligent and educated populace generally knows that it has the natural and human resources to continue climbing upward under almost any likely political system. But can it lift the shadow and end the condition of near nervous breakdown in its culture that has disoriented and partly immobilized it psychologically for more than a decade? There are essentially four ways, summarized below, that a nation can move beyond the fact of massive past complicity in unprecedented evil.

(1) *Remove the problem from public consciousness.* Collective involvement in cruelty is not such a serious practical problem for a culture that bases itself on an ethic of social conformity. This is arguably part of the reason why China, which committed under Mao even more internal genocide over a longer period than Russia under Stalin, continues to be unwilling to criticize the murderer-in-chief. A Confucian-based culture that never had a shared, transcendental religion may have helped condition an otherwise highly intelligent people to show continued deference to the many unrepentant murderers still exercising power over and among them. This may be the model that the authoritarian Eurasianists in Russia secretly aspire to emulate. They argue that a still autocratic China has earned more respect and attracted more investment from the West than a democratic Russia. Many neoauthoritarians are encouraged by the fact that the secular elite culture of the West tends to sanctify in the name of science the dissolution of any solid concern about evil into a saline solution of relativism.

(2) *Transfer the burden of evil to others.* Under this rubric, the fact of evil is not only recognized, it is made the bonding force of the nation-state through violent public acts of exorcism. Evil is located in the external enemies and internal traitors of a population that might otherwise remain divisible and confused. This is classic negative nationalism, which justifies the arbitrary exercise of autocratic power by periodic wars against nations outside and periodic purges of potential opponents inside the domain of a dictator. Expanding borders basically define such a nation's identity; and the image of righteousness combating evil justifies the unlimited exercise of power.

(3) *Evade the problem of evil in society by creating a noble personal philosophy for an elite.* This was the Stoic solution in ancient times and has been a Buddhist solution for some in the modern West. Philosophies that play a similar function have been created for the modern, utilitarian mind by John Rawls in the United States and Jürgen Habermas in Germany. Although designed for democratic societies, these and other

eminently rational and humane academic philosophies have never reached more than a small intellectual elite.

The visceral, philosophical rejection of state power and of all forms of violence enunciated by Leo Tolstoy has had a broader appeal—and was transformed into a political movement by Mahatma Gandhi. This approach influenced both the civil rights movement in the United States under Martin Luther King and the movement against apartheid in South Africa under Nelson Mandela. The success of these two movements—and of the largely nonviolent overthrow of communist dictatorships in Eastern Europe—has led some to argue that the Gandhian approach may become an even greater force for change in the future.[45]

But such an exalted and quasi-religious ethic has proven effective with a broader public mainly within societies subject to the political rule and overall cultural ambience of a controlling Christian civilization. The Tolstoyan approach has always commanded respect among the Russian intelligentsia but has never gained much of a popular following in the land of its origin.

Most Russians instinctively believe that evil cannot be *avoided* by the mere intention to do good. Still less do they think it can be *evaded* by espousing a personal philosophy that cannot be understood by, and broadly shared with, others. This psychological condition gives special salience to a fourth path away from evil. It is deeply rooted in the Orthodox Christian base of Russian culture but may seem almost inconceivable—even to most Christians—in the modern world.

(4) *Overcome evil by accepting the redemptive power of innocent suffering.* This is the basic corollary to the core Christian belief that a fallen humanity has been redeemed through the innocent suffering of God's incarnate goodness. Christ-like martyrdom was the bloody bond of the original Christians. The earliest martyrs are remembered and venerated far more in Orthodox than in most Western Christian worship. Probably the greatest number of Christians suffering martyrdom for their faith under one political jurisdiction in all of history was endured by Russian Orthodox believers within the Soviet Union in the twentieth century.

What is missing for this fact to open up broader redemptive possibilities for the Russian people is accountability, or even searching self-scrutiny, on the part of the Church itself. As an institution, it ended up in the late Soviet period accepting a defensible, but ultimately Faustian, bargain with an atheistic state. It secured a limited survival to perform liturgical rituals as long as it sought no educational role in society, supported state policies when requested, and cleared all major appointments with the state. As a result, the Russian Church played a role in perpetuating and even at times legitimizing a system bent on its destruction.

The literature on the martyrology of the Russian Orthodox clergy and devout believers is by now very large—and is growing particularly vigorously in the provinces.[46] The victimization of the Russian Church was a numerically small but ideologically central part of the horrors of Stalinism. It is now estimated that 200,000 clerics and others with religious vows and duties were killed.[47] Patriarch Alexis II characterized the twentieth century as

> an epoch of unprecedented persecution for the faith, surpassing in its scale, cynicism, insidiousness, and cruelty anything that had ever befallen the followers of Christ.
>
> In the twentieth century, Russia alone gave the world more martyrs and confessors than all of the preceding history of the entire Christian Church.[48]

Yet the Russian Church provides relatively little deep theological or philosophical analysis of the appalling experiences that have by now been richly documented. Having long failed to recognize the "new martyrs," the official church hierarchy within Russia now seems in danger of flooding the market with new canonizations without providing any deep reflection on the religious meaning of it all. The official publications of the Church often appear to assume that the fact of past suffering in and of itself imparts special virtue to the Russian Church as it is currently functioning under a hierarchy largely installed in Soviet times. Some Church spokesmen even suggest at times that Soviet antireligious persecution was only a subcategory of the ongoing, Western-inspired secularization of the modern world.

Partly because the Russian Orthodox Church is perceived by many not to have renewed itself sufficiently, many Russians now pursue their search for spiritual renewal outside of the Church.[49] But many young, well-educated priests and lay leaders within the Orthodox Church find a focus for hope in figures like the thirty-nine-year-old Hilarion Alfeev, who was for a time head of the Church's secretariat for relations with other Christians.

Alfeev combines a conservative view on faith and liturgy, reformist and ecumenical sympathy, and a desire to analyze deeply the Church's history during the Soviet period in order to move beyond its painful legacy once and for all. As a young priest serving in Lithuania, he publicly urged the Russian troops not to fire on the Lithuanians who occupied the Soviet government buildings in Vilnius in January 1991. He subsequently earned a doctorate at Oxford and became a leading advocate of improved theological education, a more accessible liturgy for the public, and the need to "reflect on and internalize the Church's entire twentieth-century experience of survival under persecution."[50]

More broadly popular—and more ambiguously consequential for Russia—has been the martyrdom of "Russia's new unofficial saint," Evgeny Rodionov, on May 23, 1996, the Feast of the Ascension and his nineteenth birthday.[51] He came from a family of carpenters in the small village of Kurilovo just west of Moscow and went off to serve without questioning as a simple private in Chechnya. Taken as a prisoner of war, both his captors and his compatriots seem to suggest that he was tortured and beheaded after 100 days for refusing to renounce his Orthodox faith and remove the cross that his grandmother had given him. His mother had to pay $4,000 to take possession of his remains (including the cross), and an additional sum to have the head returned on November 6, 1996, on the Feast of the Icon "Mother of God—joy of all who suffer." His reassembled remains have been buried on a bleak hillside of his native village.

The cult that has since developed around Rodionov's memory contains elements that support both of the contradictory impulses in contemporary Russia: democratic egalitarianism on the one hand and authoritarian nationalism on the other. The admiration for this young man is basically part of the apolitical recovery of "spiritual culture" from below. He is revered by ordinary Russians for voluntarily accepting suffering and death out of simple loyalty to family, faith, and friends. Prayers are directed to him by other soldiers who feel abandoned and abused—often by their own leaders as well as by the Chechens. Icons are painted of him locally, not ordained from above by the Church hierarchy. His veneration expresses more of the motherland ideal than that of the fatherland, and has been mainly promoted not by nationalistic politicians, but by his indefatigable and still-young mother.

Nevertheless, his personal example can be used to provide a misleading patina of sanctity for an inherently authoritarian nationalistic cause. Politicians can extol him as a heroic contemporary model for unquestioning obedience to a military unit on a xenophobic mission. Neither the boy nor his mother seem ever to have expressed any political beliefs or to have endorsed the war in Chechnya. But the brutality of Evgeny's death and the purity of his life can be used as a kind of moral justification for the continued brutalization of the Chechen population.

There has also been in post-Soviet Russia a different type of martyr: those who have died directly for democracy. They stand in the Russian tradition of the truth-tellers (*pravedniki*). They are a diverse group and have passed in and out of history in an impressive, but often inadequately noticed, parade. Nine members of the Duma and at least 130 journalists have been murdered just since 1994.[52] These have mostly been contract murders; almost none have been solved. There seems to be little prospect—in view of widespread concealment and disinformation—of compiling a full and accurate matryrology of these courageous people, let alone curtailing this "censorship by killing."

Among the many unsung and often unknown martyrs for a democratic Russia, Larisa Yudina is an impressive example. A graduate of the Moscow University faculty of journalism, she established herself in the late Soviet era as a fearless writer for the main daily newspaper in Elista, the capital of the small Kalmyk Republic north of the Caspian Sea and west of the lower Volga River. After the collapse of the USSR, she was elected editor-in-chief and became spokesperson for the democratic opposition to the dictatorial president of the republic, Kirsan Iliumzhinov.

Iliumzhinov outlawed Yudina's journal (which she continued to publish in the adjacent Volgograd region), fired her husband from his government job, and permitted, if he did not incite, threats on her life and the torching of the door to her home. She became the regional head of Yabloko, the democratic opposition party, which kept her work alive until she was brutally murdered in June 1998. She was posthumously given a minor decoration ("The Order of Courage") by President Putin, but the crime has never been solved. She has become a legendary figure as "the only little island of truth" in the small republic of the Russian Federation in which she lived and died.[53]

Two especially admired martyrs of the 1990s might conceivably point the way toward renewal within the Church as well as the broader society. First, Galina Starovoitova, the passionate and highly intelligent democratic activist in the Russian parliament, was a leader in defending national and ethnic minorities. She spoke out against Great Russian chauvinism inside and outside the Russian Orthodox Church, but she also joined that church shortly before her assassination in St. Petersburg. The witness of her short life suggested to some young Russians the validity of a core belief shared by almost all the founding fathers of the U.S. republic: that self-government depends on a moral people, and that morality will not long survive without religion. In November 2003, five years after her murder, she was publicly celebrated as being "more popular now than during the last years of her life."[54]

Second, Alexander Men was a priest of the Russian Orthodox Church who was murdered on September 9, 1990, in the shadow of the great Laura of St. Sergius and the Holy Trinity in Sergiev Posad.[55] He was the teacher and preacher most admired by the young student generation of the 1980s, but the Church permitted him to serve only in a small village on the far northern outskirts of Moscow. He was buried there on the day consecrated to the beheading of John the Baptist, who is known in Orthodoxy as "the precursor."

Men was a precursor of the post-Soviet religious renewal. He embodied and advocated a Russian Orthodox Christianity whose ecumenism would reach out not only to other Christians and to the unchurched, but also to the other, related prophetic monotheisms that needed to be honored within the Russian Federation. Of part-Jewish origin, Men fought anti-Semitism, which he felt had become one of the Church's "dominant traits" in the late Soviet period.[56] He sought to bring more of the Judaic passion for social justice into the Orthodox Church. He was planning at the time of his death to launch a dialogue on a religious basis between Christians and Muslims. He said that "the walls we erect between ourselves are not high enough to reach up to God."

Men came out of the underground branch of the Church, and he was frequently both under surveillance by the KGB and under attack by reactionary clerics. In his last interview, he lamented the triumphalism and collaboration with the Soviet state that he saw in the Church's celebration of its Millennium in 1988:

> When we believers marked the one-thousandth anniversary of the Baptism of Rus, not one word was said about the tragedy of the Russian Church, but only rapture and ecstasy about oneself.[57]

Men was killed with an axe, but he lives on for many as an icon. Embedded in his—and others'—otherwise senseless deaths is the witness left behind to the possibility of reconciliation, not just between former enemies, but also between Christian tradition and the modern world. And it is at this point that the image of a matryoshka no longer suffices. For there may be no solid wood inside the many faces of Russia, and neither an apocalypse nor an "end of history" in sight. A clear identity may be attainable only in the lives of individuals and within the smaller communities in which authentic community can be reestablished. It takes a leap of faith to believe that there can be redemptive value to innocent suffering.

It may be impossible for Russians to make a truly fresh start on the basis of their much-proclaimed spiritual values in the absence of any law on lustration or full accounting for past repression and atrocities.[58] But processes of democratization and moral engagement are noticeable within the increasingly pluralistic popular culture. Vulgar but anti-authoritarian slang (*mat*) may be transforming the Russian language from within even more than neologisms from the West are transforming it from without.[59] A popular design competition for a monument to a dog, "Mumu for the People!" effectively satirized the entire practice of publicly glorifying power figures in Russia.[60] And a new youth group called Walking Together (*Idushchie vmeste*) had by February 2003 attracted 80,000 members in sixty cities. Its program committed young members to study traditional Russian culture, accept a strict code of personal morality, and perform social services for the community.[61]

Admired by young Russians today are ideas of émigrés that were long ago generated in, but largely unnoticed by, the West: Berdiaev's version of Emmanuel Mounier's Christian personalism[62]; Frank's belief that sobornost' begins with spiritual transformation within individuals rather than material changes in society; Georgy Fedotov's suggestion that Russian Orthodoxy requires rather than opposes democracy; and the view shared by both the liberal P. I. Novgorodtsev and the conservative Ivan Il'in that establishing the uniform rule of law would be the necessary first order of business in reconstructing Russian life after communism. All of these Russian thinkers—and many others yet to be discovered—contribute not just to their own, but also to European and world civilization.[63]

The United States, which faced Russia for so long during the Cold War as the other scorpion in the thermonuclear bottle, has become a model that Russians hope to emulate rather than the rival that they once sought to overtake and surpass, if not to bury. There is continuing popular ignorance about, and growing disillusionment with, this model. But many young Russians still see the United States as the most successful and relevant example of what they basically hope to create in Russia: an inventive economy, an open society, and a more accountable government for a multiethnic, continent-wide nation. This aspiration gives Americans the opportunity, if not the obligation, to work more closely with and for the related processes of cultural self-discovery and economic-political transformation in Russia.

Accountable and participatory governments have not historically fought each other. The United States and Russia, the two large-scale nations on the Western and Eastern frontiers of European civilization, may have brought to an end the world wars of the twentieth century. These were, in fact, largely civil wars within European civilization in the Northern hemisphere. The prospects for world peace in the twenty-first century will depend in good measure on Russian democracy succeeding and becoming the norm in Eurasia. Beyond that, the question is whether the European civilizations of the North will be able to live in peace with very different, more populous civilizations to the South. This, in turn, may well depend on the United States, the only super-power and the continuing focus of world attention for better or for worse. Will the United States sustain its own tradition of keeping power accountable in a culture that values both continuing spiritual renewal and continuous self-questioning? It is that combination that has made democracy dynamic in America[64]—and gives hope now to a Russia that looks back for faith even as it moves forward in freedom.

Notes

1. The Nineteenth-Century Discovery of Identity

1. On the evolution of this project through two successive Swedish architects, Alexander Witberg and Constantine Ton, see James H. Billington, *The Face of Russia* (New York, 1998), 106–10; the exhibition catalogue *Alexander Witberg (1787–1855)* (Stockholm, 1994); and T.A. Slavina, *Konstantin Ton* (Leningrad, 1989).

   There were two comparably megalomaniacal memorial projects in the then-capital of St. Petersburg. Montferrand took twenty years to raise up the largest monolithic granite column in history in the square before the Winter Palace to commemorate the victory (see O.A. Chekanova and A. L. Potach, *Ogiust Monferran* [Leningrad, 1990]). Ton took twenty-five years to complete St. Isaac's Cathedral with a dome so large that it became the first in history to have iron reinforcement. It was a model used in designing the second such dome, the U.S. Capitol.

2. From the now immense literature on the Slavophiles, see two older, but still fundamental studies: the synthesis of A. Gratieux, *A.S. Khomiakov et le mou-*

vement slavophile, 2 vols. (Paris, 1939), stressing the central importance of Khomiakov and the Orthodox tradition; and Nicholas Riasanovsky, *Russia and the West in the Teaching of the Slavophiles: A Study of Romantic Ideology* (Cambridge, Mass.: Harvard University Press, 1952), stressing the impact of German romantic thought on their ideas. The poet-critic Nicholas Bakhtin (older brother of Michael Bakhtin) considered German influence "ruinous" for the development of Russian thought generally: "Vera i znanie," *Zveno*, no. 155 (1926): 3–4.

3. There has been much less recent scholarship on the early, liberal Westerniz-ers than on their Slavophile opponents—except for Alexander Herzen and Vissarion Belinsky, who were accepted with reservations into the Soviet pan-theon as early revolutionaries. For a balanced assessment, see the article on Belinsky by Isaiah Berlin in his series, "The Marvelous Decade," *Encounter* 1955 (December): 22–43. More generally on this period, see F. Nelidov, *Za-padniki 40kh godov* (Moscow, 1910).

4. On Herzen, see Berlin, "The Marvelous Decade," *Encounter*, 1956 (May): 20–34; Martin Malia, *Alexander Herzen and the Birth of Russian Socialism* (Cambridge, Mass.: Harvard University Press, 1961); and Herzen's own panoramic memoir, *My Past and Thoughts*, 4 vols. (New York, 1968), with an introduction by Berlin. The term "remarkable decade" was coined in an-other rich contemporary memoir of the period: P. Annenkov, *Literaturnye vospominaniia* (Moscow, 1960).

5. See L. V. Cherepnin, "S. M. Solov'ev kak istorik," introduction to vol. 1–5, in S. Solov'ev, *Istoriia Rossii s drevneishikh vremen* (Moscow 1959–1966); and the earlier and more balanced analysis of E. Shmurlo, in F.A. Brokgauz and I.A. Efron, *Entsiklopedicheskii slovar'*, vol. 30 (St. Petersburg, 1900), 798–803.

6. N. Ia. Danilevsky, *Rossiia i Evropa* (Moscow, 1991). Other re-publications of excerpts have made this book one of the most discussed treatises in post-communist Russia. See B.P. Baluev, *Spory o sud'bakh Rossii. N. Ia. Danilevskii i ego kniga "Rossiia i Evropy"* (Tver, 2001). At least six dissertations have re-cently been written on Danilevsky in Russia.

7. A ball in the Winter Palace celebrating the Romanov tricentennial in 1913 is the final tableau in the recent film *Russian Ark*, made with a single 96-minute shot entirely taken inside the Winter Palace/Hermitage of a walk through pre-revolutionary history. A lengthy epic film (not yet widely shown outside Russia), *The Barber of Siberia*, reenacts a spectacular military review inside the Kremlin with the film's director, Nikita Mikhalkov, appear-ing as Tsar Alexander III. Such images reenforce at the popular level the be-lief in pre-revolutionary national grandeur. For Ukhtomsky's "Asianist Vi-sion," see David Schimmelpenninck van der Oye, *Toward the Rising Sun* (Dekalb, 2001), 42–60.

8. See the anthology edited by I.L. Galinskaia and L.V. Skvortsov, *Samosoznanie Rossii*, vol. 1, *Drevniaia Rus' i moskovskoe gosudarstvo* (Moscow, 1999). Skvortsov (pp. 4–23) sees Russian self-consciousness emerging early from a series of cultural "shifts" (*sdvigi*) beginning with Prince Vladimir's late tenth-century conversion to Christianity. Galinskaia (pp. 24–41) discusses a little-known, pioneering scholarly attempt to establish such a lineage: M.O. Koialovich, *Istoriia russkogo samopoznaniia po istoricheskim pamiatnikam i nauchnym sochineniiam* (St. Petersburg, 1901).

9. Paul Miliukov, *Ocherki po istorii russkoi kul'tury*, vol. 2 (Moscow, 1995), part 1, 53, cited and discussed in Daniel Rancour-Laferriere, *Russian Nationalism from an Interdisciplinary Perspective: Imagining Russia* (Lewiston, N.Y., 2001), 4. Miliukov gives no reference for the quotation.

10. *Slovar' russkogo iazyka XI–XVII vv.* (Moscow, 1997), 22:258. The term *rusak* was used for everything from fish to dishes made of grain to cockroaches—all suggesting linkage with everyday peasant life. The terms *rusakovatyi* and *ruskovatyi* suggest the approximation and/or retention of something authentically Russian. See *Slovar' russkikh narodnykh govorov*, vol. 35 (St. Petersburg, 2001), 267, 269; and *Slovar' russkogo iazyka* (Moscow, 1983), 3:741.

11. *Slovar' russkogo iazyka*, 22: 217–18, 259–61.

12. *Slovar' russkikh narodnykh govorov*, 190–92.

13. Max Vasmer, *Etimologicheskii slovar' russkogo iazyka*, vol. 3 (Moscow, 1987), 521; *Slovar' russkikh narodnykh govorov*, 271.

2. The Twentieth-Century Search for Legitimacy

1. Fedor Dostoevsky, *Polnoe sobranie sochinenii*, vol. 18 (Leningrad, 1978), 37, 115, 229. Narodnost' here meant both nationality and spirit of the people. For discussion, see Vasily Vanchugov, "O 'pochve' i 'russkoi idee,'" in his *Ocherk istorii filosofii "samobytno-russkoi"* (Moscow, 1994), 121–25; and Eduard Batalov, *Russkaia ideia i amerikanskaia mechta* (Moscow, 2001), 9.

Dostoevsky coined this neologism in the prospectus for the new journal *Vremia* (Time), which he and his brother founded after his prison exile. There he moved from his early immersion in radical Western ideas to a deep respect for the faith of ordinary Russians. Hence, his juxtaposition of the ideas of Western "nationalities" with those of Russian narodnost'.

Writing about the "Russian idea" became extremely voluminous in the 1990s. In addition to works discussed elsewhere in this book, see Arseny Gulyga, *Russkaia ideia i ee tvortsy* (Moscow, 1995); T. I. Kutkovets and I. M. Kliamkin, "Russkie idei," *Polis*, no. 2 (1997): 118–40; Kh. Kh. Bokov and S. V. Alekseev, *Rossiiskaia ideia i natsional'naia ideologiia narodov Rossii* (Moscow,

1996); S. V. Alekseev, V. A. Kalamanov, and A. G. Chernenko, *Ideologicheskie orientiry Rossii*, 2 vols. (Moscow, 1998); M. A. Maslin, *Russkaia ideia* (Moscow, 1992); and N. S. Rozov, "Natsional'naia ideia kak imperativ razuma," *Voprosy filosofii*, no. 10 (1997): 13–28. See also Andranik Migranian, *Rossiia v poiskakh identichnosti (1985–1995)* (Moscow, 1997).

For thoughtful reformist versions, see V. A. Tishkov's argument for civic nationalism over ethnic nationalism ("Zabyt' o natsii," *Voprosy filosofii*, no. 9 (1998): 3–26); Vadim Mezhuev's insistence that the "Russian idea" is an extension rather than a rejection of Western civilization ("O natsional'noi idee," *Voprosy filosofii*, no. 12 (1997): 3–14); and Alexander Akhiezer's argument for simultaneously modernizing the economy and the culture, *Rossiia: kritika istoricheskogo opyta (Sotsiokul'turnaia dinamika Rossii)* (Novosibirsk, 1997).

More authoritarian, ethnic nationalist views are in Sergei Fomin, "O russkoi natsional'noi idee," *Moskva*, no. 1 (2000): 215–24; Viktor Kozlov, *Istoriia tragedii velikogo naroda. Russkii vopros* (Moscow, 1986); two lengthy discussions centered on Valentin Rasputin: "V kakom sostoianii nakhoditsia russkaia natsiia," *Nash Sovremennik*, no. 3 (1993): 148–60; and "Besedy o russkom," *Moskva*, February (1994): 112–15; and a virtual anthology of such views in "Russkaia Elita," *Zavtra*, June (1994): 6, 8.

For critical assessments of the new nationalists, see *La question russe. Essais sur le nationalisme russe*, compiled by Michel Niqueux (Paris, 1992); Kathleen Parthé, "The Empire Strikes Back: How Right-wing Nationalists Tried to Recapture Russian Literature," *Nationalities Papers*, December (1996): 601–24; Geoffrey Hosking and Robert Service, eds., *Russian Nationalism, Past and Present* (London, 1997); and Thomas Parland, *The Rejection in Russia of Totalitarian Socialism and Liberal Democracy: A Study of the Russian New Right* (Helsinki, 1993).

The entire concept of a "Russian idea" is seen as a source of moral confusion if not outright danger by Victor Ostretsov ("Russkaia ideia kak fakt falsifikatsiia," *Russkii Vestnik* (1992): 41–44); and B. S. Solodsky, "Russkaia ideia: konseptsiia spaseniia ili provokatsiia konflikta," in *Russkaia tsivilizatsiia: sobornost'*, edited by Evgeny Troitsky, 70–77 (Moscow, 1994). Igor Kliamkin and Tat'iana Kutkovets suggested in 1996 that continued Russian talk about a "special path" for Russia is basically "psychological compensation" for present woes in "a country that has not yet left its past but does not want to return to it." "Osobyi put' Rossii: mify i paradoksy," *Moskovskie Novosti*, no. 34, August 25–September 1, 1996, p. 9.

Tim McDaniel, *The Agony of the Russian Idea* (Princeton, N.J.: Princeton University Prses, 1996), is a spirited essay that sees Russians believing in a society based on ultimate values, a higher form of community, social equality, and reliance on the state—but obsessed with polarized "binary" thinking and making a seemingly irremediable mess of things in the Yeltsin era. An original approach blending in Russian folklore with the history of philosophy is taken by a scientist from Kazan, Vladimir Kurashov, in *Filosofiia: rossiiskaia mental'nost'* (Kazan, 1999).

2. Vladimir Solov'ev, "Russkaia ideia," *Sochineniia v dvukh tomakh*, vol. 2 (Moscow, 1989), 230.

3. Nicholas Berdiaev, *Dusha Rossii (voina i kul'tury)*, (Moscow, 1915); and *Sud'ba Rossii: opyt po psikhologii voiny i natsional'nosti*, (Moscow, 1918).

4. Berdiaev, *The Russian Idea* (New York, 1948), 2.

5. Ibid., 255.

6. Nicholas Berdiaev, *Filosofiia neravenstva* (Berlin, 1923. His subsequent biography of Constantine Leontiev was rediscovered and widely cited in the 1990s. Leontiev's *Vostok, Rossiia i slavianstvo* (Moscow, 1885–1886) was a blanket indictment of Western vulgarity and decadence ("The Average European as an Ideal and Instrument of Universal Destruction," in J. Edie, et al., *Russian Philosophy*, vol. 2 [New York, 1965]) and provided a prototype for anti-Western Russian nationalists in the post-Soviet period.

7. Originally published in French as *Les sources et le sens du communisme russe* (Paris, 1936).

8. The partial opening of Soviet archives has brought to light many Lenin documents that were never included in purportedly complete Soviet editions of his works. Particularly important are those showing Lenin's savage uses of terror. A characteristic telegram of August 11, 1918 instructs communists in Penza "to hang [hang without fail, so that the *public sees*] at least *100* notorious kulaks, the rich, the bloodsuckers . . . in such a way that people for hundreds of miles around will see, tremble, know and scream out. *Let's choke and strangle those blood-sucking kulaks.*" From *Revelations from the Russian Archives* (Washington, D.C., 1997), 12 (a volume of documents from the Library of Congress exhibit of June–July 1992 published in English translation). Even after the end of the Civil War, Lenin issued a secret directive to the secret police saying, "the more representatives of the reactionary clergy we manage to shoot, the better." Directive of March 19, 1922, cited in Alexander Yakovlev, *A Century of Violence in Soviet Russia* (New Haven, 2002), 160. See also the biography by the former political head of the Soviet Army who became a pioneer in opening the archives and radically revising Soviet official historiography: General Dmitry Volkogonov, "Zhretsy terrora," in *Lenin: politicheskii portret* (Moscow, 1994), 327–430.

9. Lenin, "Gosudarstvo i revoliutsiia," in his *Polnoe sobranie sochinenii*, vol. 33, 5th ed. (Moscow, 1962), 91.

10. Isaiah Berlin coined the term "artificial dialectic" to describe this systemic, rhythmic use of planned terror, which he considers Stalin's special contribution to modern politics. See his "Generalissimo Stalin and the Art of Government," *Foreign Affairs,* January (1952): 197–214, published under the pseudonym O. Utis.

11. This procedure described to me by the late General Dmitry Volkogonov seems to have paralleled, if it did not accompany, the transfer of the briefcase containing the codes to activate nuclear weapons.

12. Preface to Robert Byrnes, ed., *After Brezhnev: Sources of Soviet Conduct in the 1980s* (Bloomington, 1983), xvii.

13. Good general surveys with bibliographies of the vast literature on this subject are Gerhard Simon, *Nationalism and Policy toward the Nationalities in the Soviet Union* (Boulder, Colo., 1991), updated with a new introduction from the original German edition of 1986; and Valery Tishkov, *Ethnicity, Nationalism in Conflict in and after the Soviet Union: The Mind Aflame* (London, 1997).

   Mikhail Agursky argues that Soviet Communism was impregnated from the very beginning by a nationalism based on Russo-German hostility, in *The Third Rome: National Bolshevism in the USSR* (Boulder, Colo., 1987). On the other hand, some recent scholars (and many post-Soviet Russian nationalists) tend to conclude (or complain) that Russian nationalism was not such a central determinant of Soviet policy.

   For a good account of the various ways the Communist leadership after Stalin tried to co-opt Russian nationalist sentiments in order to perpetuate the central controls of the Soviet system, see Yitzhak Brudny, *Reinventing Russia: Russian Nationalism and the Soviet State, 1953–1991* (Cambridge, Mass.: Harvard University Press, 1998). His footnotes discuss how the general literature on nationalism applies to the specific case of Russia. The material described in the section, "What is Russia and where should it go? Political debates 1971–1985," (pp. 150–91) anticipates in some respects the broader discussion among nationalists that opened up after the Soviet collapse.

14. Kathleen Parthé, *Russian Village Prose: The Radiant Past* (Princeton, N.J.: Princeton University Press), 1992.

15. Brudny, *Reinventing Russia,* 255–56.

16. Valentin Rasputin, *Farewell to Matyora* (Evanston, 1991), with introduction by Kathleen Parthé, and his story *Fire* (1985) in *Siberia on Fire: Stories and Essays* (DeKalb, 1989). See also David Gillespie, *Valentin Rasputin and Soviet Russian Village Prose* (London, 1986).

   This school arises in reaction to an unprecedented depopulation of villages. Preliminary census results indicate that more than half of Russia's

155,290 villages have been abandoned or are populated by no more than fifty people. Eve Conant, "Ghosts of the Heartland," *Johnson's Russia List*, no. 7246, July 14, 2003.

17. In the three successive elections for president of Russia (1991, 1996, 2000), the final victor received progressively fewer votes and a progressively diminished percentage of the votes cast at each stage.

I. The Quickening Quest

1. For a detailed account of the careful preparations for the coup, which began the very day that Gorbachev left Moscow for a vacation in Foros in the Crimea, see the copy in the Library of Congress of the stenographic report of the official investigation conducted by the commission of the Russian parliament chaired by L. A. Ponomarov, *Uchastie rukovodiashchego sostava vooruzhennykh sil v gosudarstvennom perevorote 19–21 avgusta 1991 goda*, February 18, 1992, especially 110 ff.

2. James H. Billington, "Russia's Fever Break," *The Wilson Quarterly*, Autumn (1991): 58–65.

3. Viacheslav Ivanov, *Freedom and the Tragic Life: A Study in Dostoevsky* (New York, 1952), 48–50. For a recent discussion of the way in which Dostoevsky described himself as "a realist in the higher sense: that is I describe all the depth of the human soul," see V. N. Zakharov, "Khristianskii realizm v russkoi literature," in his *Evangel'skii tekst v russkoi literature XVIII-XX vekov* (Petrozavodsk, 2001), 5–20, especially 9.

3. A New Nation in Search of Identity

1. Vasily Vanchugov, *Russiaia mysl' v poiskakh "novogo sveta": "zolotoi vek" amerikanskoi filosofii v kontekste rossiiskogo samopoznaniia* (Moscow, 2000), 123–24. For many other hitherto little known aspects of the influence of William James and pragmatism well into the early Soviet period, see especially pp. 320–23.

2. Ivan Solonevich, *Narodnaia monarkhiia* (Moscow, 1991). Originally published in Buenos Aires in 1951–1954 as a five-volume set; also published in San Francisco in 1978.

3. See the collection *K. Leont'ev, nash sovremennik* (St. Petersburg, 1993).

4. For a good summary of his views and life, see Philip Grier, "The Complex Legacy of Ivan Il'in," in James Scanlan, ed., *Russian Thought after Communism: The Recovery of a Philosophical Heritage* (Armonk/London, 1994),

165–86. Kathleen Parthé is preparing a work, "Writing Russia: Ivan Il'in and Russian Identity in Diaspora."

5. Lawrence Uzzell, "Eroding Religious Freedom," *Moscow Times*, January 24, 2003.

6. See Chapter 5, note 7. Different polls indicated that ordinary Russians were at times much more receptive to liberal democracy than their ruling elites. See Stephen White, Richard Rose, Ian McAllister, *How Russia Votes*, 2d ed. (Chatham, N.J.: Chatham House, 1999).

7. Alexander Blok, *The Spirit of Music* (London, 1946).

8. E. A. Nekrasova, "Neosushchestvlennyi zamysel 1920-kh godov sozdaniia 'slovaria simvolov' i ego pervyi vypusk," *Pamiatniki kul'tury: 1982* (Moscow, 1984), 92–115.

9. Cited in Vasily Vanchugov, *Ocherk istorii filosofii "samobytno-russkoi"* (Moscow, 1994), 229.

10. Cited in Vanchugov, *Ocherk istorii*, 263.

11. Cited in Vanchugov, *Ocherk istorii*, 257–59. See also Gustav Shpet, *Ocherki razvitiia russkoi filosofii*, (Moscow, 1922), 52–53.

12. Georges Florovsky, *Ways of Russian Theology*, comprises volumes 5 and 6 of his collected works (Belmont, Mass.: Nordland Publishing, 1979). Volume 7 of the same series is *The Eastern Fathers of the Fourth Century*; and volume 8, *The Byzantine Fathers of the Fifth through the Eighth Centuries*. George Fedotov, "Russian Kenoticism," in his *The Russian Religious Mind*, vol. 1 (Cambridge, Mass.: Harvard University Press, 1946), 94–131.

13. Vladimir Vernadsky, *The Biosphere* (New York, 1998), and "The Biosphere and the Noosphere," *American Scientist*, no. 1 (1945): 1–12; and I. A. Kozikov, "Uchenie V. I. Vernadskogo o noosfere i rossiiskaia tsivilizatsiia," in *Russkaia tsivilizatsiia: sobornost'*, edited by Evgeny Troitsky, 139–45 (Moscow, 1994).

14. Leonid Leonov, *Piramida*, 2 vols. (Moscow, 1994). Leonov told me in an interview in August 1991 that he had been working on this book since World War II. Posthumously published (although still "unperfected," to use his term) after his death at age ninety-five, the novel is in three parts, consciously imitating Dante's *Divine Comedy*. It is extraordinarily pretentious, attempting to combine apocalyptical prophecy and occult symbols with allusions to many great works of world literature. Leonov describes it as an "evil obsession" (using the archaic spelling *navazhdenie*) and ends up suggesting that evil forces have totally conquered the Earth in the twentieth century, although a few virtuous Russians remain—presumably so that at least some of "those made of clay" may experience "a triumphant final return to the sun which gave birth to all of them."

Equally full of fantastic figures is Daniel Andreev, *The Rose of the World* (Hudson, N.Y., 1997), which translates three-fifths of the total. His original version was conceived during his long imprisonment, 1947 to 1957, with the aid of a prayer group composed of an Orthodox priest, a Muslim mullah, and a scholar of Indian culture (xvii–xviii). Although the original version was confiscated, he rewrote it with an outlook that is more religious and optimistic than Leonov's. He sees the "spirit of tyranny" being replaced by a "global federation of independent states" and all of the world's religions being turned "from a collage of separate petals into one single whole spiritual flower—the Rose of the World" (p. 18). This "rose" is "an upturned flower, the roots of which are in heaven and the petals here, among humanity, on earth. Its stem is revelation, through which flow the spiritual juices that feed and strengthen its petals, our fragrant chorus of religions" (58).

A considerable cult following has also developed for the painter Nicholas Roerich, who emigrated to India in 1927 and sought to relate Russian art and philosophy to Indian mystical thinking. See L. V. Shaposhnikova, *Derzhava rerikha* (Moscow, 1993). Roerich founded a museum in New York and succeeded in getting members of the Pan American Union to sign a treaty in the White House on April 15, 1935, agreeing to place "Banners of Peace" over all cultural monuments—a kind of anticipation of UNESCO. (See his biography at www.roerich.org/NicholasRoerich.html; accessed on March 7, 2002.)

Another new Russian cult sees Christianity becoming "the universal religion of Mother Earth" by absorbing Buddhism, Hinduism, and Taoism and adding a "Last Testament" to the Old and New Testaments: *A Little Grain of the Word of Vissarion Presenting the Last Testament of the Heavenly Father Who Sent Him*, an undated English translation of a pamphlet from Moscow in the Library of Congress, 1–8.

All of Roerich's transcultural syncretism is denounced as "satanism" by the prolific Orthodox writer Andrei Kuraev, in *Satanizm dlia intetelligentsii. O rerikhakh i pravoslavii* (Moscow, 1997). A contributor to another of Kuraev's books includes "the world of virtual reality" as part of the satanic undermining of Orthodox culture: *Sovremennye sekty i neoiazychestvo v rossii* (Moscow, 1998), 104–10.

15. Leonid Uspensky, *The Theology of Icons* (Crestwod, N.Y., 1976); also L. Uspensky and V. Lossky, *The Meaning of Icons* (Boston, 1952).

16. Boris Raushenbakh, *Prostranstvennye postroeniia v drevnerusskoi zhivopisi* (Moscow, 1975); and *Geometriia kartiny i zritel'noe vospitanie* (Moscow, 1994). On Zinon, see his *Besedy ikonopistsa*, Novgorod, 1993, and Billington, "Keeping the Faith in the USSR after a Thousand Years," *Smithsonian*

Magazine, April 1989, pp. 130–43. Zinon was subsequently made head of another monastery in Pskov and then dismissed for sharing communion with non-Orthodox Christians. He typifies the mixture of tradition and openness that is characteristic of a number of younger priests.

17. Stimulated by "Berdiaev's idea about modern politics as a kind of continuation of avant-garde art," Ivanov saw such harmony prefigured in the attempt of Wagner and particularly of Skriabin to unify all forms of expression in a single work of art. Skriabin's never-completed, multimedial *Mysterium* was to have been performed in India, and its text was entitled *Preliminary Act*. Real-life action had to follow such preliminaries in Ivanov's view, because of the need and obligation "to apply the intensity of the human mind to present-day problems." See Yury Lotman, *Vnutri mysliashchikh mirov* (Moscow, 1996), "Semiosfera," 163–297, and the introduction by V. V. Ivanov, "Semiosfera i istoriia," vii–xiv.

18. Citations and argument from V. V. Ivanov, "Towards Noosphere," in *Candles in the Dark: A New Spirit for a Troubled World*, edited by Barbara Baudot, 187–204 (Seattle, Wa., 2002), 187–204, especially 197–99. For the influence of Skriabin on Berdiaev and the Silver Age as well as the linkage between his attempt to synthesize all the arts with the social ideal of sobornost', see E. Kutina and E. Laushkina, "A. N. Skriabin I filosofskaia mysl' kontsa XIX-nachalo XX v. sobornost'. obshchee delo," *Gosudarstvennyi memorial'nyi muzei A. N. Skriabina Uchenye zapiski* 3 (1998): 5–17.

19. The Russian rediscovery of Bakhtin, who lived mostly in provincial obscurity in the USSR until his death in 1975, is a kind of literary reflection of the broader Russian discovery of freedom and pluralism. He is admired for seeing in prose "a type of energy . . . likely to . . . produce new freedom" through a "proliferation of voices" rather than imposing hierarchical social values and classical compositional constraints. He is praised as an optimistic "anti-revolutionary" who sees the future as open-ended and "non-finalizable." See Caryl Emerson, *The First Hundred Years of Mikhail Bakhtin* (Princeton, N.J.: Princeton University Press, 1997), 17, 35–37, 71; also Emerson, ed., *Critical Essays on Mikhail Bakhtin* (New York, 1999).

20. Yury Sokhriakov, "Rabota sovesti," in his *Natsional'naia ideia v obshchestvennoi publitsistiki xix-nachalo xx vv.* (Moscow, 2002), 183–84. Sokhriakov is paraphrasing from the newly rediscovered work of M. O. Menshikov, whom he considers "the most popular publicist . . . of the first decade of the 20th century" (p. 171). Menshikov was killed by the communists in 1918. His partly unpublished writings were discovered and published as *Iz pisem' k blizhnym* (Moscow, 1991).

21. The usually unromantic Mikhailovsky confessed that he was "entraptured" by the "astounding inner beauty" of this double meaning of the word

"pravda." "Truth in this wide meaning of the word has been the aim of my searching." N. K. Mikhailovsky, *Sochineniia*, vol. 1 (St. Petersburg, 1896); and *Literaturniia vospominaniia i sovremennaia smuta*, vol. 1 (St. Petersburg), 350–57, 447–48.

22. Likhachev is cited as the principal defender of the Old Believers by the liberal journalist Alexander Nezhny, "Na rogozhskoi zastave, u staroobriadtsev," *Moskovskie novosti*, November 29, 1987, p. 12. Likhachev valued the original martyr for the Old Belief, the Archpriest Avvakum, for his pioneering autobiography that brought personal sincerity into Russian literature. See Likhachev, *Izbrannye raboty* (Leningrad, 1987), 2:308–21, 3:146–51.

23. See the publication for the exhibit by Abby Smith and Vladimir Budaragin, *Living Traditions of Russian Faith* (Washington, D.C.: Library of Congress, 1990).

24. His lengthy memoir of this period tells of valiant effort to preserve cultural life even in this forbidding place. D. S. Likhachev, *Vospominaniia* (St. Petersburg, 1995), 112–288, 388–94.

25. Likhachev described these letters to me and showed me a number of them. I am not aware that any of them have yet been published, but they are presumably with his papers in the Pushkin House in St. Petersburg.

26. The short text of Yeltsin's speech at the burial of the tsar's family is in a Reuter's release of June 17, 1998. Likhachev played a role both in persuading Yeltsin to come and in drafting the remarks.

27. Likhachev, *Poeziia sadov. K semantike sadovo-parkovykh stilei: Sad kak tekst*, 3d ed. (St. Petersburg, 1998).

28. A. S. Pushkin, "19 oktiabria," in his *Stikhotvoreniia, 1817–1825* (Polnoe sobranie sochinenii, vol. 2, pt. 1) (Moscow: Voskresen'e, 1994), 375.

29. Boris Pasternak, *Doctor Zhivago* (New York, 1958), 493.

30. Likhachev's concept of the "ecology of culture" is most fully developed in his extended essay of 1984, *Zametki o russkom*, in his *Izbrannye raboty*, vol. 2 (Leningrad, 1987), 418–94. This is one of the two books that Putin said he was reading in his extended press conference of March 6, 2001 (the other was a history of the rule of Catherine the Great). *Johnson's Russia List*, no. 5135, March 7, 2001, p. 14.

31. Likhachev contended that "the designation of Russia as 'Scandoslavica'" is "far more appropriate than 'Eurasia'" in his contribution to Heyward Isham, *Remaking Russia* (Armonk, 1994), 51. Many Russian writers and journalists from the Silver Age such as Menshikov shared and at times fed the widespread anti-Semitism of the period. But Likhachev spoke warmly of the Jewish contribution to the cultural life of the Silver Age—and especially valued a long talk he had with Sir Isaiah Berlin when he went to receive an honorary degree in Oxford. Sir Isaiah's famous meeting with Anna Akhmatova

in Petersburg at the end of World War II was used to silence the writers and feed the anticosmopolitan, anti-Jewish purges of the high Stalin era. Likhachev seemed to want to reaffirm the link with both Western letters and the largely lost Jewish part of prerevolutionary Russia.

4. The Authoritarian Alternative: Eurasianism

1. By the time of the 1989 census, the percentage of ethnic Russians in the USSR had fallen to 50.8 percent and the percentage of Russians in the Russian Soviet Federation was 86.41 percent. *The World Factbook, 2002* (Washington, D.C.: Central Intelligence Agency, 2002), updated on January 1, 2002, estimates the ethnic Russian percentage of the shrinking overall population of the Russian Federation as 81.5 percent. The early returns from the 2002 census were greeted with so much criticism that agreed-upon statistics on these matters may not easily be achieved.

2. Paul Kolstoe, *Russians in the Former Soviet Republics* (London, 1995), 58. A. I. Vdovin, V. Iu. Zorin, A. V. Nikonov, *Russkii narod v natsional'noi politike. XX vek* (Moscow, 1998), 279, set forth a thorough academic argument that Russia, in effect, adopt a radical ethnic nationalism. The dangers of such an approach are set forth in Ernest Gellner, *Nationalism* (New York, 1997), and *Nations and Nationalism* (Ithaca, N.Y. and London, 1983), 57, where he argues that nationalism is a modern substitute for religion. It is a homogeneous "high culture" imposed on the masses, which in the end produces "the exact opposite of what nationalism affirms and what nationalists fervently believe"—"an anonymous, impersonal society" of atomized individuals held together by an artificial mythic culture (138–42).

3. P. N. Savitsky, *Kontinent Evraziia* (Moscow, 1997). Robert MacMaster, in *Danilevsky, a Russian Totalitarian Philosopher* (Cambridge, Mass.: Harvard University Press, 1967), emphasizes the authoritarianism of this precursor. Natal'ia Alevras from Cheliabinsk in Siberia traces the origins of Eurasianism to the prerevolutionary writings of the historian who later taught at Yale University, George Vernadsky, and Savitsky: "Nachala evraziiskoi kontseptsii v rannem tvorchestve G. V. Vernadskogo i P. N. Savitskogo,"*Vestnik Evrazii*, no. 1(2) (1996): 5–17.

Among those early participants who soon broke with the geopolitical Eurasianism discussed here were three great historians and philosophers of culture, Georges Florovsky, Leo Karsavin, and Peter Bitsilli. Florovsky had a rich subsequent scholarly and ecclesiastical career in France and America. The other two had the misfortune to hold academic appointments in countries overrun by the USSR after World War II. Karsavin was taken from

Lithuania to die in the gulag. Bitsilli was removed from his longtime professorship in Bulgaria, forbidden to write, and placed under virtual house arrest.

Karsavin had written before leaving the USSR "about the world mission of the Russian people, about their universality, humility, and native Christian feeling," in *Vostok, zapad i russkaia ideia* (Petrograd, 1922), 4. His early writings in emigration included organic and blood-and-soil images of society along with philological mysticism that bore some resemblance to the early, runic period of Nazism. See citations in Dmitry Mirsky, "The Eurasian Movement," *Slavonic and East European Review,* December (1927): 316–17; also Julia Mehlich, *Lew Karsawin und die russische "Einzigartigkeit"* (Cologne, 1996), and Nicholas Riasanovsky, "The Emergence of Eurasianism," *California Slavic Studies* 4 (1967): 39–72.

Bitsilli contrasted cultural with geopolitical Eurasianism in *Dva lika evraziistva* (Sofia, 1927). Florovsky wrote what is still the best history of Russian religious thought: *Puti russkogo bogosloviia* (Paris, 1927; reprint, Vilnius, 1991); translated by Robert Nichols as *Ways of Russian Theology,* 2 vols. (Belmont, Mass., 1979).

4. I. R. Shafarevich, "Pochemu russkie terpiat?," in the nationalistic Vladivostok newspaper, *Russkii vostok,* December 14–31, 2000, pp. 1–2. His major works are *Rusofobiia: bol'noi vopros* (Leningrad, 1990); and more recently, *Russkii narod na perelome tysiacheletii: beg na peregonki so smert'iu* (Moscow, 2000), and *Trekhtysiacheletniaia zagadka: istoriia evreistva iz perspektivy sovremennoi Rossii* (St. Petersburg, 2002).

5. Vladimir Zhirinovsky, *Poslednii brosok na iug* (Moscow, 1993); in English, *Last Drive Southwards* (Moscow, 1998).

6. Kozhinov cites the recently published Politburo document signed by Stalin and dated November 11, 1939, containing the instruction: "Rescind Ulianov's [Lenin's] directive of May 21, 1919, on 'The struggle against priests and religion'": Vadim Kozhinov, *Pobedy i bedy Rossii: Russkaia kul'tura kak porozhdenie istorii* (Moscow, 2000), 49. Kozhinov argues that even Marx attributed Russia's greatness to its faith (p. 33). "Russia, a unique civilization and culture" is the title of Part I (p. 355). See also Kozhinov, *Istoriia Rusi i russkogo slova: konets IX-nachalo XVI veka* (Moscow, 1999), 71.

7. Alevras, "Nachala," 12 ff. Eduard Kul'pin sees Russia's Eurasian identity confirmed by what he proclaims to be "the new scientific discipline" of "socioscientific history." "Rossiia v evraziiskom prostranstve," *Vestnik Evrazii,* no. 1 (1996): 145–53.

8. Vadim Tsymbursky, "Ostrov Rossiia (perspektivy rossiiskoi geopolitiki)," *Polis,* no. 5 (1993), discussed in Rancour-Laferriere, *Russian Nationalism,* 73–76.

9. Vadim Tsymbursky, *Rossiia—zemlia za Velikim Limitrofom: tsivilizatsiia i ee geopolitika* (Moscow, 2000), 4. He analyzes the history of imperial intrusions into the space between civilizations, with particular reference to the Caucasus and Central Asia (pp. 57–88) but with many suggestions of ways it might apply to other areas of conflict such as the Balkans and Vietnam. He suggests (p. 80) the need for "a not yet written 'world history of the borderlands of great civilizations.'"

10. Vadim Tsymbursky, "Geopolitika dlia 'evraziiskoi atlantidy,'" *Pro et contra* 4, no. 4 (1999): 172; and "Zaural'skii Peterburg," in *Rossiia—zemlia*, 107–15.

11. Anna Akhmatova, "Rekviem," *Veter lebedinyi* (Moscow, 1998), 316; full text in her *Sobranie sochinenii*, vol. 3 (Moscow, 1998): 21–30. This verse was written originally in 1938.

12. Gumilev's overall views are summarized in an interview with Wiktor Osiatynski, in Osiatynski, *Contrasts: Soviet and American Thinkers Discuss the Future* (New York, 1984), 143–51. He apparently met Savitsky in the gulag. The floodgates opened for his sudden popularity when the collapse of the USSR permitted the serial publication in Russia of his hitherto little-known works: L. N. Gumilev, *Geografiia etnosa v istoricheskii period* (Leningrad, 1990); *Ot Rusi k Rossii: ocherki etnicheskoi istorii* (Moscow, 1992); *Etnosfera: istoriia liudei i istoriia prirody* (Moscow, 1993); and *Ritmy Evrazii* (Moscow, 1993).

His influence was further magnified in the late Soviet and early post-Soviet periods by a popular television series that he co-hosted with an excellent scholar of old Russian history, the late Alexander Panchenko. See Lev Gumilev and Alexander Panchenko, *Chtoby svecha ne pogasla: dialog* (Leningrad, 1990). For a Polish perspective that relates the late Gumilev to earlier anti-European perspectives in the Russian emigration, see Lucian Suchanek, "Rossiia i Evropa. Evraziistvo: Predshestvenniki i prodolzhateli," in *Kul'turnoe nasledie rossiiskoi emigratsii 1917–1940*, vol. 1, edited by Evgeny Chelyshev, 179–90 (Moscow, 1994).

13. For the impact on Russia of the hesychast movement and its insistence that spiritual prayer could connect the believer with the "energy" (*energeia*) but not the "essence" (*ousia*) of the divine, see James H. Billington, *The Icon and the Axe: An Interpretive History of Russian Culture* (New York, 1966), 51 ff. and 644–45, note 6.

More recent writers see guidance for scientific and reformist activity in this basic insight: "God is completely transcendental with respect to the world and at the same time is immanent to the world through His energies." S. A. Gribb, "Science and Theology in the Perspective of Russian Religious Thought," *Studies in Science and Theology* 6 (1998): 42. Gribb is drawing largely on the works of one of the most original, least studied theologians of the emigration, Sergei Bulgakov, who favored constitutional monarchy and provided an Orthodox study of economics in *Filosofiia khoziaistva* (Moscow, 1912). Bulgakov's views are set out in Paul Vallière, *Modern Russian Theology* (Grand Rapids, 2000), 227–321, and bibliography, 409–24.

14. Osiatynski, *Contrasts*, 150. Alexander Barkashov, the head of the crypto-Nazi Russian National Unity, describes his conflict with opponents as the "exchange of energy strikes." Sergei Borisov, "Front v 'parallel'nykh mirakh.' Pod maskoi pravoslavnoi dukhovnosti, RNE skryvaet neoiazycheskoe litso," *NG-Religiia*, February 3, 1999, based on Barkashov, "Rossiia-imperiia dukha: beseda Aleksandra Prokhanova s liderom russkogo natsional'nogo edinstva Aleksandrom Barkashovym," *Zavtra*, no. 45, November 10, 1998.

15. Alexis Gunsky, "Istoricheskie modeli russkoi identichnosti," *Povolzhskii zhurnal po filosofii i sotsial'nym naukam*, no. 7 (2000). Gunsky is the coordinator of the University Group for Buddhist studies in Samara; the journal is an online publication of Samara University (on his personal website, http://remington.samara.ru//-buddhist/gunsky.html). For Eurasianism farther east, see the journal *Vostochnyi polius: izdanie evraziitsev Urala i Sibiri* (Ekaterinburg-Novosibirsk-Tomsk).

16. A. S. Panarin, *Rossiia v tsivilizatsionnom protsesse (mezhdu atlantizmom i evraziistvom)* (Moscow, 1995), 51, 83–84. See also the roundtable in which Panarin participated: "Evraziistvo: za i protiv. vchera i segodnia," *Voprosy filosofii*, no. 6 (1995): 3–48.

17. A. S. Panarin, *Rossiiskaia intelligentsiia v mirovykh voinakh i revoliutsiiakh XX veka* (Moscow, 1998); and *Revansh istorii: rossiiskaia strategicheskaia initsiativa v XXI veke* (Moscow, 1998).

18. Panarin, *Rossiiskaia intelligentsiia*, 108–16, 133–37.

19. Ibid., 338–42, 150–52.

20. Ibid., 339–40.

21. Ibid., 110–12.

22. Ibid., 248–52; Panarin, *Revansh*, 345, 365.

23. Panarin, *Revansh*, 29, 379. The idea of Russian Orthodoxy making common cause with Islam against the encroachment of Western pluralism had been suggested as the USSR was disintegrating by S. Dunaev, "Musul'manin v etom mire strannik," *Nezavisimaia gazeta*, November 5, 1991.

24. Metropolitan Kirill of Smolensk and Kaliningrad, "Obstoiatel'sva novogo vremeni: Liberalizm, traditsionalizm i moral'nye tsennosti ob'ediniaiushcheisia Evropy," *Nezavisimaia gazeta*, May 26, 1999.

25. Polosin had been a deputy to the Russian Supreme Soviet. The Muslim leader Geidar Jemal', who was involved in Polosin's conversion, allegedly

suggested that a union of Muslims and Orthodox Slavs could provide the beginning of a new global alignment.

In addition to its historic Muslim minority, the Russian Federation now has a small but growing body of ethnic Russian converts to Islam. There are some 20,000 Muslims in the 700,000 population of the western province of Karelia; and converts elsewhere contribute to Polosin's *Musul'manskaia gazeta*. See Dmitri Glinski, "Islam in Russian Society and Politics: Survival and Expansion," *Policy Memo Series*, no. 198 (Washington, D.C.: Council on Foreign Relations, May 2001); and *Johnson's Russia List*, no. 6351, July 12, 2002. Niiazov's party was formally registered in October 2002 as Russia's Patriot Union Eurasian Party. See *Johnson's Russia List*, no. 7009, January 9, 2003. See also the apparent attempt to forge a common front in 1999 called "Orthodox Christianity and Islam"; Nikolas Gvosdev, "The New Party Card? Orthodoxy and the Search for Post-Soviet Russian Identity," *Problems of Post-Communism*, November/December (2000): 34.

Among Russian Muslims themselves, a minority of younger, fundamentalist Wahhabites are challenging the older, more moderate Muslim leaders, which could have the effect of moving more of Russia's 20 million Muslims in a more militantly anti-Western direction.

A cultural and scientific association called "The Eurasian Forum" was formed in Moscow in 1992, but appears to have developed a more activist agenda for its second Moscow conference in June 2001, which was opened by academician G. V. Osipov and Zhirinovsky, and included academic and political figures from a wide range of Eurasian cultures. They called for "strengthening the integrative processes" in "Eurasia—our common home." *Igotovoe reshenie Evraziiskoi sotsiologicheskoi assotsiatsiia* (Moscow, June 29, 2001) and *Programma "Evraziia—nash obshchii dom* (Moscow, June 29, 2001); copies of these documents were provided to me by one of its participants, Timur Timofeev.

26. Alexander Dugin, *Osnovy geopolitiki. Geopoliticheskoe budushchee Rossii. Myslit' prostranstvom*, 3d ed. exp. (Moscow, 1999), 488, 821.

27. Panarin, *Revansh*, 11, 345–49, 366–69.

28. A. S. Panarin, *Iskushenie globalizmom* (Moscow, 2000).

29. Mikhail Bakhtin, *Problems of Dostoevsky's Poetics*, ed. and trans. by Caryl Emerson (Minneapolis, 1984); Panarin, *Rossiiskaia intelligentsiia*, 110–12.

30. Panarin, *Revansh*, 341–84.

31. Evgeny Trubetskoi, cited by Nicholas Lossky in *Slavonic and East European Review* June (1924): 95. See also B. Ishboldin, "The Eurasian Movement," *Russian Review*, Spring (1946): 64–73. The desirability of a more moderate Eurasianism for post-Soviet Russia was suggested by the young deputy

mayor of Moscow, Sergei Stankevich, in the early 1990s and more recently by Dmitri Glinski, in "O soblaznakh I pogibeliakh, ili prevrashcheniia evraziiskoi idei," *Oppozitsiia*, no. 35 (2001): 3.

32. Dugin, *Osnovy*, 211–13, 485 ff. Members of the organization called Russian National Unity (for which Dugin served as an instructor) believe that Russian Orthodoxy itself is the sum of "Eurasian Nordic mysteries." See Borisov, "Front v 'parallel'nykh mirakh'.".

33. Dugin, *Osnovy*, 488.

34. Ibid., 339 ff., 689, 821.

35. *Programma i ustav politicheskoi partii "Evraziia"* (Moscow, 2002); discussed by Stephen Shenfield in *Johnson's Russia List*, no. 6535, November 6, 2002.

36. A rationale for the radical Eurasian belief that they might bring many religions into their fold can be found in the analysis of B. V. Dubin. He suggests that Russians in the 1990s moved beyond their traditional *dvoeverie* (duality of belief in both the Christian God and pagan spirits) to *mnogoverie* (multiplicity of beliefs). Since the objects of faith are vague and shifting, religion and other forms of belief have tended to become "more and more identified with the idea of Russian exclusiveness and xenophobia" rather than with "positive feelings of belonging to a valued confraternity." Dubin, "Pravoslavie, magiia i ideologiia v soznanii rossiian (90-ie gody)," in *Kuda idet Rossiia?* (1999), especially 366–67 and ff.

Alexander Dugin, however, was clearly fantasizing when he suggested in August 2003 that the Old Believers would provide mass support for his movement; see Dugin, "Evraziistvo gorazdo shire kakikh by to ni bylo partii, 'Evraziia v bloke'," *Novosti*, September 9, 2003.

37. Reprinted in Dugin, *Osnovy*, 491–549, with more texts added to the expanded third edition (pp. 825–97) along with a glossary of terms (pp. 898–914).

38. Yury Pivovarov and Andrei Fursov, "'Tserkov' i orda na puti k pravoslavnomu khanstvu," in "Russkaia sistema," *Politicheskaia nauka: teoriia i metodika*, vol. 2 (Moscow, 1997); and Chapter 5, notes 87 to 89.

39. Gleb Nosovsky and Anatoly Fomenko, *Rus' i Rim: Pravil'no li my ponimaem istorii Evropy i Azii?*, vol. 2 (Moscow, 1999), 291–93; following analysis in their *Novaia khronologiia Rusi* (Moscow, 1997). There is more detail in their *Bibleiskaia Rus': russko-ordynskaia imperiia i Bibliia*, 2 vols. (Moscow, 1998); and a popularized version with illustrations in their *Rus'-orda na stranitsakh bibleiskikh knig* (Moscow, 1998).

40. Nosovsky and Fomenko, *Novaia khronologiia*, 12–19. Gleb Nosovsky, Anatoly Fomenko, and V. V. Kalashnikov, *Geometrical and Statistical Methods of Analysis of Star Configurations: Dating Ptolemy's Almagest* (Boca Raton, Fla., 1993).

41. Nicholas Morozov, *Khristos (istoriia chelovechestva v estestvenno-nauchnom os-veshchenii)*, 7 vols. (Leningrad, 1924–1928). The discovery by Nosovsky and Fomenko of the manuscript of Morozov's unpublished eighth volume on Russia (*O russkoi istorii*) in the archive of the Russian Academy of Sciences added a host of philological arguments for fusing the two empires. Morozov fancifully suggested that the word Mongolian came from the Greek word for "great" *megaleion* (although classical Greek already had a distinct word for Mongols: *mougoulioi*). This word was then allegedly adopted to describe the "great empire" of Rus, which, in turn, was said to have taken its name from the Turkish mispronunciation of the Mongol term for a political district (*ulus-urus*). Nosovsky and Fomenko, *Novaia khronologiia*, 12, 95, 236–48.

Morozov moved from revolutionary activism to a massive study of the natural sciences in prison. Before his incarceration, he wrote his ground-breaking *Terroristicheskaia bor'ba* (London and Geneva, 1880); after his release, he turned to apocalyptical and prophetic writings: *Otkrovenie v groze i bure: vozniknovenie apokalipsisa* (St. Petersburg, 1907); and *Proroki: istoriia vozniknoveniia bibleiskikh prorochestv* (Moscow, 1914). A condensed translation of *Otkrovenie* was published as *The Revelation in Thunder and Storm* (Northfield, Minn., 1941). For more biographical and bibliographical information on Morozov, see the lengthy introduction by Sergei Valiansky to N. A. Morozov, *Novyi vzgliad na istoriiu russkogo gosudarstva* (Moscow, 2000), v–liv.

Morozov worked in astronomical and scientific institutes during the Soviet period until his death in 1946. He seems to have remained an atheist (Nosovsky and Fomenko, *Novaia khronologiia*, 244) despite his fascination with biblical prophecies. In the introduction to the first volume of his *Khristos*, he suggests that his title (the Russian word for Christ) is meant to refer to the generic phenomenon of the anointed leader in history; and he seems especially to admire the pre-Christian model of a leader who is anointed to power only after demonstrating his knowledge. *Khristos: Pervaia kniga*, (Leningrad, 1924), vi.

The West allegedly turned the great Mongolian-Russian empire away from its hitherto tolerant Eurasian identity after the crusaders' sack of Constantinople in 1204; Nosovsky and Fomenko, *Novaia khronologiia*, 236–37. The retrospective mythology pitting Russia against the Mongols was allegedly created under the Westernizing Romanov rulers who were unduly influenced by the Germans that they brought in as empresses and wives to their emperors; *Novaia khronologiia*, 16 ff.

42. Gary Kasparov, "Istoriia s geografiei," *Ogonek*, nos. 21/22 (2001); and replies in *Ogonek*, no. 23 (2001). Kasparov was far from being a Eurasian national-

ist, however. He was harshly critical of Putin from a liberal and human rights position. See his "KGB State," *The Wall Street Journal*, September 18, 2003.

43. V. L. Yanin, "Ziiaiushchie vysoty' akademika Fomenko," available at: http://www.hist.msu.ru/Science/DISKUS/FOMENKO/Janin.htm, accessed on September 11, 2003, 5.

44. Gennady Zyuganov, "Rossiia i mir," in *Sovremennaia russkaia ideia i gosudarstvo*, edited by Zyuganov, 25–26, 10, 21 (Moscow, 1995). See also his *Rossiia—rodina moia* (Moscow, 1996) and *Geografiia pobedy: Osnovy rossiiskoi geopolitiki* (Moscow, 1997), a geopolitical treatise that uses little rhetoric from the communist past but expresses nostalgia for Soviet success in the Third World. See "Da, Aziaty my?" *Geografiia*, 169–71. Zyuganov's links with National Bolshevism are suggested by Wayne Allensworth, *The Russian Question: Nationalism, Modernization and Post-Communist Russia* (Lanham, Md., 1998), 161–79.

Tsymbursky sees an "axis" forming among Ukraine, Moldova, and Karabakh, and another among Turkey, Georgia, and Azerbaijan (*Rossiia—zemlia*, 84). He fears future threats to Russia from such incursions into "its own other" part of the "limitrophe" (87). Alexis Podberezkin sees an "axis" of Turkey, Ukraine, Georgia, and Azerbaijan moving Western power into Central Asia. Podberezkin, *Iskusstvo zhit' v Rossii* (Moscow, 1997), 38 ff.

A more moderate Eurasianism invokes economic arguments for learning from noncommunist Asia. See Dmitri Glinski, ed., *Rossiia v tsentro-perifericheskom miroustroistve* (Moscow, 2003). In this collection, Victor Krasilshikov sees a model for Russia in the Asian capitalism of South Korea, Taiwan, and Singapore ("'Modernizatsionnaia lovushka' v post-industrial'nuiu epokhu: sravnitel'nyi analiz rossii i aziatskikh 'tigrov,'" 151–66); and Sergei Lunev suggests that "the prospects for developing the Russia-India-China triangular relationship" envisaged by then Prime Minister Evgeny Primakov in 1998–1999 as a counter to American power are brighter in the economic than in the political sphere ("Global'nye tendentsii v perspektivy razvitiia otnoshenii v treugol'nike 'Rossiia-Indiia-Kitai,'" 190–205). In his introduction, Glinski suggests that inner contradictions in the modern West and its "pax Americana" as well as the rising power of Asia may lead to a geopolitical shift comparable to "the 'orientalization' of the pax Romana in late antiquity" (pp. 11, 20 ff.).

45. Zyuganov, "Rossiia," 26. This volume, issued in the name of the Governmental-Patriotic Union "Spiritual Heritage" (*Dukhovnoe Nasledie*), suggests that the purpose of religion in Russia has always been to support state power, noting that "the Russian government is a full century older than the Russian Orthodox Church" (p. 51). In December 2002, Zyuganov allegedly

praised a plan to teach Russian Orthodoxy in state schools. "Manifestation à Moscou pour les cours de 'culture orthodoxe' à l'école," Agence France Presse, December 15, 2002.

46. Interview of Igor Froianov conducted for the news service Russkaia Liniia by Sergei Stefanov, in *Pravda*, February 5, 2003, cited in *Johnson's Russia List*, no. 7050, February 6, 2003, p. 2. Polozkov had described the Russian Orthodox Church in an unprecedented way for a Communist leader as the party's "natural ally in the struggle to enforce morality and prevent interethnic conflict." "Bol'she dela," *Sovetskaia Rossiia*, July 1, 1990, cited in Yitzhak Brudny, *Reinventing Russia: Russian Nationalism and the Soviet State, 1953–1991* (Cambridge, Mass.: Harvard University Press, 1998), 251. Shortly thereafter, an antireformist manifesto written in catechistic style by Alexander Prokhanov and signed by Zyuganov and other Communists as well as Valentine Rasputin and other nationalists included the following: "We address ourselves to the Russian Orthodox Church, which having passed through Golgotha is now slowly, after all the massacres, rising from the grave . . . [and needs] the support of a strong, directing power (opory v sil'noi derzhavnoi vlasti)." "Slovo k narodu," *Sovetskaia Rossiia*, July 23, 1991 (front page).

47. Oleg Platonov, *Sviataia Rus': Otkrytie russkoi tsivilizatsii* (Moscow, 2001), 6; for paganism, 13–19, 37–55; and V. A. Shnirel'man, *Neoiazychestvo na prostorakh Evrazii* (Moscow, 2001). For Orthodoxy, see Platonov, *Sviataia Rus'*, 56–90, 158–297.

48. Platonov, *Russkaia tsivilizatsiia* (Moscow, 1995), 130 and ff. The term "okaiannaia Nerus'" was originated by Ivan Il'in in the 1920s as an epithet directed at the Soviet system. See Kathleen Parthé, "Russia's Unreal Estate: Cognitive Mapping and National Identity," Kennan Institute Paper no. 265 (Washington, D.C.: Woodrow Wilson Center, 1997), 16.

49. Title of the final section of Platonov, *Sviataia Rus'*, 480 ff.; see also 396.

50. Ibid., 481, 499.

51. Ibid., 502.

52. Ibid., 500. Platonov is quoting the priest Dmitry Dudko.

53. Ibid., 3. There has been no highly placed clerical successor to Ioann propagating this apocalyptical-conspiratorial view; but the authoritarian and xenophobic nationalism expressed by Metropolitan Mefody of Voronezh is representative of a substantial number of older bishops in the synod, which some liken to a Soviet-type institution by calling it the "Mitropolitburo." The radio station of the Radonezh society speaks for the authoritarian-xenophobic side of the Orthodox Church. See the interview with its president, Evgeny Nikiforov, and criticism of him in *NG-Religiia*, February 21, 2000; and the arguments advanced against religious pluralism by Metropolitan

Kirill in the society's journal, "Rossiia-pravoslavnaia, a ne 'mnogokonfessional'naia' strana," *Radonezh*, no. 8 (2002).

54. *Zagadka sionskikh protokolov* (Moscow, 1999); *Rossiia pod vlast'iu masonov* (Moscow, 2000); and *Taina bezzakoniia: Iudaizm i masonstvo protiv khristianskoi tsivilizatsii*, (Moscow, 1998).

55. The last two phrases are the titles of the first two sections of Platonov, *Pochemu pogibnet Amerika: tainoe mirovoe pravitel'stvo* (Moscow, 1999), 13, 24.

56. Ibid., 3.

57. Alexis Moroz, *Rossiia pered vyborom. Dukhovnost' istinnaia i lozhnaia*, St. Petersburg, 1998, 12. See also *Ternovyi venets Rossii* ("Russia's crown of thorns"), the title of the general series for which Platonov's *Zagadka*, *Taina*, and *Sviataia Rus'* were all written.

58. *Tainaia istoriia Rossii XX vek: epokha Stalina* (Moscow, 1996), 317. A poll of 1,500 on the eve of the fiftieth anniversary of Stalin's death indicated that more Russians felt that Stalin had done more good than bad for the country: 36 percent, compared to 29 percent who thought the opposite. *Johnson's Russia List*, no. 7082, February 28, 2003.

59. Gennady Zyuganov, "Rus' griadushchaia," *Nash sovremennik*, no. 1 (1999): 158, 160–63. Like much of the terminology used by post-Soviet authoritarians, the term *derzhavnost'* (literally "power-ism") is a new invention, although the adjectival form can be traced to the crudely propagandistic Soviet poet Demian Bedny's praise of "steely worker-power will" (*volia stal'naia, rabochederzhavnaia*). D. N. Ushakov, *Tolkovyi slovar' russkogo iazyka*, vol. 5 (Moscow, 1935), 691.

60. Zyuganov, "Rus' griadushchaia," 161, 163.

61. Susan Glasser, "Russia's Muslims Become Target," *Washington Post*, December 23, 2002, p. A12.

62. Dugin, "Imperializm ili 'imperiia,'" available at: www.izvestia.ru/politic/article_37691, accessed on September 11, 2003; and "Ot kakoi matritsy my otkazyvaemcia," *NG Ex-libris*, September 11, 2003, an argument from and with Michael Hardt and Antonio Negri, *Empire* (Cambridge, Mass.: Harvard University Press, 2000). For Zyuganov's Eurasian bloc, see his "Rus' griadushchaia," 165.

63. Concluding words of an interview with Alexander Dugin, "Polet nad propast'iu," *Rodnaia gazeta*, April 18, 2003, p. 8.

64. Alexander Dugin, *Tampliery proletariata: natsional-bolshevizm i initsiatsiia* (Moscow, 1997).

65. Alexander Dugin, *Konets sveta. eskhatologiia i traditsiia* (Moscow, 1997), 17, 8 ff. 52. Cited in *Johnson's Russia List, Research and Analytical Supplement*, no.

10 (2002), edited by Stephen Shenfield, available at: www.cdi.org/russia/
johnson/6350-8.cfm, accessed December 3, 2002.

66. Andrei Zolotov, Jr., "Antichrist Fears Put Church in Crisis," *Moscow Times,*
February 21, 2001, reprinted in *Johnson's Russia List,* no. 5108, February 28,
2001.

67. V. K. Kantor, concluding summary of "Evraziistvo: za i protiv," 38–48.

68. A. Ignatov, "Evraziistvo i poisk novoi russkoi kul'turnoi identichnosti," *Voprosy filosofii,* no. 6 (1995): 62–63.

69. Sergei Glazev, *Kto v strane khoziain?* (Moscow, 2001). Glazev, like Yakovets
and many other post-Soviet economists, believes that because of long-term
cycles on the Kondrat'ev model and because of Russia's unique experiences
and geographical location, "Russia can enter into the new historical epoch
as a leading world power" (p. 62). A combination of twenty-year projections, long-term plans for twelve years, medium-term plans for five years
and yearly indicative plans can save Russia from its dependence on "the ar-
bitrariness of monopolists" (pp. 76–77).

70. Sergei Glazev, "Kakaia Rossiia nam ne nuzhna," *Rodnaia gazeta,* April 18,
2003, p. 6.

71. Glazev's latest work is *Blagosostoianie i spravedlivost' i kak pobedit bednost' boga-
toi strane* (Moscow, 2003). His Rodina party was rapidly organized with support by President Putin on the eve of the December 2003 parliamentary elections in a successful effort to weaken the communist vote. Some saw in this
new left-right bloc an attempt to move the communists toward a social democratic position. Others saw it as a dangerous move toward a "red–brown"
authoritarianism.

72. Platonov's "Encyclopedia" co-sponsored a pro-Nazi international conference on "The Global Problems of World History" in Moscow on January
26–27, 2002, which was largely devoted to denouncing a variety of alleged
Jewish conspiracies. See Mina Sodman, "Revisionists Gather in Moscow,"
Searchlight, March 2002, available at: www.searchlightmagazine.com/sto-
ries/RussiaRevisionistsGather.htm, accessed on December 6, 2002.

73. This analysis is in Sergei Kurginian's contribution to a roundtable discussion on February 10, 2000. *Nezavisimaia gazeta,* March 23, 2000.

74. Sergei Kurginian, "Kogda my govorim 'gosudarstvo'—pod kakie obshch-
estvennye zadachi gosudarstvo?" *Nezavisimaia gazeta,* March 22, 2001; cited
here from the website of the Special Project of the National Information Service, www.strana.ru, accessed on March 22, 2001. Kurginian's authoritarian
nationalist views, already evident in his speech, "Tseli i tsennosti" of November 1991 to the Club Postperestroika in Moscow, are intensified in his
Rossiia vlast' i oppozitsiia (Moscow, 1994) (English version, *Lessons of Bloody*

October [Moscow, 1994]), which accuses Russia's post-Soviet leadership of repudiating Russia as well as the Soviet system.

75. Kurginian, "Kogda."

76. Ibid.

77. Sergei Kurginian, "Ia—ideolog chrezvychainogo polozheniia" (also translatable as "extraordinary position"), available at: www.russ.ru/antolog/1991/kurginian.htm. Accessed in 1999.

78. Speech at a St. Petersburg conference on "Globalization and National Self-Determination," cited in *RFE/RL Newsline*, January 23, 2003, p. 3.

79. John Dunlop, *The Rise of Russia and the Fall of the Soviet Empire* (Princeton, N.J.: Princeton University Press, 1993), 165, cited by Brudny, *Reinventing Russia*, 254, in a general discussion of Kurginian during this period (pp. 251–56), citing writings other than those referenced here.

80. Kurginian, "Kogda," and "Ia ideolog." Elsewhere, he argues that Russia can be "a balance wheel on the scale" (*gir'ka na vesakh*) of world politics if it can solve the three problems of "self-identification": "Who am I?" "Where am I?" and "Where am I going?" Kurginian argues that such problems are not being solved in the outside world or by the current government of Russia, but he does not himself provide answers. "Kliuchevye problemy i neobkhodimye resheniia rubezha tysiacheletii," available at: www.millennium.ru/2000/frontier/kurgin.htm, accessed in 2001. See also his interview conducted in Krasnoiarsk, "Poslednii 'pevets' imperii," available at: www.lebed.com/art276.htm, accessed in 2001.

5. The Travails of a Democratic Identity

1. Stanislav Govorukhin, *Velikaia kriminal'naia revoliutsiia* (Moscow, 1993), one of the most popular works of the early post-Soviet period, is the concluding volume of a trilogy.

2. Personal discussion with Yakovlev in Moscow, May 25, 2002. For an opposite view on the two words for freedom that denigrates the Western-type freedoms then being introduced by Gorbachev, see the article by the authoritarian nationalist Stanislav Zolotsev, "O vole ili o svobodakh," *Moskovskii literator*, December 8, 1989. For a different perspective closer to Yakovlev's, see D. I. Fel'dshtein and E. V. Saiko, *Svoboda ili volia: k probleme natsional'nogo opredeleniia i samoopredeleniia* (Kishinev, 1994).

3. L. E. Shepelev, *Chinovnyi mir Rossii XVIII—nachalo XX v* (St. Petersburg, 2001), 449. It is surprising that such an important phenomenon in Russian history has not been studied in more detail. Shepelev's study provides a

good account of the organization of government service and its supporting bureaucratic structures in the last two centuries of Romanov rule. Oksana Gaman-Golutvina, *Politicheskie elity Rossii: vekhi istoricheskoi evoliutsii* (Moscow, 1998), 172–393, describes the replacement of the aristocracy by the imperial bureaucracy in the nineteenth century and stresses its continuing role in social mobilization and elite formation (*elitoobrazovanie*) up to the post-Soviet period.

Relatively little work has been done on how bureaucratic institutions worked in specific cases or on how bureaucracy impacted either popular psychology or government policies. And there is still no archivally-based study of the functioning of either the substantial bureaucracy that predated Peter the Great or the gargantuan bureaucracy of the Soviet era.

V. B. Pastukhov suggests that Russia cannot experience a transition to democracy unless it is able to move from a "bureaucratic state" to a "national government." "Ot gosudarstvennosti k gosudarstvu: Evropa i Rossiia," *Polis*, no. 2 (1994): 6–25. Viktor Aksiuchits sees the crucial step in Russia's further development as the necessary move from "bureaucratic capitalism" (a term he prefers over "criminal capitalism") to "popular capitalism." This he defines as "capitalism for the people as a whole, with property for the middle class and small proprietors." James H. Billington and Kathleen Parthé, compilers, Colloquium on Russian National Identity, Istra, Russian Federation, June 11–12, 1998 (Washington, D.C.: Library of Congress, 1999), 21.

4. Citations from the transcript of a roundtable conducted by the Liberal Mission Foundation, originally published in *Nezavisimaia gazeta*, no. 1 (2001), and translated as "Putin: Preliminary Results. The Liberal View. Russian Authorities in Search of Political Strategy and Development," *Johnson's Russia List*, no. 5058, January 30, 2001. Individuals cited in the latter include Alexis Kara-Murza (p. 16), Igor Kliamkin (p. 19), and Lilia Shevtsova, "Whither Putin after the Yukos Affair?" *Moscow Times*, August 27, 2003.

5. Billington and Parthé, Colloquium on Russian National Identity, 19.

6. Alexander Yakovlev has been head of the Presidential Rehabilitation Commission since the last days of Soviet rule. His disappointment with the slowing down of the process is discussed by Richard Beeston, "Russia Shies Away from Confronting Stalinist Horrors," *The Times* (London), March 2, 2002.

Yakovlev's publication series, *Rossiia, XX vek: dokumenty*, is produced through his International Democracy Foundation in Moscow and has published ten titles in fourteen volumes of a projected thirty- to forty-volume series. The extent and sweep of Stalin's atrocities against his own people and of the precedence for such practices in Lenin's work have been laid out with new documentary material in Alexander Yakovlev, *A Century of Violence in Soviet Russia* (New Haven, Conn.: Yale University Press, 2002).

7. The description and analysis provided here are derived from the statistics and some of the commentary in the two valuable reports of the commission given to me by Satarov: Georgy Satarov and Vladimir Rimsky, *Tsennosti i idealy rossiiskikh grazhdan: sotsiologicheskii analiz ideologicheskogo diskursa*, and the subsequent study (which has no designated author), *Analiz vospriiatiia rossiiskim naseleniem ideologo-politicheskogo diskursa*. No date or place of publication is listed for either study.

Satarov has subsequently focused his Indem (Information for Democracy) Foundation on a massive study of corruption in Russia, which he finds most pervasive in the political sphere, requiring citizens to pay the equivalent of $2.8 billion in annual bribes to officials. See *Reshenie est' vsegda!* (Moscow, 2002), and his interview on the report's submission to the World Bank: "Ot pervogo litsa: partii—nash rulevoi," *Rossiiskaia gazeta*, August 7, 2002. Satarov saw "pragmatic advantages in quarrelling with Bush" at the onset of the war with Iraq (*Johnson's Russia List*, no. 7084, March 20, 2003) and made a sweeping indictment of bribery and corruption among officials in the Putin administration (*Johnson's Russia List*, no. 7290, August 15, 2003).

8. Richard B. Dobson, "Young Russians' Lives and Views: Results of a May 1998 USIA Survey" (Washington, D.C.: United States Information Agency, September 1998); and Dobson and Alex Bratersky, "Russia's Generation 'Nyet' Finds Nothing to be For," *Christian Science Monitor*, November 24, 1998.

Viktor Aksiuchits, *Ideokratiia v Rossii* (Moscow, 1995), uses the term "ideocracy," depicting communism as the climax of the "ideomania" for utopian Western theories, which continues to threaten Russian traditional values even in the present age of "communo-democracy." As a longtime dissident from Siberia and founder of the short-lived Christian Democratic movement in Russia, Aksiuchits sees a combination of political democracy with Russian Orthodoxy as the only cure for Russian "ideocracy" and believes with "tragic optimism" that such a synthesis will eventually emerge. See also the introduction to this work by Alexander Vodolagin, author of *Ontologiia politicheskoi voli* (Tver, 1992). The Soviet government was described as "ideocratic" already in 1935 by N. S. Trubetskoi. See L. V. Ponomareva, ed., *Evraziia. istoricheskie vzgliady russkikh emigrantov* (Moscow, 1992), 177.

9. Gury Sudakov, "Shest' printsipov russkosti," *Rossiiskaia gazeta*, September 17, 1996, p. 4. On December 31, 1996 (p. 1), the same governmental jour-

nal later revealed that Sudakov was a philologist-historian who had been a
"permanent representative of the President of the Russian Federation in
Vologda" from 1991 to 1995 and thereafter a deputy in the Vologda regional
legislature.

10. I am especially indebted to Dmitri Glinski for his identification and analysis of these two phenomena, for a number of the citations, and for locating
and summarizing most of the articles presented in notes 11 to 17.

11. Viktor Cherepkov, "Vozvrashchenie zastoia," available at: http://cherepkov-
part.narod.ru/paty-index.htm.

12. Alexis Kara-Murza, "Mezhdu Evraziei i Aziopoi," in *Inoe: Khrestomatiia
novogo rossiiskogo samosoznaniia*, vol. 3, edited by S. B. Chernyshev, 165–84
(Moscow, 1995). This is part of an excellent four-volume collection of essays on different aspects of the search for a new identity by a wide variety of
Russian scholars. See also Kara-Murza, "Russkaia Aziopa," in his *Kak vozmozhna Rossiia?* (Moscow, 1999), 190–93.

Alexander Zinoviev also sees postcommunist Russia combining the
worst of both East and West, creating "a hare with horns"—an unnatural
monster that grafts artifical Western institutions onto yet another form of
"monolithic unity" coming out of a corrupt Kremlin leadership. Zinoviev,
"Gibel' utopii: Rogatyi zaiats," *Literaturnaia gazeta*, November 28, 2001. In
his prolific journalism since returning from the emigration, he sees Russia
wobbling its way "from Sovietized Westernism to Westernized Sovietism"
with a system that is "a hybrid of the remains of Sovietism, parts of Westernism and memories of pre-revolutionary years." See his interview in "U
kremlia bol'shie trudnosti," *Vek*, January 26, 2001.

13. O. N. Yanitsky, "Rossiia kak obshchestvo vseobshchego riska," *Kuda idet
Rossiia?* 6 (1999): 127–34. As with many such concepts, that of a "risk soci-
ety" is taken directly from a Western thinker writing about the West: Ulrich
Beck, *Risk Society: Towards a New Modernity* (New York, 1992).

14. V. A. Yadov, "Rossiia kak transformuiushcheesia obshchestvo: reziume mno-
goletnei diskussii sotsiologa," *Kuda idet Rossiia?* (2000): 383–90.

15. L. D. Gudkov, "Strakh kak ramka ponimaniia proiskhodiashchego," *Kuda
idet Rossiia?* (2000): 429–47. This is an analysis of Russian fears during the
decade since 1989.

16. L. D. Gudkov, "Reformy i protsessy obshchestvennoi primitivizatsii," *Kto i
kuda stremitsia vesti Rossiiu?* (2001): 283–97. (This is a retitled continuation
of the same annual survey cited in notes 14 and 15.) Gudkov sees the
process of reform in effect facilitating the "primitivization" of society and
the numbing of any will or capacity for change.

Kathleen Parthé called to my attention an early analysis that located the root of all problems in post-Soviet Russia in the very adaptability and ambition of young Russians who find no "framework in which to place themselves or their own successes." Anthony Solomon, "Young Russia's defiant decadence," *New York Times Magazine*, July 18, 1993, p. 41. For a later study on the "vacuum of conscience," which produces "naive dreams about the moral rebirth of Russia" in the entire public culture, see Vladimir Stupishin, "Vakuum sovesti," *Literaturnaia gazeta*, February 2–8, 2000, p. 5.

The statistics on television watching are in B. V. Dubin, "Strana zritelei: massovye kommunikatsii v segodniashnei Rossii," in *Kto i kuda* (2001): 297–310. He reports that (1) the number of people who do not have a personal collection of books has increased from 24 percent in 1995 to 34 percent in 2000; (2) the average number of printed copies of a book fell from 38,000 in 1990 to 8,000 in 2000; and (3) the most popular surviving magazines by far are those that publish the most about television programming.

Dubin concludes that the new national television culture is inculcating values antithetical to those needed in the democratic society that Russians are supposed to be building: personal responsibility, independent reflection, and innovative achievement.

17. From the conclusion of a study of high school seniors and of other polls of youth by O. M. Zdravomyslova, I. I. Shurygina, "Vyzhit ili preuspet: predstavleniia starsheklassnikov o svoikh zhiznennykh shansakh," *Kto i kuda* (2001): 366–74. They conclude that the main tendency among educated youth is a resigned moving toward "an accommodation to perpetual poverty."

18. Viktor Pelevin, *The Yellow Arrow* (New York, 1996), 36; interview by Dmitri Glinski of Yury Boldyrev, "Nedeesposobnoe obshchestvo mozhet lishit sebia budushchego," *Oppozitsiia*, no. 36 (2002): 1–2.

19. Vladimir Vysotsky, Leonid Monchinsky, *Chernaia svecha* (Moscow, 1992), 4–5.

20. Yury Nagibin, *T'ma v kontse tunnelia* (Moscow, 1996), 157–58.

21. Alexander Rekemchuk, biographical note to Nagibin, *T'ma v kontse tunnelia*, 532.

22. Nagibin, *T'ma v kontse tunnelia*, 160.

23. I am indebted here to the characterization presented by Sophia Kishkovsky in her review of this book, *New York Times*, August 25, 2000, p. 10.

24. The article in a Far Eastern electronic journal by Oleg Kopytov ("Kliuchevye slova russkoi kul'tury," *Dal'nii Vostok Rossii*, previously available at: http://dvr.dvtrk.ru, is no longer on the Internet but is retrievable from the Rambler search system) evokes untranslatable key Russian words (*dusha, toska, sud'ba*) to suggest this kind of Russian resignation to failure.

25. Title of an interview with the pollster Yury Levada, *Johnson's Russia List*, no. 7140, April 20, 2003. For the earlier poll, see Vitaly Golovachev, "The Year which Russia Did Not Live for Nothing," *Johnson's Russia List*, no. 6003, January 3, 2002, translated from an article in *Trud* analyzing the results of polls carried out by the All-Russian Center of Public Opinion Studies.

The ousting of the widely respected Yury Levada from the government-owned polling agency on the eve of the 2003 elections ended the independence of this hitherto independent agency and followed the prior pattern of extending state control over the media. See Julius Strauss, "Kremlin Loyalist to Run Polling Agency," *Daily Telegraph*, September 13, 2003, p. 21.

26. For the central importance of the concept of God's "energies" to the Orhodox spiritual revival of the fourteenth century, see the excellent study by this Athonite monk Basil Krivoshein, "The Ascetic and Theological Teaching of Gregory Palamas: II Substance and Energy," *Eastern Churches Quarterly* 2 (1938–1939): 138–56. For the monastic role in colonization, see Sergii Shirikov, *Valaamskii monastyr' i amerikanskaia pravoslavnaia missiia* (Moscow, 1996).

27. Igor Chubais, *Ot russkoi idei k idei novoi Rossii* (Moscow, 1996), 34.

28. Ibid., 83.

29. Ibid., 84, 50, 96.

30. A. V. Gordon, "Arkhetipy rossiiskoi vlasti," in *Kuda idet Rossiia?* 2 (1995). See also Yury Lotman and Boris Uspensky, "Otzvuki kontseptsii 'Moskva—Tretii Rim' v ideologii Petra Pervogo," in Boris Uspensky, *Izbrannye trudy*, vol. 1 (Moscow, 1994), 60–74.

31. Dubin, "Strana zritelei."

32. Vera Heifits, Rosbalt report on the research project, "Russia from the Baltic to the Pacific Ocean: National Characteristics and Regional Peculiarities in the Russian Identity," *Johnson's Russia List* no. 7013, January 11, 2003.

33. From an abridged version of the Rosbalt report by the St. Petersburg sociologist Zinaida Sikevich, "Ten Years of Russia's Reforms as Seen by her Citizens," *Johnson's Russia List*, no. 6157, March 26, 2002, pp. 1–2.

34. Oleg Kharkhordin, *The Collective and the Individual in Russia: A Study of Practices* (Berkeley: University of California Press, 1999).

35. S. N. Baburin, *Rossiiskii put': utraty i obreteniia* (Moscow, 1997), 75–89, 201.

36. See, for instance, V. B. Pastukhov, "'Novye Russkie': poiavlenie ideologii," *Polis*, no. 3 (1993): 15–26. "Most difficult of all for our society will not be the political choice between democracy and authoritarianism, but the ideological one between nationalism and chauvinism." See also the first part of this article published as "Ot nomenklatury k burzhuazii: 'novye russkie,'"

Polis, no. 2 (1993): 49–56. Baburin believes "the absence of a national ideal" is Russia's "most serious problem." *Rossiiskii put'*, 132.

37. Igor Zevelev, "The Unfinished Quest for Russian Identity," *The Russian Journal*, June 14–20, 1999.

38. Yury Yakovets, "Per Aspera Ad Astra," in his *At the Sources of a New Civilization* (Moscow, 1993), 222. Subsequent citations are from Yakovets, *Ekonomika Rossii: peremeny i perspektivy* (Moscow, 1996), 104–105. See also Yakovets, *Predvidenie budushchego: paradigma tsiklichnosti* (Moscow, 1992), for his theory of "cyclism" developed from the work of N. D. Kondrat'ev and V. I. Vernadsky.

39. Yakovets, *At the Sources*, 145, 152, 155; for his scenarios, see 203–13. For a later version, see Yakovets, *Tsikly krizisy, prognozy* (Moscow, 1999), 430–35.

40. *Tsikly*, 395. Yakovets develops an elaborate theory relating a distinctive Russian place in history both to world historical cycles (*tsiklizm*) and to the development of the natural world (*kosmizm*).

This type of broad analysis of the rise and fall of civilizations is widespread in post-Soviet Russia. The general tendency is to trace a lineage from Danilevsky through Oswald Spengler and Arnold Toynbee to Fernand Braudel—and then to take strong exception to Samuel Huntington's thesis about the "clash of civilizations" and Francis Fukuyama's idea of "the end of history." The stated or implied conclusion is that Russia can somehow play a key role in transcending the clashes and/or in beginning a new stage of history.

The analyses often seem designed simply to support a "third way" between capitalism and communism, but sometimes seem to be aspiring to establish a new kind of science (often by drawing on long-proscribed social scientific ideas from the West). See, for instance, E. B. Cherniak's treatise on "civilography," in *Tsivilografiia. nauka o tsivilizatsii* (Moscow, 1996).

Yakovets seems to believe that a new science of "socio-genetics" can be derived from a close study of the interaction between natural, political, and economic cycles. *At the Sources*, 223–33. He provides an abundance of ingenious tables and charts (mainly in *Tsikly*). But when he comes to explaining how this science will guide humanity to the happy future he foresees, he begins with a turgid sentence of eighty-two words (p. 230) and never provides a clear explanation.

41. The polling in early 2003 for the project "Russia from the Baltic to the Pacific Ocean" reported that 43 to 57 percent of those polled in each region and age group identified themselves by region and 25 to 45 percent as Russians. Heifits, "Russia from the Baltic to the Pacific Ocean." A report in the online version of *Pravda*, March 26, 2003, reported that—in marked con-

trast to Soviet times—"Russians prefer to read the press published in the regions, not that issued in the capital. . . . [T]he share of regional, republican, local newspapers is over 80 percent." Cited in *Johnson's Russia List*, no. 7118, March 27, 2003.

42. Yury Perfiliev, "Regional'naia simvolika i ideologiia," in *Regiony Rossii v 1999 g.*, annual supplement to *Politicheskii almanakh Rossii*, ed. by N. Petrov (Moscow: Carnegie Center, 2001). He estimates that about forty of the eighty-nine political regions of Russia started from scratch, that a third of them chose their symbols through competitions, and that by 1999, fourteen regions still had none.

Debates over public architectural monuments in post-Soviet provincial cities such as Yaroslavl have been important in determining "what does the adjective Russian mean? How can the Russian Federation secure an emotional bond with the people . . . [when] the present regime lacks an ideological center?" Blair Ruble, "Architecture, Urban Space, and Post-Soviet Russian Identity," in *Architectures of Russian Identity*, edited by James Cracraft and Daniel Rowland (Ithaca, N.Y.: Cornell University Press, 2003), 212.

43. In sharp contrast to Soviet times, 80 percent of newspaper readership was in the local, regional, or republican press. Report in the online version of *Pravda*, March 26, 2003, cited in *Johnson's Russia List*, no. 7118, March 27, 2003.

44. T. F. Shubina, "Identichnost' kak kharakteristika territorial'noi obshchnosti," in his *Rossiia na poroge XXI veka: strategicheskie interesy i aktual'nye problemy Rossii na evropeiskom severe* (Arkhangel'sk, 2000), 409.

45. Statistics provided in Rostislav Turovsky, "Regional'naia identichnost' v sovremennoi Rossii," in *Rossiiskoe obshchestvo: stanovlenie demokraticheskikh tsennostei?*, edited by Michael McFaul and Andrei Riabov, 87–136 (Moscow, 1999). Even in regions that are overwhelmingly ethnically Russian, large numbers identify their region as their "motherland," including 42 percent in Krasnoiarsk krai and 37 percent in Sverdlovsk oblast.

46. Emil Pain, "Razocharovanie opasno ne menee, chem sotsial'nye volneniia," *Rossiiskaia gazeta*, April 1997; and Pain, "Separatizm i federalizm v sovremennoi Rossii," *Kuda idet Rossiia?* vol. 1 (1994): 170. According to the report by Adam Ellick (Jewish Telegraphic Agency, September 1, 2003), only 5 percent of Birobidzhan's 88,000 residents are Jewish.

47. Phrase of the then-governor of St. Petersburg, Vladimir Yakovlev, cited by Andrei Petrenko, "Arktika—zona osobogo riska," *NG-Regiony*, May 9, 1999, p. 34. *NG-Regiony*, an appendix to the Moscow newspaper *Nezavisimaia gazeta*, seems to be the only national Russian periodical that systematically covers provincial issues throughout the federation in a serious way.

48. The governor of Sakhalin Island, Igor Farkhutdinov, cited by Alexis Baiandin, "Tsel' ekonomicheskoi politiki—chtoby nishchikh regionov bylo men'she," in *NG-Regiony*, 30, no. 5, March 10, 1999.

49. Vadim Tsymbursky, *Rossiia—zemlia za Velikim Limitrofom: tsivilizatsiia i ee geopolitika* (Moscow, 2000), 76–77, 115, 139. In developing the anti-Moscow line first set forth by V. Mironov in *Nezavisimaia gazeta*, September 27, 1994, Tsymbursky is clearer about what he rejects than what he affirms. He argues for a new "counter-elite" to combat the Moscow elite of "inertially pro-reform Eurorussians" (p. 139), and for a new geopolitical strategy to reconstitute Russian authority in the borderland "limitrophe" between civilizations in Eurasia. He objects to the reformers' idea of a "common European home" for Russia. But he never makes clear what would be the nature of the new elite and new political system. See pp. 107–41 for his summary of the discussion of an "alternative capital" centered on Novosibirsk and largely launched by the collection *Rossiia, Moskva, i al'ternativnaia stolitsa* (Moscow, 1995).

A cultural roundtable from the Ural region suggested that since Muscovites have moved either physically or psychologically to the West, the traditional capital is now open to a provincial "takeover without a fight." Vitaly Kalpidi, "Provintsiia kak femomen kul'turnogo separatizma (liricheskaia replika)," *Ural'skaia nov'* (Cheliabinsk), 6, no. 1 (2000).

50. Yakovlev's plan is presented in Petrenko, "Arktika," as supporting an idea proposed by Mikhail Nikolaev. For the use of the term "northern capital" to describe Petersburg and "northern alliance" to describe Putin's coterie of fellow Petersburgers in the top leadership, see Christian Caryl, "St. Petersburg's Revenge," *Newsweek International*, March 11, 2002. For the ambitious "Petersburg Project," see the account of Viktor Terentiev in *Parlamentskaia gazeta*, August 28, 2003.

51. Pavel Zaidfudim, "Na kraiu zemli," *NG-Regiony* 24, no. 21, December 9–11, 1998.

52. This is a key element in the passionate and often ingenious argument of Vladimir Makhnach, "Russkii sever: krov' i dukh," *Moskva* (1999): 157–66, that there was a distinctive culture in the Russian north from the time of "pagan proto-Russianness (*prarossianstvo*)" through the proliferation of chapels in places of great natural beauty on to the development of a great dairy culture in the late nineteenth century.

Gury Sudakov from the northern city of Vologda, winner of the state competition for defining "Russianness" in 1996, stressed the Russians' innate preference for the organic products of nature over things manufactured with minerals.

53. Makhnach, "Russkii sever."

54. Even more astonishing than this claim is the seriousness with which journalists took it, particularly in the provinces. See Alexis Ulianov, "Solnechnyi
    chelovek: Rossiia spaset mir. V etom pomozhet Solntse," *Viatskii nabliudatel'*, no. 41, October 6, 2000; and the statement of the Russian E. Berezikov
    living in Tashkent, Uzbekistan, that "the time is coming when this museum
    will enrapture the world," in Gennady Kustov, "'Solnyshki Valeriia
    Lipenkova," *Akademgorodok* (Novosibirsk), no.1 (1997): 43. Lipenkov is described as conducting archaeological research on ancient Eastern mythology near the Mongolian border and gathering in materials from Switzerland, Italy, Egypt, and China.

55. Fedor Tumusov, "Novyi rossiiskii federalizm dlia 21 veka," *NG-Regiony*, February 9–10, 1999. For discussion of the rivalry among, as well as the democratic tendency within, regions particularly in Siberia, see the supplement
    on provincial politics edited by Stephen Shenfield, *Johnson's Russia List*, no.
    6535, November 6, 2002.

56. Cited by Stephen Watrous, "The Regionalist Conception of Siberia, 1860 to
    1920," in *Between Heaven and Hell: The Myth of Siberian Culture*, edited by
    Galia Diment and Yury Slezkine (New York, 1993), 121. The term *oblastnik*
    first came into use for proponents of regionalism in the 1890s (p. 117). Watrous cites the magisterial work of S. G. Svatikov, *Rossiia i Sibiri, K istorii
    sibirskogo oblastnichestva v XIX v.* (Prague, 1930), 5, for the judgment that
    "comparing the destiny of North Asia with the fate of North America played
    no small role in the development of regionalism" (p. 121). Potanin's crowning work was *Oblastnicheskaia tendentsiia v Sibire* (Tomsk, 1907).

57. James H. Billington and Kathleen Parthé, Second Colloquium on Russian
    National Identity: Final Report, November 5–6, 1998, American Center,
    Tomsk, Russian Federation, and Library of Congress, Washington, D.C.
    (transcript, 1999), 48.

58. Putin's remarks cited in Interfax report of January 16, 2001, in *Johnson's Russia List*, no. 5023, January 17, 2001; Vitaly Tsepliaev, Alexander Kolesnichenko, "How to Promote the Motherland," *Argumenty i fakty*, September
    11, 2002, *in Johnson's Russia List*, no. 6439, September 16, 2002; Simon
    Saradzhian, "Glazyev's Homeland Goes after Oligarchs," *Moscow Times*,
    September 16, 2003. "Motherland" is a better translation of *rodina* than
    "homeland."

59. For the roots of the "movement to the people" in the early 1870s, see James
    H. Billington, *Mikhailovsky and Russian Populism* (Oxford, 1958), 53–98.

60. Cited in Yury Afanasiev, *Opasnaia Rossiia: tragediia samovlastiia segodnia*
    (Moscow, 2001), 342.

61. Nicholas Nekrasov, "Rus'," in his *Sobranie sochinenii*, vol. 2 (Moscow and Leningrad, 1930), 579.

62. Cited in Daniel Rancour-Laferriere, *Russian Nationalism from an Interdisciplinary Perspective: Imagining Russia* (Lewiston, N.Y., 2001), 41.

63. Boris Pilniak, "Rossiia, rodina, mat'," cited in Agursky, *The Third Rome: National Bolshevism in the USSR*, (Boulder, Colo., 1987), 271.

64. Alexander Shestakov, "Kontroverzy identichnostei: rodina i otechestvo v post-kommunisticheskoi kul'ture," *Povolzhskii zhurnal po filosofii i sotsial'nym naukam* (Samara), no. 1 (1998). See also Joanna Hubbs, *Mother Russia: The Feminine Myth in Russian Culture* (Bloomington, 1988), especially 52–86, on the cult of the Damp Mother Earth.

65. I. A. Reibandt, "Mentalitet russkoi kul'tury," *Povolzhskii zhurnal*, no. 8 (2000).

66. Rancour-Laferriere, *Russian Nationalism*, 47. In *The Slave Soul of Russia: Moral Masochism and the Cult of Suffering* (New York, 1995), Laferriere argues more extensively that the patriarchal exterior of Russia conceals a "matrifocality" (pp. 137–38) and that the image of the suffering woman exemplifies the masochistic "slave soul" of Russia (pp. 134–80, especially 144–59, 163–68).

There is a recurrent tendency to invoke psychological concepts to explain Russia's uniqueness. Vasily Rozanov wrote already in 1903 about "the purely womanish sentiment of spineless obedience" he felt watching a military parade; and Nicholas Berdiaev later spoke of Russia's "eternally womanish" servility before power.

Geoffrey Gorer traced the absence of freedom in Russia to the tight swaddling clothes that confine babies' movements (Gorer and John Richman, *The People of Great Russia: A Psychological Study* [New York, 1949], discussed in Rancour-Laferriere, *Slave Soul*, 116–21). Robert Tucker effectively used psychological categories to explain Stalin in a number of his works. As a young researcher in the Office of National Estimates in the mid-1950s, I remember reading a specially commissioned psychological study of Khrushchev that sought to explain his actions by diagnosing him as a "psychothenic personality." More recently, an art critic has used French psychological studies to develop an approach called terrorology in explaining the implanting of violence in Soviet and European thinking. See Mikhail Ryklin, *Terrorologiki* (Tartu and Moscow, 1992).

67. Maxim Shevchenko, "Vo chto verit prezident?" *Nezavisimaia gazeta*, September 12, 2000, pp. 1, 3; and the profile by Karen House, *The Wall Street Journal*, February 12, 2002.

His reluctance to speak publicly about his own religious beliefs was generally accepted in the West in the terms he explained it: as the desire not to mix religion with politics. Many Russians, however, saw Putin in the tradition of former communists, as hypocrites in church "standing with candles" (*podsvechniki*).

68. Fedotov, cited in V. V. Serbinenko, "O 'Russkoi idee' v perspektivakh demokratii v Rossii," in *Vestnik Moskovskogo Universiteta* (Seriia 12), sotsial'no-politicheskie issledovaniia, no. 6, (1993): 38.

69. Nicholas Lossky, *Dostoevskii i ego khristianskoe miroponimanie* (New York, 1953), cited in Serbinenko, "O 'Russkoi idee,'" 39, juxtaposes the instinctive democratic life of the Russian lower classes to the artificial constitutionalism of aristocratic intellectuals.

70. Sister Maria Borisova described her remarkable experiences in "Nurturing a Cherished Garden: the Growth of a Youth Community," at a conference in February 1999, sponsored by the John Templeton Foundation at the Library of Congress, published in William vanden Heuvel, ed., *The Future of Freedom in Russia* (Philadelphia, 2000), 107–29.

Starovoitova, who was assassinated in 1998, was that rare phenomenon in Russian history: a passionate evolutionary. "We are in a very natural, slow process of growing our values. . . . The solution is not building an official idea, but in continuing to build a civil society that will generate [its own ideas]." Cited in James Rupert, "In Search of the Russian Meaning of Life," *The Washington Post*, August 4, 1996.

71. I describe this in Billington, *Russia Transformed: Breakthrough to Hope, August 1991* (New York, 1992); and, with more detail about the religious element, in my speech on the 200th anniversary of the introduction of Russian Orthodoxy into North America in September 1994.

72. Olga Volkogonova, "Est' li budushchee u russkoi idei?", *Mir Rossii* 9, no. 2 (2000): 28–52. See also her "Russkaia ideia, Mechty i real'nost'," March 26, 2000, available at: www.philosophy.ru/library/volk/idea.html. Accessed in early 2001.

73. Serbinenko, "O 'Russkoi idee,'" 41.

74. Andrei Parshev, "Nash pobratim v Afrike," in his *Pochemu Rossiia ne Amerika: kniga dlia tekh, kto ostaetsia zdes'* (Moscow, 2000), 270–73, for all citations in the next two paragraphs. A tendency to wallow in how deservedly bad things are in Russia recurs almost as frequently as the opposite tendency to idealize how marvelous life once was and/or is about to become. See the lament by Alexander Rubtsov, a member of Satarov's commission in Colloquium on Russian National Identity transcript (p. 23): "[W]hat we have now is all extremely repulsive. . . . Actually we deserved worse."

75. Parshev, "Nash pobratim v Afrike," 405.

76. L. V. Milov, *Velikorusskii pakhar' i osobennosti rossiiskogo istoricheskogo prot-sessa* (Moscow, 1998); and discussion in Parshev, "Nash pobratim v Afrike," 391 ff.

77. Parshev, "Nash pobratim v Afrike," 400.

78. I have drawn these scenarios out of the articles in the English-language version of the report on the project directed by Vladimir Preobrazhensky, *2015 Scenarios for Russia*, no place of publication or date is given, but the report was released and discussed at a conference in Moscow on November 7, 1999.

79. Sergei Glazev, *Russia and the New World Order: A Strategy for Economic Growth on the Threshold of the 21st Century* (Washington, D.C., 1999), translated from the original Russian of 1998, 248–49.

80. A recurrent theme of James H. Billington, *Fire in the Minds of Men: Origins of the Revolutionary Faith*, (New York, 1980); see especially, "The Symbiosis of Extremes," 469–81. Volkogonova, in "Russkaia ideia," 17–20, sees the same convergence of extremes in the parallel insistence by both the Communist leader Gennady Zyuganov and the conservative writer Alexander Solzhenitsyn that Russia's identity depends on rejecting contemporary Western models and reuniting with Russia at least the Slavic republics (Ukraine and Belarus) of the former USSR. See Solzhenitsyn, *Rossiia v obvale* (Moscow, 1998); and Zyuganov, ed., *Sovremennaia russkaia ideia i gosudarstvo* (Moscow, 1995).

81. For a balanced assessment of the protofascistic tendencies in post-Soviet Russia, see Stephen Shenfield, *Russian Fascism: Traditions, Tendencies, Movements* (Armonk, 2001). For additional material, particularly on the links of these groups with the Russian security forces, see Viacheslav Likhachev, *Natsizm v Rossii* (Moscow, 2002).

82. Yury Afanasiev, *Opasnaia Rossiia* (Moscow, 2000), and *Rossiia na rubezhe tysiacheletii: imperiia mertva, da zdravstvuet imperiia?* (Moscow, 2000).

83. Afanasiev, *Rossiia na rubezhe*, 10.

84. Ibid., 12.

85. Ibid., 39; full discussion, 36–39.

86. Ibid., 9. See also Afanasiev, *The Dangerous Russia* (Moscow, 2000), for an alternate version of the same argument. There is far more material and argumentation in his *Opasnaia Rossiia*, and even more in the extended introduction to the French edition, *De la Russie* (Paris, 2002), 7–49.

87. Yury Pivovarov and Andrei Fursov, "Tserkov' i orda na puti k pravoslavnomu khanstvu," in "Russkaia sistema," *Politicheskaia nauka: teoriia i metodika*, vol. 2 (Moscow, 1997), 151–57, 165. The authors point out that beginning in 1265, Russians prayed for the Tatar tsar in Sarai; and "that Tsar, who was

neither Russian nor Orthodox, nevertheless became the first Russian tsar
and remained so for nearly 200 years" (p. 144). They find it appropriate
that the Tatar capital of Sarai was later renamed both for the Muscovite
Tsars (Tsaritsyn) and for Stalin (Stalingrad) (p. 143). They do not specu-
late on whether there might be a subliminal hint of the motherland ideal
in the present name Volgograd.

88. Pivovarov and Fursov, "Russkaia sistema i reformy," *Pro et Contra* 4, no. 4
(1999): 176–97. The authors identify centralized "power" and the atomized "population" as the enduring basic actors in the "Russian system"—
with the "superfluous man" as a third force belonging to neither.

89. Pivovarov and Fursov, "O demokratii," *Politicheskaia nauka* (Moscow,
1995), 6–32.

90. Igor Kliamkin and T. I. Kutkovets, "Russkie idei," *Polis*, no. 2 (1997):
118–40, especially the chart on 120.

91. Ibid., 129, 140.

92. Ibid., 139.

93. Ibid., 138.

94. Ibid., 140.

95. Yury Afanasiev et al., *Rossiia v XX veke: uchebnyi kompleks po istorii, kontury,
kontseptsii* (Moscow, 2000). For more detail and the overall historical approach, see Afanasiev et al., *K kontseptsii universal'noi komponenty obrazo-
vaniia* (Moscow, 1999).

96. A. I. Fursov, "Na zakate sovremennosti: terrorizm ili vsemirnaia voina?"
Russkii istoricheskii zhurnal 2, no. 3 (1999): 225–31.

97. Afanasiev, *Opasnaia Rossiia*, 163–65. He argues that the Soviet system not
only pitted power against the population but also skillfully cultivated civil
conflict within the population itself, right down to the perpetual "communal warfare" (*kommunal'naia voina*) over the use of shared facilities in apart-
ments.

98. Ibid., 75, 193.

99. Ibid., 174, 375.

100. Ibid., 172, 382.

101. Ibid., 374.

Conclusion

1. According to a nationwide poll of more than 1,300 people living in cities
in May 2002, cited in *Johnson's Russia List*, no. 6281, May 31, 2002. Only
35 percent disagreed with the proposition that it was necessary to impose
censorship on the Russian media. Both the Cultural Commission of the

Duma and President Putin's Language Council took steps in 2002 to control (and devise penalties for) the "aggressive Americanization" of the Russian language in the media. (See Fred Weir, "Russian Lawmakers Try to Stamp Out Foreign Slang," *Christian Science Monitor,* June 4, 2002.) On February 5, 2003, the Duma passed a law prohibiting the use of foreign expressions that have Russian-language equivalents in public documents. *RFE/RL Newsline,* February 5, 2003, p. 2.

2. Cited by Liudmila Telen from an interview with Glazev in *Moscow News,* May 15, 2003, reproduced in *Johnson's Russia List,* no. 7182, May 15, 2003. Glazev further contends (pp. 8–9) that many noncommunist politicians secretly vote for the communists, since they represent "not so much a party as a coalition of patriotic forces."

3. Such a progression was foreseen already in 1999 by Leonty Byzov, "Stanovlenie novoi politicheskoi identichnosti v post-Sovetskoi Russii," in *Rossiiskoe obshchestvo: stanovlenie demokraticheskikh tsennostei?,* edited by Michael McFaul and Andrei Riabov, 43–86 (Moscow, 1999).

4. Available at: www.kprf.ru/history/party.shtml and www.ediros.ru/. Detailed registration listings are available in *Johnson's Russia List,* no. 7009, January 9, 2003. Two of the five next largest minor parties registered about 40,000 nominal members, but this second tier had far fewer past electoral results or seeming future prospects than any of the five leaders. Almost all of the eight additional small parties that registered and of the twenty-eight new parties formed since the 1999 Duma elections registered about 10,000 members.

5. In a key debate late in 2002, the mayor of Moscow, Yury Luzhkov, advocated restoring the giant, fifteen-ton Soviet-era statue of Felix Dzerzhinsky, founder of the communist secret police, to the prominent place it had long occupied in front of the infamous Lubianka prison and headquarters of the KGB. The removal of this statue on August 22, 1991, had been a major celebratory event after the collapse of the communist coup attempt (described in James H. Billington, *Russia Transformed: Breakthrough to Hope, August 1991* [New York, 1992], 57–70).

A poll of Muscovites taken by the NTV television station showed that 41 percent favored Luzhkov's proposal and 50 percent opposed it. The restoration did not take place, but the question seemed to remain open and openly worrisome to liberal politicians and journalists. They, however, found consolation in the apparent decision to erect a statue of the reformist Tsar Alexander II inside the Kremlin. See reports in *RFE/RL Newsline,* September 16, 2002; *Johnson's Russia List,* no. 6500, October 19, 2002. Alexander Yakovlev proposed putting a monument to Tsar Nicholas II on the still-empty spot where Dzerzhinsky's statue had stood. *Agence France Presse*, December 24, 2002.

6. "Russian Middle Class Not as Large as It Seems," *RFE/RL Newsline*, July 1, 2003, p. 5, based on an interview with Tatiana Maleva, director of the Independent Institute for Social Policy in *Komsomol'skaia Pravda*, April 16, 2003.

By the mid-1990s, 45 percent of the Russian people believed that the current intelligentsia did not in any way express the concerns of the majority of the Russian people, and the percentage of highly educated people expressing the same sentiment was even higher. See L. D. Gudko, "Konets intelligentsii i massovoe chtenie," in V. D. Stel'makh, ed., *Biblioteka i chtenie v situatsii kul'turnykh izmenenii* (Vologda, 1998), 90. This is a valuable analysis of how the Soviet degradation of intellectuals corroded respect for the intellectual enterprise itself and how the postcommunist mass culture has undercut the appeal of the dissident culture.

The sociologist N. E. Pokrovsky of Moscow State University relates the demise of the historic Russian intelligentsia to its "social-group egocentrism," in which "legitimate criticism in its attitude to the system as a whole was somehow combined with a completely uncritical and utopian attitude toward its own place in the system of social relations." In A. I. Studenikin, ed., *Intelligentsiia v usloviiakh obshchestvennoi nestabil'nosti* (Moscow, 1996), 31.

Pokrovsky describes six "paradigms" of how the intelligentsia tried to cope with the totalitarian regime that destroyed it: emigration, catacombs, attempts at dignified partnership, moderate collaboration, self-oblivious servility, and dissidence (pp. 15–30). He asks, in conclusion, "How to make Russia 'part of the world community' and not destroy within it the spiritual ground for future Dostoevskies and Tolstoys?" He suggests that the best chance lies in incorporating foreign, particularly American, writers into Russian culture itself so that Russia can have a chance not only to create a "normal" society but also to preserve the spiritual striving of its own "abnormal" intelligentsia (pp. 39–40).

The dissident emigre writer, Andrei Siniavsky, suggested wearily (in an interview that he and his wife gave to a reactionary nationalistic journal inside Russia) that "the place of the intelligentsia will always be in the opposition," expressing some nostalgia for even the creativity engendered by his time in the gulag. "Mesto intelligentsii vsegda v oppozitsii," *Zavtra*, nos. 43/48 (1993): 6.

7. V. V. Ivanov, "Epilogue: Will Russia's Terrible Years Be Repeated?" in *Russia's Fate through Russian Eyes*, edited by Heyward Isham (Boulder, Colo., 2001), 401.

8. Ibid., 412, 417. See Mikhail Prusak's own account: "Reform in Russia's Region: The view from Novgorod," in *Russia's Fate*, 43–64.

   In "Towards Noosphere," in *Candles in the Dark: A New Spirit for a Troubled World*, edited by Barbara Baudot, 187–204 (Seattle, Wa., 2002), 192, Ivanov foresees "a possible catastrophe of the near future" in the likelihood that "no more than 600 languages out of 6,000 that exist in the world may survive in the next generation."

9. Alexander Solzhenitsyn, for all his conservative fear of pluralism and the destruction of traditional authority, endorsed this view in criticizing the Russian government after his return to Russia. See his "What Kind of 'Democracy' Is This?" *New York Times*, January 4, 1997; and his televised proclamation that Russia can overcome its problems only through "genuine self-government of the people . . . building the power system from the bottom to the top," in *Johnson's Russia List*, no. 3649, November 29, 1999. See also his excellent interview on March 28, 1997, by Evgeny Kiselev, who was later dismissed when NTV lost much of its independence.

10. See Peter Barenboim, *Pervaia konstitutsiia mira: bibleiskie korni nezavisimosti suda* (Moscow, 1997), with an introduction by the chief justice of the Russian Supreme Court, V. M. Lebedev. The author relates (p. 99) that the original title was "The divine nature of judiciary power: three thousand years of the doctrine of the separation of powers from the Old Testament to our days." He traces this genealogy from 1 Samuel 1:25 (120) through a host of Old Testament passages (pp. 91–96).

11. This idea was advanced by Nursultan Nazarbaev, the president of Kazakhstan, the largest of the newly independent Muslim republics, at a conference in Moscow and in two conversations with Boris Yeltsin. See Nazarbaev, *Evraziiskii soiuz: ideia, praktika, perspektivy 1994–1997* (Moscow, 1997). Nazarbaev proposed a new type of "cultural and economic union" that would replace the former "monarchical" and "totalitarian" models for unity. It would involve in the first instance "the economic and humanistic integration of Belarus, Kazakhstan, and Russia," but would be open to all in Eurasia (p. 273).

   A more aggressive plan was apparently advanced by Eduard Limonov, a former dissident and leader of the cryptofascist National Bolshevik Party. He allegedly planned a series of terrorist attacks designed to create a "Second Russia" among ethnic Russians in Northern Kazakhstan, presumably to trigger both the expansion of Russian power and a turn toward authoritarian leadership. See the report by Tom Parfitt in *Johnson's Russia List*, no. 7074, February 23, 2003.

12. When asked following a speech in Moscow if there could be a national idea for Russia, the leader of the liberal Yabloko Party, Grigory Yavlinsky, replied: "Once, Academician Likhachev told me that there cannot be a single national idea in Russia because people in our country are too different. But I think that there can be. And I want to tell you what I think about what kind of national idea can be in Russia. It can be described in one word: respect." Speech at Moskabelmet Company, November 12, 1999, available at: www.yabloko.ru/Publ/Speach/Moskabel/zavod-991112.html, accessed in late 2001.

13. The official Soviet style of socialist realism was challenged at the core by the surreal, often abstract style of the films of Sergo Paradjanov, and the officially propagated belief in the self-corrective power of the Soviet system without Stalin was punctured by Tengiz Abuladze's *Repentance*, the last part of his trilogy of films, which became probably the most important single document in delegitimizing Soviet communism during the 1980s.

Also important was the film *Land in Desolation* (*Zemlia v bede*), unofficially produced over a period of years by members of the Soviet Academy of Sciences. It used documentary footage to take the viewer from the headwaters of the Volga to its outlet in the Caspian Sea, showing how the river had been polluted and its villages flooded by senseless central planning. This film has never to my knowledge been publicly shown. I saw it in Moscow in the mid-1980s and later heard that it was shown with devastating impact to members of the Gorbachev politburo on the eve of perestroika.

For a chronicle of the rising tide of criticism in the late Soviet cinema, see Anna Lawton, *Kinoglasnost': Soviet Cinema in Our Time* (Cambridge, 1992). The history is brought up to 1999 in Christine Engel, *Geschichte des sowjetischen und russischen films* (Stuttgart, 1999). The Russian film industry was seriously depleted financially after the fall of the Soviet state. It had to rely on co-productions with France for its most important retrospective movies critical of the Soviet era, including *Burnt by the Sun* (1994) and *East-West* (1999), but it began to revive at the beginning of the new century.

14. Leonid Zhukovsky and Nadezhda Azhgikhina, *V Rossii chto-to proiskhodit...* (Moscow, 2000). In discussing the future of Russia, the liberal leader Grigory Yavlinsky said, "I am reminded of the fairy tale when a knight comes up to a boulder on which are written three different directions. If you go to the left, you lose your head; if you go to the middle or to the right, other things will happen because there are dangers in each direction. But before Russia can choose one of three directions, we need to learn how to walk . . . to focus on fundamentals and take small steps." James H. Billington and Kathleen Parthé, *The Search for a New Russian National Identity: Russian Per-*

spectives (Washington, D.C.: Library of Congress, March 2003), available at: www.loc.gov/about/welcome/speeches/russianperspectives/index.html. compilers, p. 28.

15. S. L. Frank, *The Spiritual Foundations of Society* (Athens, Ohio, 1987), 54–67; Frank, *Russkoe mirovozzrenie* (St. Petersburg, 1996), 180–81, and the entire section, "Sushchnost' i vedushchie motivy russkogo mirovozzreniia," 103–210; and Philip Boobbyer, *S. L. Frank: The Life and Work of a Russian Philosopher, 1877–1950* (Athens, Ohio, 1995).

16. I. A. Esaulov, *Kategoriia sobornosti v russkoi literature* (Petrozavodsk, 1995), 16–17, 28–29. Within this collection of essays on the penetration of the idea of *sobornost'* into the Russian literary imagination, Esaulov's own introduction and conclusion provide a good overall assessment of the history and recent revival of this concept along with ample references. See also Esaulov's earlier discussion of *sobornost'* in the collection edited by V. N. Zakharov, *Evangel'skii tekst v russkoi literature vekov,* vol. 1 (Petrozavodsk, 1994), 32–60. The many contributors to this and to the two subsequent volumes published in this series under the same title (1998, 2000) suggest that more of modern Russian literature has been penetrated in more ways by Orthodox religious ideas than has been previously contended by all but a very few scholars. See also Pavel Tulaev, "O sobore i sobornosti," *Narod i intelligentsia* (Moscow, 1990).

V. N. Sagatovsky sees sobornost' representing the world as a "temple"— not (as the West sees it) as a "conveyor" along which individuals seek the endless "satisfaction of increasing demands and not as a stage on which soloists perform." "Sobornost' i svoboda," in *Russkaia tsivilizatiia i sobornost',* edited by Evgeny Troitsky (Moscow, 1994), 169.

17. Statement of the original formulator of the concept, in Alexis Khomiakov, *Polnoe sobranie sochinenii,* vol. 2 (Prague, 1867): 282, cited in Esaulov, *Kategoriia,* 16.

18. Esaulov, *Kategoriia,* 268–69. A writer sympathetic to market reforms, P. I. Smirnov, nevertheless insists that it is essential not to lose Russia's "domestic type of civilization" focused on familial-type obligations to others: "'Domashnii' tip tsivilizatsii Rossii i russkii natsional'nyi kharakter," *Vestnik Moskovskogo Universiteta,* series 12, Sots-pol issledovaniia, no. 5 (1993).

19. See V. N. Trostnikov, "Ot gorbachevshchiny do el'tsinizma," in his *Put' Rossii v dvadtsatom stoletii* (Moscow, 2001), 36–40. This work is an original religious reflection on the twentieth century by a devoutly Orthodox mathematician from Irkutsk. The word for "cynicism" in Russian is contained in the word for "Yeltsinism."

20. A poll by the University of Chicago's National Opinion Research Center in-

dicated that 30 percent of Russians under 25 converted from atheism to belief in the 1998–1993 period. See Billington, "The Case for Orthodoxy," *The
New Republic,* May 1994, 24–27.

21. A poll of nearly 2,000 respondents (Agence France Presse, October 6, 2001)
    indicated that only half of those who identified themselves as Orthodox
    said that they believed in God and that less than 10 percent attend church
    regularly. Other polls show that most Russians now identify themselves sim-
    ply as Christian even if they are Orthodox. On the growth of Christian plu-
    ralism in general, see the collection of essays published by the Keston Insti-
    tute, *Religiia i obshchestvo: ocherki religioznoi zhizni sovremennoi Rossii*
    (Moscow, 2002).

22. *RFE/RL Newsline,* August 21, 2001, p. 2. Putin became the first Russian pres-
    ident to visit the Solovetsky camp, on which see the comprehensive, illus-
    trated volume by Yury Brodsky, *Solovki: dvadtsat' let osobogo naznacheniia*
    (Moscow, 2002).

23. V. P. Rossikhina, *Opernyi teatr S. Mamontova* (Moscow, 1985), 37.

24. Alexander and Barbara Pronin assert the Japanese origin in *Russian Folk Arts*
    (South Brunswick, 1975), 119. Elena Khell'berg accepts this view in
    "Zagadki matryoshki," *Scando-Slavica* 37 (1991): 84–100. The most lengthy
    study, Larisa Solov'eva, *Matryoshka* (Moscow, 1997), concludes (pp. 5–12)
    that the first such doll in Russia was made in the 1890s by a toymaker
    Vladimir Zvezdochkin in Sergiev Posad, where the Monastery of St. Sergius
    is located and where the dolls were first mass produced. Illustrations of both
    the Japanese model and the Russian adaptation are on pp. 7–9. The popu-
    lar study by Vera Polyakova and Gennady Kryukov, (*Russkaia matryoshka,*
    Moscow, 1995, 3–4) suggests that the model was of a Buddhist saint and
    may have come via Paris rather than directly from Japan.

25. "Suicidal Russia," available at: http://english.pravda.ru/main/18/87/347/
    10835-suicide.html, accessed on September 3, 2003.

26. Fazil Iskander, "Who Are We?" in *Remaking Russia,* edited by Hayward
    Isham, 44, 47–48.

27. Ibid., 47–48.

28. V. N. Chugreev, "Pochva i sud'ba," in A. I. Studenikin, ed., *Intelligentsiia v
    usloviiakh obshchestvennoi nestabil'nosti* (Moscow, 1996), 73, sees the edu-
    cated class of Russia split between a *katastroficheskaia* and a *domostroitel'naia*
    approach.

29. Yury Lotman, *Kul'tura i vzryv* (Moscow, 1992), 265.

30. According to the posthumously published work of a careful historian, W.
    Bruce Lincoln, *Sunlight at Midnight: St. Petersburg and the Rise of Modern Rus-
    sia* (New York, 2000), 320.

31. A more balanced view of Peter is created in the discussion about his legacy in the novel by the leading literary figure in contemporary St. Petersburg in anticipation of the 300th anniversary of the city's founding: Daniel Granin, *Vechera s Petrom Velikim*, 2d ed. (St. Petersburg, 2001).

32. Years ago, I stressed the discontinuities between Kievan and Muscovite Russia ("Images of Muscovy," *Slavic Review*, March [1962]: 24–34, which was questioned by two of my most esteemed colleague-mentors: Georges Florovsky and Dmitry Likhachev. I expressed skepticism in 1966 in *The Icon and the Axe: An Interpretive History of Russian Culture* (New York, 1966), 631–32, note 24, about the authenticity of the epic *Lay of the Host of Igor* (*Slovo o polku Igoreve*), which also attracted their criticism. Edward Keenan has now provided fresh argumentation for André Mazon's original contention that it was an eighteenth-century rather than a medieval composition. Keenan attributes it to the Czech scholar Josef Dobrovský, who called himself a *slavofil* long before the term became popular in Russia. "Was Iaroslav of Halich Really Shooting Sultans in 1185?" *Harvard Ukrainian Studies* 22 (1998): 313–27.

The failure of Likhachev and other leading Russian scholars fully to engage (and at times even to publish) the arguments of dissenters on authenticity is an indication that even the most enlightened and cosmopolitan of Russian scholars occasionally become overprotective of works with nationalistic appeal.

33. Nikita Moiseev, *Byt' ili ne byt'. . . chelovechestvu?* (Moscow, 1999), is a wide-ranging prophecy of impending global catastrophe by a retired applied mathematician who has turned to ecology. This book amplifies themes from his *Chelovek i noosfera* (Moscow, 1990), and was the subject of a round-table with hundreds of participants (reported in *Voprosy filosofii*, no. 9, [2000]: 3–28).

Alexis Kara-Murza, *Kak vozmozhna Rossiia?* (Moscow, 1999), is a penetrating set of essays by a democratic modernizer. Vladimir Onopriev, *U Rossii est' budushchee!* (Krasnodar, 2000), is (in the words of its subtitle) "an optimistic prognosis on a scientific basis" by a prominent surgeon.

Even authoritarian nationalists who seek to imitate Japan and China rather than Europe use similarly florid titles such as "It is an art to live in Russia." See Alexis Podberezkin and Igor Yanin, *Iskusstvo zhit' v Rossii* (Moscow, 1997). Yanin begins his part of the book by asking four pages of anguished rhetorical questions, beginning with the historic Russian ones: What is to be done? and Who is to blame? (pp. 40–45).

34. S. B. Chernyshev, "Kal'dera Rossiia," *Inoe: Rossiia kak ideia*, vol. 3 (Moscow, 1995), 477–542, especially 478–79.

35. A. Fadin, "Modernizatsiia cherez katastrofu?," in *Inoe: Rossiia kak predmet* (Moscow, 1995), 323–42, especially 342.

36. E. Ia. Batalov finds almost nothing in common between the two sociocultural myths, "the Russian idea," and the more individualistic "American dream." They both accommodate immigrants; but Russia functions "not like the U.S. melting pot, but as a rug-weaving shop where a huge multicolored carpet is being woven with original designs." *Russkaia ideia i Amerikanskaia Mechta* (Moscow, 2001), 63, 67, 70.

37. There are less sublime aspects of these passions. Gorbachev chairs the environmental organization Green Cross International, which he founded in 1993. He planned to donate to it his fee for participating with former President Clinton and Sophia Loren in a new recording of Prokofiev's *Peter and the Wolf* and a sequel, *The Wolf and Peter*, by a French composer, "to see the story from the point of view of the wolf." See Kevin O'Flynn, "Gorbachev, Clinton, Loren to Record Classic," *St. Petersburg Times*, February 7, 2003. People turn to astrology as well as to the Bible for predictions. A 1996 poll conducted with Finnish scholars by the Russian Academy of Sciences revealed that only 20 percent of respondents who affirmed a belief in God believed in the resurrection of the dead while 41 percent believed in astrology. See Mark Elliott, "What Percentage of Russians Are Practicing Christians?" *East-West Church Ministry Report*, Summer (1997): 2.

38. See the remarkable account by the founder of the multicity post-Soviet private charity organization Nochlezhka ("overnight hostel") and its newspaper by and for the homeless, *Na dne* ("at the bottom"): Valery Sokolov, "Caring for the Homeless in St. Petersburg," in *Russia's Fate*, edited by Heyward Isham, 250–57. The entire section "Civil Society Building Blocks" (pp. 193–295) illustrates what young participants in the Library of Congress's Open World program regularly attest to: the cardinal importance of building a nongovernmental civil society if democracy is to succeed.

39. The literal translation of Alexis Tolstoy's Soviet trilogy, *Khozhdenie po mukam*, written between 1920 and 1941 and published in various English editions usually under the title *Road to Calvary*. See also the account and statistics on the repression of all religions in the 1920s by M. Odintsov, "Khozhdenie po mukam," *Nauka i religiia*, no. 5 (1990): 8–10.

40. See the interview with Georgy Satarov, "I Think Putin Is to be Blamed," in *Johnson's Russia List*, no. 7180, May 13, 2003. On Glazev's People's Patriotic Union and other attempts at a red–brown political bloc prior to his electorally successful Motherland group, see "Glazev Will Lead the Patriotic Forces," *Johnson's Russia List*, no. 7189, May 20, 2003.

41. Gennady Zyuganov, "Rus' griadushchaia," *Nash sovremennik*, no. 1 (1999): 162. He sees a traditional *zemsky sobor* (council of the land) as the way out of the current Russian smuta (p. 163); and he redefines "collectivism" as *sobornost'* (pp. 159–62).

42. Alexander Dugin, "Evoliutsiia Natsional'noi Idei Rusi (Rossii) na raznykh istoricheskikh etapakh," the lead article in the symposium of the Museum of Anthropology and Ethnography in St. Petersburg: *Lev Nikolaevich Gumilev. Teoriia etnogeneza i istoricheskie sud'by Evrazii*, vol. 2 (St. Petersburg, 2002), 34.

43. This is a remarkable inversion of the established terminology. The period that is usually described as brutally subjugating ancient Rus' with a "Mongol yoke" is covered more positively in a section called "Rus' Mongol'skaia" (Ibid., 18–21). The period usually described as a progressive opening of Russia to the West is characterized as that of a "Romano-German yoke" (pp. 27–32), which split the elite from the masses and left them with a "mute nostalgia" for the preexistent Mongol-Muscovite period.

44. Ibid., 34. The capitalization is in the original.

45. This was a conclusion suggested by Judith Brown and Jonathan Spence and endorsed by other participants at the Library of Congress Bicentennial Conference on the Frontiers of the Mind in the 21st Century, June 15–16, 1999. Text available on cybercast, at www.connective.com/events/libraryof-congress/schedule061599.html.

46. The main source is an eleven-volume collection edited by Hieromonakh Damaskin (Orlovsky), of which the first six volumes have appeared: *Mucheniki, ispovedniki i podvizhniki blagochestiia Russkoi Pravoslavnoi Tserkvi xx stoletiia* (Tver, 1992–2002). (The first volume used the term *Rossiiskoi* in the title.) Although blessed by the Patriarch, the series is being published in Tver; and the print runs have declined from 100,000 for the first volume to 10,000 for the sixth. The most telling testimony is now coming from the provinces. From the small village of Osa in Perm comes pictorial evidence of a mass grave of more than 2,000 and of a crucified priest (Orlovsky, *Mucheniki*, 2:114–15). From the village of Saraktash in Orenburg comes a substantial clerical martyrology. Of the 238 churches and five monasteries active in the Diocese of Orenburg prior to the Bolshevik Revolution, none were functioning in 1938 (Nicholas Stremsky, *Mucheniki i ispovedniki Orenburgskoi eparkhii xx veka* [Orenburg, 2000], book 3: 11–12). From the Pskov Spiritual Mission comes a martyrology covering Latvia and a small section of Northwest Russia, where more than four hundred churches were functioning prior to the Revolution and none remained at the beginning of World War II (Andrei Golikov and Sergei Fomin, *Krov'iu ubelennye* [Moscow,

1999], ii). Itemization of the martyrs in Simbirsk (Lenin's birthplace) reveals 304 clerical names: Vladimir Dmitriev, *Simbirskaia golgofa. 1917–1938* (Moscow, 1997). Alexis Zhuravsky compiles a substantial dossier just for the year 1918 in Kazan: *Zhizneopisaniia novykh muchenikov kazanskikh. god 1918* (Moscow, 1996).

The new martyrs in a number of other regions are described and celebrated for "cleansing Rus" through their sufferings in the collection *Ikh stradaniiami ochistitsia Rus'* (Moscow, 1996). Other works, published and in process, are itemized in *Ikh stradaniiami*, 262.

47. Anton Zhogolev, in *Novye mucheniki i ispovedniki samarskogo kraia* (Samara, 1996), 7, estimates (on the basis of material presented at a press conference in December 1995 by Alexander Yakovlev) that 200,000 clerics were killed and another 500,000 repressed in various ways in the Soviet period.

The analysis of statistics assembled up to May 1998 on repression and martyrdom in the Russian Orthodox Church by N. E. Emil'ianov, "Otsenka statistiki gonenii na Russkuiu Pravoslavnuiu Tserkov' (1917–1952 gody)," available on www.pstbi.ru/cgi-bin/code.exe/mstatist.html?ans, is based on a computerized program operating since 1990. It concludes that of 60,000 churches operating in 1917, less than 100 remained active in 1937 with only four bishops not in prison (p. 1). Using the somewhat broader category of "those who serve in church" (*sviashennosluzhiteli*), the study cites a 1988 estimate of 320,000 martyrs and concludes that between 500,000 and 1 million Orthodox believers "suffered for Christ" and were killed for their faith (p. 4).

The most extensive official inventory of martyrdom had compiled more than 9,000 biographies by the end of 1996. Vladimir Vorob'ev, *Za khrista postradavshie. goneniia na russkuiu pravoslavnuiu tserkov' 1917–1956. kniga pervaia A–K* (Moscow, 1997), 17. Year-round readings from the new saints have been compiled (with the blessings of Bishop Veniamin of Vladivostok and the Primorskii Krai) by M. B. Danilushkin and M. B. Danilushkina, *Zhitiia i zhizneopisaniia novoproslavlennykh sviatykh i podvizhnikov blagochestiia, v Russkoi pravoslavnoi tserkvi prosiiavshikh*, 2 vols. (St. Petersburg, 2001). For additional material and a 365-day calendar of new martyrs, see Romano Scalfi, *I testamoni dell'agnello. Martini per la fede in USSR*, 2d ed. (Bergamo, 2001).

48. Patriarch Alexis II, introduction to the second volume of Orlovsky, *Mucheniki*, 3. For the several hundred new saints canonized in the General Councils of the hierarchy in 1988 and 2000, see *Zhitiia i zhizneopisaniia novoproslavlennykh sviatykh i podvizhnikov blagochestiia*.

The idea that the Bolshevik Revolution precipitated martyrdom from the beginning is suggested in a remarkable novel written by Leonid Monchinsky in Irkutsk in 1982 but first published only in 1991. "Proshchenoe voskresen'e," *Literaturnaia ucheba* no. 1 (1991): 4–39; no. 2 (1991): 3–51. Priests figure prominently in the sufferings inflicted by the revolutionaries, and the coincidence of these events with "forgiveness Sunday" (the title of the book and the popular name for the last Sunday before Lent) may suggest that the only way ultimately to move beyond the horror is through the kind of forgiveness that Orthodox Russians are supposed to extend to one another before entering the Lenten fast.

49. Some idea of the proliferation of religions in post-Soviet Russia can be gained from the study of "more than 630 religious communities" now active in Leningrad Oblast by Vladimir Sharov, *Religioznye ob'edineniia Sankt-Peterburga i leningradskoi oblasti* (St. Petersburg, 2001). Although the number of Orthodox communities doubled to 300 in the 1990s, the number of Protestants rose much more rapidly, with Lutherans alone increasing from nine to forty communities between 1990 and 1997 (p. 60). Apart from numerical increases everywhere, the author notes a general tendency toward "the spiritualization of scientific knowledge and the broadened application of eastern religions" (Sharov, an undated English-language communication to me about the book).

50. Hieromonakh Hilarion (Alfeev), "Reviving the Russian Orthodox Church: A Task both Theological and Secular," in *Russia's Fate*, edited by Heyward Isham, 235–49.

51. The characterization of Rodionov as "unofficial saint" is by Seth Mydans, "From Village Boy to Soldier, Martyr and, Many Say, Saint," *New York Times*, November 21, 2003. Most of my account is based on the fifth edition of the booklet compiled by A. I. Shargunov, *Novyi muchenik za Khrista voin Evgenii* (Moscow, 1999), provided to me by Kathleen Parthé. See particularly the account of his life written by his mother, Liubov' Vasil'evna Rodionova (pp. 18–41), which contains simple, moving poetry that he included in letters to her (pp. 32–33); and the interview of a local priest conducted by a correspondent of the ultraconservative Orthodox radio station Radonezh (42–53). Although there is no indication that the Orthodox Church has even begun to consider the many steps that could lead to canonization, this laudatory memoir is blessed by Patriarch Alexis II.

52. According to the report on the assassination of the human rights activist and head of the Liberal Party, Sergei Yushenkov, in *RFE/RL Newsline*, April 18, 2003, pt. 1.

53. She is cited as calling herself the little island of truth "without any bravado, almost as an aside" in the last interview she gave before her murder. See the powerful account of her life and impact in "Pamiati Larisy Yudinoi," avail-

able at: www.peoples.ru/state/correspondent/yudina/. For overall statistics on killings of journalists and an analysis centered on the successive murders within eighteen months of the two editors-in-chief of a reformist journal in the city of Togliatti on the lower Volga, see Peter Baker, "In Russian City, Publish and Then Perish," *Washington Post*, October 24, 2003, p. A20.

54. The judgment of Galina Stolyarova, "Slain Democrat's Popularity Grows," *St. Petersburg Times*, November 21, 2003, which describes the testimony at the presentation on November 20 of the commemorative book, *Galina Starovoitova: The Continuation of Her Life*. In the Duma elections that followed, however, Deputy Speaker Irina Khakamada, whom Starovoitova's sister Olga considered "the closest to Galina," was defeated for reelection from Galina Starovoitova's former district in St. Petersburg. See Irina Titova, "Seleznyov Beats Khakamada in Starovoitova's Old District," *St. Petersburg Times*, December 9, 2003.

55. There is still no authoritative, scholarly study of the remarkable life and extraordinary influence of Father Alexander Men in the late Soviet era. He wrote a prolific number of devotional and pedagogic works of Orthodox evangelism. But he also completed a seven-volume study of world religions.

See the anthology edited by Elizabeth Roberts and Ann Shukman, *Christianity for the Twenty-first Century: The Prophetic Writings of Alexander Men* (New York, 1996). In addition to works referenced in their bibliography, see the biographies written by two of his disciples: the priest Andrei Eremin, who served Men in his parish at Novaia Derevnia, *Otets Aleksandr Men'. Pastyr na rubezhe vekov* (Moscow, 2001); and the poet and sculptor Zoya Maslenikova, *Zhizn' otsa Aleksandra Menia* (Moscow, 1995), which includes the first three chapters of a historical novel given to her from the Men archive.

56. Cited by Pilar Bonet, *Figures in a Red Landscape* (Baltimore, 1993), 107. Bonet noted his fear that "cultural narcissism" and closed societies might appear in the Soviet republics if the USSR disintegrated. She cites him as saying, "Only self-confident societies are strong enough to be open to others" (p. 108).

57. Pilar Bonet, "Poslednee interviu Aleksandra Menia," *Panorama*, no. 13 (1990): 2.

58. See Gary Kasparov and Therese Raphael, "When Red Is Not Dead: What a Refusal to Face the Communist Past Does to Russia," *National Review*, April 8, 2002, 31–34; and Nikita Petrov (a researcher at the Memorial Society), "A Measure of Suspicion: The 'cheka-ization' of Society," *New Times*, March 2001, 17–19.

59. Victor Erofeev, "Dirty Words: The Unique Power of Russia's Underground Language," *The New Yorker*, September 15, 2003, 42–48. *Mat* in the words of this popular writer, has "transformed Russian into a language of desire, irony, coercion, and pragmatism," appropriate for a contentious free soci-

ety. He cites Anatoly Baranov, director of the Institute of the Russian Language of the Russian Academy of Sciences as saying, "In the Soviet period the status of the high lexicon was devalued—such as *fatherland, motherland, truth.* . . . In this situation, obscene words began to function as markers of authenticity. . . . Russian political language came under pressure from Russian colloquial language. This is a historic fact of democratization."

60. The contest to create a monument to the dog in Turgenev's short story is fully and humorously reported in "Vernite mumu narodu!!!" *Ogonek*, October 25, November 8, November 22, 1999.

61. Steven Myers, "Russian Group Is Offering Values to Fill a Void," *New York Times*, February 16, 2003.

62. On this linkage see the chapter, "The Philosophy of Personalism," in James H. Billington, "Nicholas Berdiaev" (undergraduate honors thesis, Princeton University, 1950), 48–71. For the strength of personalism in the Russian emigration, see V. V. Vanchugov, "Russkaia filosofiia i evraziistvo," *Vestnik RUDN, Ser. filosofiia*, no. 1 (1997): 64–75. He notes that "Personalism in Russia has been a poorly studied theme" (p. 70).

The Russian word *lichnost'* is seen as implying the whole person and, like sobornost', was praised as a distinctively Russian idea by Leo Karsavin in *O lichnosti* (Kaunus, 1929), and by other Russians, discussed in Georgy Pocheptsov, *Istoriia russkoi semiotiki* (Moscow, 1998), 165–68. Creating and serving *lichnost'* is also central to the vision of a new information-based identity for Russia suggested by Vladimir Skrypnik, *Rossiiskaia natsional'naia ideia tselostnogo garmonichnogo obshchestva* (Moscow, 1997), 22.

For a sympathetic, appreciative reappraisal of Berdiaev's outlook by a leading philosopher from a totally different tradition, see Ludwig Wittgenstein's literary executor, the late Georg von Wright, "Filosofiia tekhniki Nikolaia Berdiaeva," *Voprosy filosofii*, no. 4 (1995), 65–78.

Perhaps the most ranging and rigorous attempt to develop a Russian personalist philosophy rooted in Eastern Orthodox tradition has been made by the distinguished Czech Jesuit scholar, Tomáš Špidlík, in *L'idée russe. Une autre vision de l'homme* (Paris, 1994). He makes the case for continued belief in the existence of a "Russian idea" as both a distinctive historical reality and a view of the world with broader and continuing validity. In many ways, he echoes and amplifies the original vision of Vladimir Solovev, the spiritual father of the Silver Age (who also first introduced this idea to a non-Russian audience with his *L'idée russe*, Paris 1888). Špidlík provides an outstandingly rich bibliography that documents (347–94) Western interest in this "idea" and line of thought. A five-day international conference in Moscow in September 2003, for the 150th anniversary of

Solovev's birth, indicated renewed interest in his ideas from many regions of the Russian Federation.

63. A five-day international conference in Moscow on "The rebirth of religion and the birth of democracy in Russia" in May 2000 suggested that (1) the Russian Orthodox Church could make "spirituality and politics reinforce each other, and orthodoxy and pluralism exist in harmony"; but that (2) the Church leadership was not willing to honor its own rules (and protodemocratic tradition of sobornost'), not having convened an inclusive council (*pomestnyi sobor*) since 1990. See the interim report of June 19, 2000, by David Hoekema on www.calvin.edu/news/releases/russia.htm.

   In December 2003, a school textbook, *Russiology* (*Rossievedenie*) was scheduled for publication to promote both "the common religious values of all Russians" and the need for "a transition to democracy." Endorsed by both the liberal democrat Satarov and the conservative traditionalist Solzhenitsyn, this text was to be introduced for instructional use in Kaliningrad in 2004. The prospectus speaks of the "evolution" of the "Russian idea," emphasizing literature (*Russkaia slovesnost'*) and seeming to suggest an emerging civic consensus among all citizens of Russia (*rossiiskikh*). (*Novaia naachnaia shkola "Preemstovo,"* Moscow, 2003, copy in the Library of Congress.) The more ethnically inclusive term *rossiskost'* (all-Russianness) is sometimes used by proponents of democracy rather than the more exclusive *russkost'*. See Iosif Diskin, "Ideologiia 'novoi Rossii': pochva I rostki," *Segodnia*, April 4, 1996, 5.

64. The central importance of recurrent religious "great awakenings" in the transformation of a representative republic into a more egalitarian democracy in the United States has received new recognition from the study of Nobel laureate Robert Fogel, *The Fourth Great Awakening and the Future of Egalitarianism* (Chicago, 2000).

Bibliographical Postscript

Recent works received too late for inclusion in the text widen the variety of approaches. Nicholas Ostrovsky (*Sviatye raby. o russkikh i Rossii*, Moscow, 2001) suggests (p. 334) that "the power of culture" will control Russia's future more than economics or politics. Alexander Gudzenko (*Russkii mentalitet*, Moscow, 2001) sees Russia producing an original model for development and Europeanization in the Third World. G.G. Beliaev and G.A. Torgashev (*Dukhovnye korni russkogo naroda*, Moscow, 2002) see Russian spirituality relinking earth with heaven as the "world tree" did in ancient Slavic mythology. Sergei Domnikov (*Mat'-zemlya i tsar-gorod. Rossiia kak traditsionnoe obshchestvo*, Moscow, 2002) stresses the persistence of Russia's agrarian mentality and pre-Christian beliefs, which are also lauded in

Vadim Kozhinov's posthumous *O russkom natsional'nom soznanii*, Moscow, 2002. Sergei Glazev, S. G. Kara-Murza, and S.A. Batchikov, *Belaia kniga. Ekonomicheskie reformy v Rossii 1991–2001* (Moscow, 2003) is a statistical-laden study from the nationalistic left contending that post-communist reforms have created an economy that in some respects is worse than after World War II—sometimes even declining to pre-revolutionary levels. (4) They express preference for the Chinese model (8).

V.S. Zhidkov and K.B. Sokolov, *Desiat' vekov rossiiskoi mental'nosti. kartina mira i vlast'* (St. Petersburg, 2001), argue that popular, often irrational "pictures of the world" have historically limited the possibilities for change open to those in power. They provide four variant options for establishing a "unifying normative basis" for the new Russia (630–33). *Kto my v sovremennom mire* (Moscow, 2000) is a collection of essays from an academic conference for the millennium of which Nikita Moiseev is the general editor. It laments the "political, economic and cultural cataclysms" of the 20th century, but sees hope for Russia in the growth of the "infosphere" and a "culture of non-violence" (*nenasiliia*).

A modernizing suggestion that Russia will find itself by recognizing and correcting its traditional way of managing activities is provided by A. P. Prokhorov, *Russkaia model' upravleniia*, Moscow, 2002. M. Iu. Alekseev and K.A. Krylov provide a business perspective, arguing for "managed democracy" as the best way of accommodating the latent potential as well as the limiting features of Russian reality: *Osobennosti natsional'nogo povedeniia*, Moscow, 2001.

V.V. Bushuev (*Ia-my-oni. Rossiianstvo*, Moscow, 1997) sees the revival of Russia accomplished by a blend of technological skills and the "communal-familiality" (*sobornoi semiestvennosti*) (p. 219) nature of Russian and the other Eurasian peoples. A.I. Zimin (*Evropotsentrizm i russkoe kul'turno-istoricheskoe samosoznanie*, Moscow, 2000) critically assesses the historical impact of Eurocentric and particularly Christian perspectives on Russian identity. A.A. Gorsky and E. Iu. Zubkova have edited a series of essays that are particularly good on the subject of applying the concept of "mentalities" to Russian history (*Rossiiskaia mental'nost: metody i problemy izucheniia*, Moscow, 1999). Valentina Oxen ranges widely in considering folklore and popular habits in her *Über die Eigenschaft, russisch zu sein: kulturspezifische Besonderheiten der Russinnen und Russen*, Stuttgart, 2001.

The formation of a Russian postcommunist identity is examined in a broad comparative context by M. Lane Bruner (*Strategies of Remembrance: The Rhetorical Dimensions of National Identity Construction*, Columbus, South Carolina, 2002), and with regard to the parallel process in Ukraine by Mikhail Molchanov (*Political Culture and National Identity in Russian-Ukrainian Relations*, College Station, Texas, 2002).

Other works that would seem to be relevant but that I have not been able to consult are the collection of essays edited by Wendy Helleman, *The Russian*

Idea: In Search of a New Identity, Bloomington, 2003; Iu. V'iunov, *Slovo o russkikh,* Moscow, 2002; Iu. G. Fedoseev, *Russkie sredi drugikh,* Moscow, 2002; the three-volume textbook assembled for the "Association for the Complex Study of the Russian Nation" by Evgeny Troitsky, *Russkaia etnopolitologiia,* Moscow, 2001–3; V.B. Avdeev and A. N. Savel'ev, eds., *Rasovy smysl russkoi idei,* Moscow, 2002; G. V. Akopov, *Rossiiskoe soznanie: istoriko-psikhologicheskie ocherki,* Samara, 1999; and V. I. Bol'shakov, *Grani russkoi tsivilizatsii,* Moscow, 1999.

Index